For ten months before the Second World War, there was an organised movement of mainly Jewish children out of Nazi Europe.

The children were bundled onto trains, waved goodbye to their parents and set off across Germany and Holland to the ferries which took them to England.

Only a few spoke English, most had no family or friends here. Almost none ever saw their families again.

The first memory of the children arriving at dawn in Harwich after their long trek was 'the policeman smiled', a telling witness to the authoritarian regime they were escaping from.

Based on previously unpublished records and extensive interviews, ... *And the Policeman Smiled* traces the poignant story of the *Kindertransporte,* those who helped organise the transports, the families who took them in, but above all the often painful adjustments of the young refugees to a strange country and often lonely life of billeting, fostering, evacuation and even deportation.

By turns moving and amusing, the book captures the lives of both those who came to terms with their new existence and those who were unable to.

. . . AND THE POLICEMAN SMILED

Barry Turner

BLOOMSBURY

First published in hardback by Bloomsbury Publishing Limited, 2 Soho Square, London W1V 5DE

This paperback edition published 1991

Copyright © 1990 by Central British Fund for World Jewish Relief and Barry Turner

British Library Cataloguing in Publication Data
A CIP catalogue for this book is available from the British Library

ISBN 0 7475 0958 1

10 9 8 7 6 5 4 3 2 1

Photoset by Rowland Phototypesetting Limited, Bury St Edmunds, Suffolk

Printed and bound in Great Britain by Cox & Wyman Limited, Reading

It is not a small thing, in these years of suffering without parallel, to have given to ten thousand children the opportunity to grow up in an atmosphere of decency and normality, to work, to play, to laugh and be happy and to assume their rightful heritage as free men and women.

Dorothy Hardisty,
General Secretary of the Refugee Children's Movement.

Acknowledgements

Seldom has one writer owed so much to so many. Where to start? Pride of place must go to the veterans of the *Kindertransporte* who allowed themselves to be interviewed, often for hours on end. Their memories together with the records of the Refugee Children's Movement held by the Central British Fund for World Jewish Relief are the main source material for this book. Where I have used first names only, it is to protect anonymity, either because interviewees have requested it or because I have been unable to trace certain individuals mentioned in the records.

Grateful thanks go to Cheryl Mariner, executive director of the CBF, her honorary archivist, Dr Amy Zahl Gottlieb and all the CBF staff for their kindness and generosity. Also to Dame Simone Prendergast, chairman of the Jewish Refugees Committee of the CBF, for her long standing commitment to preserving CBF records. The CBF is the leading relief organisation for Jewish refugees and has a dramatic history stretching back to the early days of Nazism. The Refugee Children's Movement was just one of the many subsidiary groups which at the time of greatest crisis owed their survival to the financial support of the CBF. Today, CBF responsibilities are world wide and serve as a painful reminder that the refugee problem is still a long way from a solution.

If the CBF archive has been a prime source of material, a huge amount of support documentation has come from the Board of Deputies of British Jews, the Chief Rabbi's Archive, the Lambeth Palace Archive, the Wiener Library, the London Museum of Jewish Life, the London Library and, in the Netherlands, the Rijksinstituut Voor Oorlogsdocumentatie where Madelon d'Aulnis de Bourouill was not only kind enough to act as guide and translator but also made available to me material she had gathered for her forthcoming PhD thesis.

The inspiration for . . . *And the Policeman Smiled* came from Eva Mitchell, former executive director of the CBF, who ten years ago decided that the story of the Kindertransporte should be told. During that time she has remained an enthusiastic supporter of the project, offering advice and practical assistance far beyond the call of duty. Inevitably, though I hope willingly, Eva's husband Felix has become involved. His enviable knowledge of German and Dutch combined with an eye for detail makes him a superb proof reader. His careful study of the manuscript has led to the removal of numerous errors. I need hardly add that those remaining are the responsibility of the author.

Thanks also to Alan Dein and Mark Burman for their skilled interviewing; to Lucie Kaye for invaluable research and advice on the sections bearing on religion and education; to Thea Bennett for sifting material and reducing it to manageable proportions; to Jill Fenner for transferring my nearly indecipherable scribble into a readable manuscript; and to Kathy Rooney, ever the constructive and sympathetic editor. And many thanks to Peter Morgan for his permission to use the cover photograph.

There is one more credit, the most important one of all. It belongs to the late Margot Pottlitzer, a journalist in pre-war Germany and herself a refugee and internee who subsequently joined the CBF Jewish Relief Unit in Germany to help survivors of the Holocaust. Margot left the greater part of her estate to the CBF. In financing the research and travel for . . . *And the Policeman Smiled*, Margot's executors have chosen a fitting, and I hope, a worthy tribute to her memory.

CONTENTS

1

Beginnings

'At school the class no longer stood up and chorused: "Good morning, Fräulein Ratchen!" when the teacher came in; instead we had to stand up, thrust out our arms and shout, "Heil Hitler!" I never quite knew whether to join in or not. I knew Hitler was evil and the cause of all our troubles, but felt afraid not to raise my hand.'

First memories are of the railway station. Few of the children can immediately recall what happened in the days and weeks before the journey. It is as if their parents deliberately made life as ordinary as possible in a vain attempt to ease the inevitable trauma, or simply as a way of holding off reality.

They gathered in small groups, usually in the early morning when there were few other travellers about, the boys fidgeting in thick tweed suits, the girls more comfortable in woolly dresses and long coats buttoned up to the neck. Each child had a suitcase.

Little was said. The parents were tongue-tied by emotion, the children bewildered into silence. Only the teenagers had any clear idea as to why they were going away. The youngest were mostly consoled by fantasy – that they were off on holiday, or to stay with relatives for just a few weeks. Some were not told anything. It was worst for them. They were angry with their parents for packing them off and refused the final hug as they clambered aboard the train. The hurt was to stay with them always.

The jostle for a seat by the window took up the last few minutes. Those left on the platform waved and shouted through the billows of steam and, as the engine pulled forward, craned their necks for a last glimpse.

In the crowded compartments, the bitter sickness of loneliness took hold and there were many tears. 'Never mind,' said the older ones. 'It won't be long. You'll soon see your families again!' But few of them ever did.

This scene, repeated at least a hundred times in the year up to the beginning of the war, was of a *Kindertransport* – a random selection of young people, from infants to early teenagers, who were sent away to Britain by their parents as a last resort against Nazi persecution.

Some ten thousand children were saved in this way. They came from Berlin, Hamburg, Munich, Frankfurt, Düsseldorf, Vienna and Prague. A few had relatives in Britain ready to take them in but the rest went to hostels, or were farmed out to foster parents or boarding schools. It was a new beginning with a new language; the start of a mounting succession of powerful and often bewildering demands on their capacity to adapt and survive.

The first transports arrived in the early days of December 1938. The *De Praag* docked at Harwich on 2 December with over two hundred children, mostly survivors of a Berlin orphanage burnt down by stormtroopers. Ten days later a transport arrived from Vienna with another two hundred children. Thereafter there were at least two children's transports a week until the movement reached its peak in June and July 1939, with transports arriving daily and all but overwhelming the organisers. Bea Green, from Munich, remembers her escape:

> I am fourteen years old and I am wearing a suit, a raincoat, a hat on the back of my head and gloves. I feel quite grown-up and excited. I have already made friends with two girls in my compartment, one older than I and one little orphan, a pretty girl. There is some shouting and waving and slowly the train moves forward. I see my mother stepping behind my father so I shouldn't see her take out her handkerchief and put it to her face. I see the gesture and suddenly feel hollow in my stomach and my knees. But I cannot cry and we are off. Goodbye, Munich.
>
> And now the excitement of travel and the anticipation of arrival. My tall travelling companion says she will be met by a couple who have already suggested she should call them Mummy and Daddy. I am puzzled by this. She has her own parents. I don't know who will collect me. I do know that I am going to a lady who already has Margot Alsberg from Hamburg.

We spend what is left of the night in some big hall in Frankfurt where a lot more children join us and then we're off to the Hoek van Holland. We come to the border of Holland and before leaving Germany we have to show our passports with the letter 'J' stamped on the front page in red. Also I have been given another name. I am now Maria Beate Sarah Siegel. I rather like it. I think it's nice that all the other girls are also called Sarah. The border guards look at our passports. I am a bit nervous because my mother has hidden a couple of extra ten mark notes wrapped up in one of my sandwiches. It's all right. The border guard is not interested in my sandwiches. More puffing and hissing of the engine and we are in Holland.

At our first stop there a team of big and very kind ladies comes on to the train with fresh orange juice and very white bread and butter. The bread is soft and delicious. I am surprised that the ladies are so very kind. I don't know any of them. The train moves on and I see my first windmill. I am pleased that they are real and not just in story books. I must tell my mother, I think. And then it hits me – I won't be seeing her to tell her these things.

It's night time when we get to the ship. We sleep in bunks and arrive in Harwich at dawn. I cannot find all my luggage. I have more cases than originally stipulated. I don't know why the Munich authorities let me take more. I have to use my English now to ask an official about these cases. I wish I didn't have to. But I find them in another hall and feel triumphant and – and tired, both. A little girl cries and keeps repeating 'Mutti, Mutti'. I put my arm round her and tell her she'll see her soon. Then we have to get on to our train bound for London, Liverpool Street. Funny name, I think: *Leberteich*.

*   *   *

The exodus from Germany started within weeks of Hitler coming to power in January 1933. At first it was no more than a blip in the demand for extended holidays abroad. Most Germans, including most Jews, discounted Nazi racism as part of the overblown rhetoric of reawakening nationalism. Even after the April boycott of Jewish shops and businesses and numerous well-reported acts of unprovoked violence, a mood of hope prevailed in some Jewish circles.

Listening to his parents and their friends, young Philip Urbach, not then dreaming that within four years he would be on his way to England, leaving his home near Leipzig for ever, recalls a general conviction that 'the old shame of defeat had been erased and that a bright future of economic and political improvement was beckoning the Germans'. This view was echoed abroad where Jewish leaders urged patience and restraint. Speaking at a London rally in October 1933, Leonard Montefiore, one of the aristocrats of Anglo-Jewry and soon to be a prime force in the Refugee Children's Movement, refused to believe that Nazism was 'only composed of hatred and prejudice'. He identified some worthy elements in National Socialism such as 'a certain austerity and readiness for self-sacrifice, a spirit of patriotism', and concluded: '. . . were it not for the anti-semitic plank in the Nazi programme there is no doubt that a large proportion of young German Jews would be enthusiastic followers of the movement.' (Naomi Shepherd: *Wilfrid Israel*, 1984.)

The popular feeling among German Jews that they could some-how contain the wilder side of Nazism was rooted in a strong sense of national identity with national aspirations. There was no way in which they could be judged as essentially different from other Germans. After all, they shared a history going back a thousand years. German industry, law, medicine, science, litera-ture and art drew heavily on Jewish talent. Defeat in the Great War led to a predictable hunt for scapegoats, but meanwhile, the Weimar Republic removed the last barriers against Jews entering the highest ranks of the civil service. Surely, it was argued, the Nazis would not sacrifice so much proven achievement.

But the dogma of National Socialism dictated otherwise.

In March 1933, Sir Horace Rumbold, British ambassador to Berlin, reported on the mounting hostility to leading Jewish citizens.

> Thus, today's papers state that Professor Einstein's house has been searched for explosives by SS and SA troops. Herr Bruno Walter, the celebrated conductor, was recently prevented from conducting a concert at Leipzig, and then one at Berlin, on the now classical excuse that such a proceeding on his part would result in the disturbance of public order. The house of Herr Feuchtwanger, the author of *Jew Süss*, was searched by SA troops, who carried away the manuscript of a novel. One of the most eminent physicians in

the country, of Jewish persuasion, who is head of a well-known clinic, was forced to sign a paper agreeing to leave Germany. His assistants who were of the same persuasion were likewise dismissed.

There are many instances of musicians and officials of Jewish race having been dismissed from orchestras and theatres, and in one town in Silesia the Nazis invaded the law courts and summarily forced judges and lawyers of Jewish race to cease their activities.

There was no more euphemistic talk of vacations abroad as an antidote to Nazism. Now, those who seriously thought of getting out knew that they had to plan a long way ahead. Even if, as one observer commented, 'they stand with one foot in Germany' the lengthening queue of visa applicants accepted that it would be years rather than months before they could return.

In a sense, this made the decision easier for the wealthier families who had to balance the likelihood of the Nazis staying in power against the legal requirement to hand over twenty-five per cent of their capital as a condition of taking the remainder out of the country. Introduced in 1931 to prevent the collapse of German currency, the 'escape tax' (*Reichsfluchtsteuer*) was a powerful argument against emigration only so long as Nazism was seen as a temporary phenomenon. When that illusion was crushed, the exit charge was acknowledged as a bargain.

The moneyed class, particularly those with business connections overseas, had the best chance of leaving Germany without fuss. Along with leading academics, and well-known actors, singers and writers they were best equipped to re-establish themselves without causing their host country any financial embarrassment.

The prospects for the ordinary run of Jewish citizens were far less promising. Europe and America were still struggling to climb out of a massive trade recession which had cut living standards and caused heavy unemployment. The last thing any government wanted was a huge influx of German refugees. If they were unable to fend for themselves they would be a drain on overstretched resources; if they lived up to their reputation for enterprise and hard work they would take jobs from those already in possession. A third possibility, that if the incoming Jews were so industrious, far from diminishing the pool of employment they would actually create jobs, was studiously ignored.

Another factor counting against emigrating Jews was the fear of importing anti-Semitism. If it can happen in Germany it can happen here, went the argument. There was a case to be made on these lines, as subsequent events were to prove, but it was not one that was strong enough to justify shutting out the problem. Yet this is precisely what happened. In one country after another the barriers went up.

The British law on immigration allowed for special treatment 'in the case of an immigrant who proves that he is seeking admission to this country solely to avoid prosecution on religious or political grounds', and the 1905 Aliens Act promised that 'leave to land shall not be refused on the ground merely of want of means or the probability of his becoming a charge on the rates'. But in the early thirties, the government was unwilling to extend these provisions to German Jewry. Instead, all Continental refugees were lumped together under a general rule which allowed them to enter the country if they could support themselves and their dependants or if they had jobs to go to which did not appeal to the British. In effect, this meant domestic service or nursing for women and agriculture or the coal mines for the men.

German Jews in middle-class occupations – teaching, medicine, the law – who were among the first to be ostracised, naturally resisted the offer to take up manual labour. Instead they tried to persuade immigration authorities that they were self-supporting, hoping, once they were in, to find a niche in their own professions. The strategy worked well in the early days of Nazi rule when the refugees were so few as to be easily absorbed, but when their numbers increased to a point where chauvinistic politicians could raise the scare of an invasion by stealth, the restrictions were tightened and stronger evidence was demanded of every immigrant who claimed to be able to pay his way.

It was the same throughout Europe.

The one bright spot was the Netherlands where a liberal policy towards refugees went beyond a friendly welcome to practical help in resettlement, notably by creating training centres like the *Wieringen* farm, a large acreage of reclaimed land in the Zuider Zee. Having set the example, the Dutch were in a strong position to demand a concerted effort to solve the refugee problem. This they did at the League of Nations in Geneva where intense lobbying by Jewish groups helped towards the appointment of a high commissioner to negotiate with the German government on behalf of refugees and to plan for their resettlement. To avoid the threat of veto by the Germans, who were then still holding on to their League membership, the high commissioner was given the League blessing, but not actually made part of the League administration. He was to have an office outside Geneva, though not too far away, at the Lausanne Palace Hotel, to be financed mainly by Jewish funds, with a staff wise in the ways of international politics but not directly accountable to the League.

But as soon as the plan was formalised, the need for it disappeared. The Germans marched out of the League. In theory the way was clear to rehabilitate the high commissioner. On the other hand, this would have meant another round of negotiations with inevitable time-wasting. In September 1933 it was decided to leave the high commissioner in limbo, of but apart from the League, prestigious but utterly powerless.

The man chosen for this impossible task was the very un-Jewish James Macdonald, a fair, blue-eyed American who was director of a privately funded organisation for international understanding. One of his chief lieutenants was Norman Bentwich, a lawyer academic, a pillar of the Anglo-Jewish community, a Zionist who had lived and worked in Palestine as a high ranking civil servant and a spirited promoter of good causes.

By now, a large part of German Jewry was only too happy to consider any proposal for releasing them from their terrible predicament. As more were thrown out of work or suffered other brutal forms of discrimination the numbers wanting to emigrate increased rapidly. Those without relatives or friends in high places, at home or abroad, turned to an organisation set up by Leo Baeck, the leading Berlin rabbi and an early advocate of organised emigration. He managed to persuade the various religious, social and political groups to work together in the *Reichsvertretung der Juden in Deutschland* (the representative body of German Jewry), which had complete authority to negotiate with the German authorities while keeping the lines open to sympathisers overseas. At the heart of the organisation was a committee for relief and reconstruction which also prepared young people for the day when they could start their lives afresh.

Leo Baeck's initiative sparked off a response in other European countries. In Britain the lead was given by a veteran campaigner for refugees whose experience of directing relief work went back to the Great War. Born in Germany, Otto M. Schiff was a wealthy City stockbroker who diverted much of his time and resources to the Jews' Temporary Shelter in Whitechapel. Founded towards the end of the last century to provide for the thousands of near-destitute families who fled the Russian pogroms, the Shelter was well regarded by the Home Office, the officials who held command over the destiny of foreigners seeking to enter Britain. Otto Schiff was a severely practical man who could distinguish between what might be achieved in an ideal world and what could be realistically expected in real life.

Schiff's priority was to make the powers in Whitehall realise that the German Jews were facing more than a little local difficulty. Reflecting earlier impressions in Germany, many politicians and senior civil servants had yet to be persuaded that Hitler was other than a tough operator who just might be capable of pulling Germany into shape.

There were still Jewish leaders who believed that Hitler was open to reason. Sir Herbert Samuel, one time high commissioner for Palestine and Home Secretary in the 1931 'National Government', Lionel de Rothschild, MP, whose banking family was said to be the sixth great power of Europe, and Lord Reading among others had frequent meetings with the German ambassador in the fond expectation of softening the Nazi line. In April 1933 there was talk of an all-Jewish Parliamentary delegation to Berlin – a proposal which did not go down well with the Foreign Office, where the visit was interpreted as interference in matters beyond British jurisdiction.

Hardly a day passed without some notable figure sounding forth on Hitler as 'a man of peace' and his party as a 'great stabilising force'. Alone among the national press the *Manchester Guardian* consistently denounced Nazi persecution. Other papers found much to admire. 'Whatever one may think of his methods,' opined *The Times*, 'Hitler is genuinely trying to transform revolutionary fervour into moderate and constructive effort and to impose a high standard of public service.'

To argue the case for those German Jews who did not see the future of their country in such rosy terms, Otto Schiff founded the Jewish Refugees Committee. (It was later to become the German Jewish Aid Committee, to get away from the idea that refugee status was permanent, and later still to revert to the original title to escape from the abhorrence of all things German.)

His first move was to gain the sympathy of the Home Office. Schiff knew that it was not enough to argue his case on humanitarian grounds alone. Against the sufferings of the German Jews had to be set the prior claims of the British unemployed, not to mention the vocal protests of British taxpayers.

Somehow, concessions to German refugees had to be made to seem trouble-free so that the civil servants and their political masters could have the pleasure of feeling generous without appearing to give too much away. In March 1933 Schiff hit on a way of achieving this by promising that, in return for a relaxed interpretation of entry regulations, his committee would guarantee that no Jewish refugee would become a charge on public funds. In a sense this was merely a restatement of existing regulations. But Schiff's offer assumed a change of emphasis from individual to community responsibility, allowing wider discretion to immigration officials to let in immigrants who had little evidence to show that they could care for themselves. In effect, Schiff was saying that the Jewish community would look after its own. The burden was a heavy one but, at the time, even Schiff himself had no idea just how heavy. He thought in terms of perhaps four to five thousand refugees entering Britain over several years and assumed that a high proportion of these would be able to bring some money with them.

He was quickly disillusioned. Within weeks the Jewish Refugees Committee was overwhelmed by appeals for help. More staff was taken on and the Committee moved out of its cramped accommodation in the Temporary Shelter to larger accommodation at Woburn House, in Bloomsbury.

Of greater concern was the Nazi clampdown on the export of capital. Theoretically, the twenty-five per cent escape tax still applied but, since all other money had to go into blocked funds to be released at Government discretion and always at a heavily depreciated rate, the real escape tax was nearer one hundred per cent. It was clear that the work of the Jewish Refugees Committee could not be sustained without a massive fund raising campaign.

In May 1933 Lionel de Rothschild and Simon Marks, patriarch of the Marks and Spencer empire, led the way in setting-up the Central British Fund for German Jewry. With a call for a 'united effort of all British Jews in aid of their German brethren', the CBF brought in no less than £250,000 (close to £10 million by current values), in under a year. Through the CBF, the Jewish Refugees Committee set up lines of communication to American Jewry in the hope of raising more money and to the high commissioner for refugees at the League of Nations who was still the best prospect for finding countries where refugees could be resettled.

In both directions the going was hard. Moving with the national inclination towards isolationism, American Jewry was slow to respond to appeals for funds and unwilling to lobby the administration to adopt a more liberal policy on refugees. At the same time, cleverly thought-out schemes for giving the Germans some commercial advantages in return for releasing Jewish capital were rejected on the grounds that such manoeuvres would merely support an unsavoury dictatorship. Nor did it help that 1934 was a relatively quiet period in German–Jewish relations which lulled all but the most pessimistic into a sense of false security.

As for the League of Nations, James Macdonald and Norman Bentwich were away on their travels, busily getting nowhere. Received courteously in all countries except Poland, where anti-Semitism was a way of life long before Hitler had anything to say on the subject, they were never short of advice on where to send the refugees. New Mexico was highly favoured, being suitably remote and unspoiled, but in the event of unforeseen objections there was always Central or South West Africa, North China, Central America, Northern Australia and Alaska. 'The more remote and emptier the region,' noted Bentwich, 'the more detailed were the plans. It proved an ineradicable fallacy that the greatest number of persons could be put into the empty places. A knowledge of colonisation was much rarer than that of geography.'

Given a free choice most of those fleeing Germany would have opted to resettle in another European country or in America. But there was a growing counter-attraction in the Middle East. While Zionism had never been a strong movement in Germany, Palestine was an increasingly powerful draw for young people.

Administered by Britain acting as a mandatory power on behalf of the League of Nations, Palestine was the designated Jewish National Home and had been so since the Balfour Declaration of 1917. But no one, including Chaim Weizmann, the leader of the World Zionist Movement, could say if the National Home was to be self-contained or simply a Jewish state in a predominantly Arab land. Having for years pussy-footed with Jewish nationalist aspirations, the current British policy was to restrict Jewish immigration in the forlorn hope of pacifying the Arab majority.

With the annual limit on refugees from all countries set at 40,000, it was clear that Palestine could only be a part solution to the German problem. The total population at risk was over half a million. But there was reason to believe that pressure could be brought to persuade Britain to relax her grip. After all, there was, or so it seemed to Zionist leaders, a moral commitment to the National Home which Britain would find all but impossible to abrogate.

Meanwhile, the call that went out to young people to come to Palestine found a ready response in Germany as Nazi legislation aimed specifically against Jewish youngsters began to bite. As early as April 1933, German state schools were ordered to limit the number of Jewish pupils to under five per cent of their total intake. With the crazed logic of all racial legislation, exemptions were granted to those Jewish children whose fathers had been front line soldiers in the Great War and to children who had one Aryan parent or two Aryan grandparents.

More invidious than the restriction on numbers was the prejudice against Jewish children by teachers who were also Nazi sympathisers. Their bigotry was given full rein by the 1935 Nuremberg Decrees which deprived all non-Aryans of German citizenship – no state employment, no access to the professions, no vote and no right to the ordinary decencies of life.

Johnny Blunt, then Johnny Eichwald, aged twelve, was at a school in north Germany, just twenty-eight miles from the Danish border. His father was a tobacconist, the only Jewish trader in the small town of Kappelin.

> Teachers started calling me 'Jewboy' in front of the class. And even my friends in the class got so used to it, they didn't even know what it meant. We accepted. I accepted the same as my friends. Then there was this yearly occasion – I don't know what you call it in English – it's like a sports day which is once a year where everybody shows their prowess in various fields and we used to have shooting. Now in this particular year I was the best shot. I had three shots right into the bull's-eye, but when the prizes were

given out I was put in second place. I heard one of my schoolfriends tell a teacher: 'There must have been a mistake, surely Johnny had three.' And the reply was: 'We can't have a Jewboy as king of the shots.' I was very upset about it.

Even the youngest children were not immune to persecution. Edith Taylor, then Birkenruth, was born in Neustadt, near Bremen. Her family, of Dutch descent, had lived there for more than a hundred years.

I was supposed to go to nursery school at the age of five and there was such a hue and cry that they wouldn't take me so I went to a Catholic nunnery. They were very kind and nice to me. Then at the age of six I had to go to the regular school and the first thing that greeted me was the children saying that I was a dirty Jew and I must eat in the toilet. My brother and I were the only Jewish children in the school and we had to eat our sandwiches in the toilet – the teachers were aware of this but did nothing. Sometimes I would eat my sandwiches near the toilet so that if one of them came along I could dash into the toilet and not get bashed over the head. We were at this school for three years and this sort of thing went on all that time. Classes were all right at first but then here and there would be a very anti-Semitic teacher who would do things such as send me out of the classroom saying I was a Jew and I didn't have to learn this and then call me back in and ask me questions. She would then say to the others: 'You see, the Jews aren't all that clever, they don't know everything.' She liked to make fun of me and my brother. The children would laugh, they thought it was very funny.

Occasionally, a teacher showed a little sensitivity, as Hannele Zürndorfer remembers:

At school the class no longer stood up and chorused: 'Good morning, Fräulein Ratchen!' when the teacher came in; instead we had to stand up, thrust out our arms and shout, *'Heil Hitler!'* I never quite knew whether to join in or not. I knew Hitler was evil and the cause of all our troubles, but felt afraid not to raise my hand. Fräulein Ratchen, with her customary perspicacity, told me quietly one day that I need not do it. Instead of the little hymn or folksong with which we used to start the day, we now had to sing 'Deutschland, Deutschland über Alles', 'Horst Wessel' or other patriotic Nazi songs.

In 1936, discrimination against all Jewish children was made official; they could no longer mix with Aryan children. Peter Praeger was at school in Berlin:

Things were getting difficult for Jewish boys. Encouraged by their attendance at Hitler Youth group evenings, many boys refused to sit next to Jews. Also, some teachers were outright anti-Semitic. Our PE teacher, Herr Neumann, would make the entire class do punishment PE drills 'because one of the Jew-boys didn't pay attention'. Our music teacher taught us Nazi songs, one of which had the refrain: *Wenn's Judenblut vom Messer spritzt, dann geht's nochmal so gut.* (When Jewish blood gushes forth from your knife, you can work much better.) The teacher would kindly tell us Jewish boys that we did not have to join in the refrain.

We had special lessons, called National Politics. One topic was called 'Racial Theory'. According to our teacher, who was a professor of biology, the world was divided into a number of races which could be distinguished by the shape of their skulls. The highest development occurred in the Germanic Longheads. In order to prove his point, the professor made us three Jewish children stand up. He asked me to come to the front of the class. The teacher explained that my skull was several inches shorter than that of others, which meant that I was inferior. How well do I still remember my feelings when I stood there while the teacher measured my head. At first I was terribly frightened, but soon gathered up my courage when the teacher patted me on the back and said: 'There is no need to be afraid. I shall not do you any harm. After all, it is not your fault that you are inferior.'

Such lessons served a double purpose: they gave a sense of superiority to the majority, and at the same time inculcated a sense of inferiority in Jewish children. This feeling began to develop within me, and when the boys played games in the playground I asked meekly whether I was allowed to participate. More often than not I was told, 'Jews may not join.' I accepted this as normal and on the few occasions when no objection was raised, I was only given minor roles in the game. However, I was pleased, and accepted this minor role as normal. I regretted being Jewish and thus inferior, and secretly wished I was 'Aryan' like my peers.

The humiliation of sitting apart in lessons, of being excluded from games and ignored in the playground was too much for some children. For them, it was a short step from depression to suicide. Others, like Johnny Blunt, fought back:

We had an Aryan school round the corner and very often on the short distance from the school back to the orphanage we were attacked by them [Aryan children]. And that went on for months and months. Many times I came home with a stiff lip or a black eye until I started to learn how to box. And I remember one occasion there was a small child – he was much younger than we were. He was on his own. And he was shouting obscenities at us. Of course, I think there were four of us and we tried to have a go at him and he disappeared round the corner. But what we didn't know was that there were about twenty of them waiting round the corner. So you can imagine how we came home.

While there was a big expansion of Jewish education, the demand was too great to satisfy in full. Before Hitler came to power, barely fifteen per cent of Jewish children went to schools outside the state system. There was not the staff or the accommodation to provide for all those who now wanted an alternative. Desperate strategies were called for, as in the case of young Leslie Brent, whose parents sent him to an orphanage in what is now East Berlin:

This was certainly one of the more traumatic experiences of my life because I was suddenly in an institutional environment; I was with boys of various ages, some late adolescent, some younger than I was, many of them orphaned and therefore with all kinds of emotional problems, some very disturbed. Although it was a humane kind of school it was nevertheless rather a shock coming from a small family into this environment. I was not bullied at all but it was distressing for me to see boys who were having great screaming fits and who were clearly very badly disturbed.

For those who missed out on formal education there was the chance of joining one of an increasing number of initiation courses for a pioneering life in Palestine. The Nazis were not averse to these enterprises, partly because they were paid for by others – notably the Central British Fund and its transatlantic offshoot, the Council for Germany Jewry – but more particularly because, as a *quid pro quo*, Jewish businesses in Palestine offered preferential trade deals.

The inspiration for transfusing Palestine with German enterprise and energy came from *Youth Aliyah*, a singularly well named organisation since the Hebrew word *Aliyah* can be interpreted as 'uplifting' or 'immigration'. Founded in 1932, *Youth Aliyah* was the brainchild of Recha Freier, wife of a Berlin rabbi. Searching for a response to a group of unemployed teenagers who wanted advice on their future, she consulted Wilfrid Israel, head of a large departmental store who was later to be instrumental in saving thousands from the gas chambers. He came up with the idea of a training camp in Palestine. It started with the emigration of twelve Berlin boys.

> There were several hitches; a friend of Mrs Freier's pawned some jewellery to raise funds, and, at the last moment, the parents raised an unexpected objection: the boys had no overcoats. In the semi-tropical conditions of Ben Shemen in the Palestinian coastal plain there was no need for heavy overcoats in any season, but parents in chilly autumn Berlin were worried. Twelve tweed overcoats, with velvet collars, were taken off their hangers in W. Israel's junior clothing department and presented to the apprehensive pioneers, and Recha Freier and Wilfrid Israel, together with the children's parents and a small choir, sent them on their way from the Anhalter station in Berlin on 12 October 1932.
>
> (Naomi Shepherd: *Wilfrid Israel*, p. 70)

The popularity of *Youth Aliyah* owed much to the Jewish Youth Movement, from which it took many of its ideas. By linking physical work in the open air and other country pursuits with Zionist values, Recha Freier gave many Jewish boys and girls what they needed most – a sense of purpose. Not that it was easy going, as Philip Urbach recalls:

> For me the most memorable thing was a gigantic hole in the ground which was, of course, a cesspit. I was detailed to empty this – along with several others – into a big wagon. I was basically a town boy – I was interested in reading, in music, I wrote stories of my own. I loved theatre and films. I had no real experience of this but I had no choice. The cesspit must have held thousands of gallons and we had long ladles with something like maybe nine- or ten-foot handles to get down there, and lift the stuff into a great big container. Of course, as you can imagine, the stuff, as you were trying to get it in, ran down you and you were covered in it. By the end of the day you began to enjoy it. It took me, it seemed to me, weeks to get rid of the smell. This was my most memorable experience.

Strong support for *Youth Aliyah* came from Britain where the CBF targeted for the training and resettlement of one hundred thousand young refugees in four years. Nods and winks from friends in government suggested that a way might be found to bend the rules on emigration to Palestine. The signals were sufficiently encouraging for Sir Herbert Samuel and Simon Marks to set off to America to raise two-thirds of the three million pounds needed to finance the project. A separate fund was opened to buy land in Palestine.

The general sense of urgency was intensified by the knowledge that little help could now be expected from the League of Nations. In late 1935 James Macdonald gave up the unequal struggle to advance the interest of refugees against the forces of retrenchment and appeasement. Before sailing home to America he urged the League to take a stand against Germany 'in the name of humanity and of the principles of the public law'. But the League council ignored the appeal, choosing instead to refer the matter to the next meeting of the Assembly – several months ahead, this being in line with the well-established Geneva principle, to touch nothing which it did not adjourn. Sir Herbert Emerson was eventually appointed as new High Commissioner. He had the advantage over his predecessor in that he reported directly to the Secretary-General, but his brief was limited to refugees outside Germany. He was told to concentrate on judicial matters; relief and settlement were not his concern.

A measure of the growing Jewish disillusionment with the League of Nations was the hurried withdrawal from Geneva of Norman Bentwich who, after his stint as chief aide to James Macdonald, came home to take charge of CBF training and emigration. He shared this job with Sir Wyndham Deedes, an old Palestinian hand and convinced Zionist who was also a non-Aryan Christian. As such, he was able to speak on behalf of those in Germany who were of Jewish blood but not of the Jewish faith. Being half-Jewish was no protection against persecution and, though it was difficult to estimate the numbers, some indication of how many were at risk could be gleaned from the marriage statistics which showed that of all the marriages in the Jewish community nearly a third were mixed.

While Bentwich and Deedes were both to be closely involved in the Refugee Children's Movement, they had little in common. Bentwich was urbane and sophisticated, a man of radical views who nonetheless enjoyed the good life. Deedes was a workaholic and a dedicated aesthete who gave much of his life to social work in London's East End. His frail health caused his friends some worry, although it was Bentwich's view that there was nothing wrong with Deedes that could not be fixed by a square meal.

The money to support the emigration programme came in large part through the efforts of Rebecca Sieff, an indefatigable promoter of twin causes – the independence of the Jews in Palestine and, on a wider front, the liberation of women from male hegemony. She was the sister of Simon Marks and the wife of Israel Sieff, who shared with Simon the credit for putting Marks and Spencer on the map. But as a strict feminist, Becky Sieff preferred to be known as a founder member of the Federation of Women Zionists and president of the Women's International Zionist Organisation (WIZO). From this vantage point she launched out on a campaign trail which took her to every major city in Britain.

From 1933 to 1936 some 80,000 German refugees of all ages were successfully resettled (though many who stayed too close to home in Austria, Poland or Czechoslovakia were soon to relive the Nazi nightmare). In the next two years alone, 60,000 German refugees found new homes, at least a third of them in Palestine. Of those under the age of eighteen, by 1937, Palestine was taking in upwards of 1000 a month. Impressive though it is, this achievement fell a long way short of the CBF target. Finance was undoubtedly a problem. Education and training, travel, accommodation in Palestine, not to mention the weary process of documentation, were all a heavy draw on funds. Optimistic expectations of somehow tapping into Jewish capital in Germany were consistently disappointed, but while hope of gaining this obvious source of income remained it was bound to inhibit other efforts to raise funds.

On the administrative side the main problems centred on Jerusalem, where the British authorities were made nervous by the influx of young idealistic workers eager to make the Jewish National Home an early reality. A sharp brake was put on the further release of immigration papers. Nonetheless, violence against Jewish settlers increased, leading to fears of an Arab uprising which the administration would be unable to contain.

As ever in these situations, the British government responded by setting up a royal commission to inquire into the causes of the unrest and to suggest remedies. Earl Peel, who was given the unenviable task of leading the team of inquiry, reported back in July 1937, having concluded that 'the policy of conciliation, carried to its furthest limits, has failed'. His solution was to partition the country.

The principle was welcome to Zionists but they were less keen on the practicality as envisaged by Peel, allowing them a tiny area albeit with the most fertile land, but already occupied by a hostile Arab population. Nor was there much enthusiasm for the proposed limitation on immigration to 12,000 a year for five years – an arbitrary attempt to keep some sort of ethnic balance.

The government blew hot and cold on the proposals which encouraged Arab nationalists to further acts of terrorism and increased Jewish distrust of the mandatory power. The only firm decision was to clamp down on immigration – a self-defeating policy which simply led to a sharp increase in the number of illegal immigrants.

Then in March 1938, the Nazis marched into Vienna. They brought with them the full panoply of anti-Jewish laws and a practised bureaucracy to enforce them. The environment was conducive to their work. In comparison with Germany, anti-Semitism in Austria had a head start. From the days of the Empire, the clash of nationalist minorities – Czechs, Poles, Croats, Slovenes and Serbs – had left the Jews isolated; distrusted on all sides. It was in Vienna that the young Hitler had learned to engage in the oratory of hate.

For 200,000 Austrian Jews and other non-Aryans, every semblance of ordinary life disappeared as if by some appalling wizardry.

'It is impossible for you to imagine,' wrote G. E. R. Gedge, the Central European correspondent of *The Times*, 'what it means for one-sixth of the population of Vienna to be made pariahs overnight, deprived of all civil rights, including the right to retain property large or small, the right to be employed or to give employment, to exercise a profession, to enter restaurants, cafes, bathing beaches, baths or public parks, to be faced daily and hourly, without hope of relief, with the foulest insults which ingenious and vicious minds can devise, to be liable always to be turned overnight out of house and home, and at any hour of every day and every night to arrest without the pretence of a charge or hope of a definite sentence, however heavy – and with all this to find every country in the world selfishly closing its frontiers to you when, after being plundered of your last farthing, you seek to escape.'

Norman Bentwich was one of the first into Vienna after the Nazi takeover. Reporting home on a 'position more catastrophic even than we had judged', he calculated:

> The number of persons who have to be fed in the communal soup kitchens has risen to about 25,000 a day. It should be larger, because 40,000 are in great need; but they have not the money to feed more.

Children were bewildered and frightened though many, like Richard Grunberger, then just turned fourteen, had seen the warning signs:

> In 1937, the third year, we had a history master by the name of Prochasker. He was a monarchist and yearned for the days of the Austo-Hungarian empire. He was very embittered by what the allies had done to Austria and Germany after the First World War which put him in agreement with the illegal Hitler Youth leader in my class. I could tell by the way in which the Hitler Youth character was asking certain questions and making certain points, which the history teacher was not really courageous enough to refute, that something was really going on under the surface. For example, I remember one lesson about the setting-up of the United States, where the history teacher merely told us how the Declaration of Independence was drawn up and so on, and this Hitler Youth character said: 'Isn't it a fact that among the founding fathers of the United States there was only a majority of one who voted in favour of making English the language of the new country rather than German?' and I was rather amazed at this but the history teacher said: 'Yes, this is so.'

For Jews, Vienna became a city of fear and destitution. The risks of offending what was ludicrously described as the law were endless. 'No Jews Here' signs were everywhere. Cafes and cinemas carried warnings: 'Gypsies and Jews Keep Out'; children were told to stay away from public parks; a little girl who was brave enough to attend school found 'Cursed be the Jew' scrawled across her desk. Magda Chadwick recalls her mother having to stand in front of her shop with a placard: 'Jews must not buy or come in here'.

One obvious target was Judenstrasse – Jews' Street – where Rosina Domingo lived. On the night they wrecked her local synagogue:

> It had two galleries. At the top one was a huge tablet of the ten commandments with the sun rays coming from it. The Nazis threw everything down, but probably because the tablet was too heavy they couldn't move it and it was left. It was so symbolic when you went in there. Everything was destroyed but the tablet still stood.

The demands on youngsters was not easily understood. For Angela Carpos, who is half-Jewish, the pain of not knowing who she was or how she was supposed to behave started with the order for her to attend Jewish school in the morning and state school in the afternoon. It was not long before she encountered Nazi rule head on.

> When I was still living with my mother the Nazis were burning books and they came and snatched out of my hand my one and only lovely teddy bear and burnt it in front of me. They didn't hit us – but what really terrified me were the scrubbings that went on. I saw neighbours and friends being humiliated, scrubbing windows and scrubbing streets. Absolute fear ran through everybody. You cannot understand it unless you have experienced it. The fear of walking the streets, the fear of every door. You are not aware of it. When I was in one of my foster homes in Scotland I lived in a bungalow with some very nice people. They had a gravel driveway with a little gate. Apparently, they told me years later, every time someone came along the gravel, I took a kitchen knife and sat under the table. I don't remember – which is interesting. What must have gone into us children is beyond belief.

And over all there was the feeling of utter loneliness, of having no one to turn to. In the tenement block where Richard Grunberger lived:

> . . . everybody was asked to put out swastika flags. Across the landing from us was a veteran social democrat. In the weeks preceding the *Anschluss*, when the political climate had got ever more intense, he had come over and spent a few evenings chatting to my mother and proclaiming his social democrat convictions and reminiscing about the old days. Well – I thought a man with those

convictions would refuse to put out swastika flags. But on that Saturday morning we found ourselves the only flat on the block that was totally denuded of flags.

In charge of the Jewish emigration office in Vienna was a thirty-two-year-old SS *Obersturmbannführer*. Described as 'a painstaking bureaucrat', Adolf Eichmann was soon to prove his value to the Reich as the unrivalled expert in handling what were known as 'technical and organisational problems' connected with the treatment of Jews. His declared aim was to make Austria *judenrein*, 'free of Jews'.

His victims were only too happy to comply. Thousands besieged the *Kultusgemeinde*, the central Jewish organisation, begging for visas. An emigration bureau set up by a Dutch philanthropist collected 20,000 names in a matter of days. Outside the United States embassy, the queue stretched for a quarter of a mile, day and night. In London, the Jewish Refugees Committee received up to 1000 calls a day.

But the supply of visas was a long way short of demand. Embassy officials of all nationalities had to reconcile orders from their governments to examine every application for an excuse to reject with the threat of annihilation hanging over the entire community.

Demand for places on the Palestinian immigration quota intensified, the very opposite of what the British intended. Meanwhile, German shipping companies discovered a profitable sideline in charging high prices for berths in clapped-out steamers which sailed the Mediterranean, crowded with Jewish families hoping to be smuggled ashore in Palestine or to be accepted by the authorities because there was nowhere else for them to go.

Those who still had some faith in Europe took any chance of refuge, even if it meant splitting up families to allow for children to escape ahead of their elders. In Britain there were several groups of well-wishers ready to care for young people, though the numbers sponsored by charitable enterprise were pitifully small.

Concerned for Jewish and non-Aryan Christian children alike, the Children's Inter-Aid Committee brought in some 150 children up to the beginning of 1938 and another 300 by the end of the year. Founded in 1936 by two unsung heroines – Mrs Skelton and Mrs Francis Bendit – of whom little is known except their sympathy for young people in need, the Inter-Aid Committee was supported by the CBF and the Save the Children Fund. A link across to the CBF was provided by Sir Wyndham Deedes, who was chairman of the Committee. Another valuable link was with *B'nai B'rith*, a Jewish fraternal society which maintained several hostels in the London area.

From Inter-Aid it was but a short step to The Society of Friends (their headquarters were in a neighbouring street). The Quakers numbered less than 23,000 in Britain and only 160,000 world wide, yet, of all the non-Jewish bodies who might have been expected to take an active interest in the refugee problem, they were alone in having a network of contacts in the European capitals.

Their German Emergency Committee was active from 1933. In its first two years, 600 families and individuals were helped to escape. Among them were numerous political dissidents – socialists, communists and pacifists – who were even worse off than the Jews, since they had few friends at home and even fewer abroad.

As early as 1934, Bertha Bracey and two other members of the German Emergency Committee gathered support for a school at Stoatley Rough near Haslemere in Surrey, primarily for German children. But the work by Quakers on behalf of young people only really took off after the *Anschluss*. By November 1938, the Vienna centre had arranged for over 300 children to go to other countries.

Stoatley Rough was not unique. Another was at Bunce Court, a manor house in Kent. The head teacher of Bunce Court was a remarkable woman called Anna Essinger. In 1925 she founded Herrlingen School near Ulm, but when the Nazis came to power she decided that 'Germany was no longer a place where children could grow up in honesty and freedom'. Taking advantage of a loophole in the immigration laws which allowed for children to be admitted for educational purposes, she removed herself, several of her staff and some of her pupils to Britain. Predictably, the loophole was closed in 1936, preventing others from following her example.

Herrlingen was handed over to Hugo Rosenthal, a teacher who had returned from Palestine, and who ran the school on progressive lines until it was shut down in 1939. The house was eventually transformed into a luxury home for Field Marshal Rommel, a reward for military success that he was unable to sustain. It was in the woods close by the house that he committed suicide.

The history of Bunce Court followed a different if hardly less eventful route, but in the pre-war years, when Anna Essinger was allowed to pursue her ideals, the school was a children's refuge that came closest to a real home. Bunce Court was progressive in that it stressed the virtues of self-discipline and self-help; but Anna Essinger was not a Zionist, nor was she particularly interested in the formalities of religion.

On quite another level was Rabbi Solomon Schonfeld, director of the Chief Rabbi's Religious Emergency Council and, not insignificantly, the Chief Rabbi's son-in-law. Courageous and single-minded to the point of fanaticism, Schonfeld made several trips to Germany and Austria to bring back refugee children for his two hostels – Avigdor House in Bedford Row for boys and Northfield on Stamford Hill for girls. The life they led was orthodox in every particular; there was to be no compromise with liberalism or free thinking. This devotion to a single cause was soon to put Schonfeld at odds with the mainstream refugee movement.

Finally, there were local groups of individuals who operated outside the refugee organisations. In Cambridgeshire, for example, 55 Hills Road was made available by Jesus College to house seventy German teenagers. The job of organising their education (mostly at private schools on reduced fees) went to Greta Burkill, who gathered about her a committee of sympathisers ready 'to deal with a great amount of heartbreak and difficulties of adjustment'.

Greta, the daughter of a left-wing journalist, spent her childhood in Germany. When she married Charles Burkill, a Cambridge don, she brought to her adopted country a healthy distrust of conventional politics and an inextinguishable desire to help the victims of fascism. She was not Jewish, but from the mid 1930s on she sought out jobs in the university for Jewish boys who could not otherwise have got visas. A boy who was suffering at a German school because his father was in a concentration camp, she made one of her own family. He was followed by an Austrian boy who adopted the name of Burkill by deed poll. Not surprisingly, Cambridge was soon to become one of the most active centres of the child refugee movement.

The collapse of democracy in Austria did have one positive benefit. It stirred the conscience of the United States, and brought the administration to the point of asking if there was anything to be done about the refugee problem beyond hoping that if it was ignored long enough it would go away.

In June 1938 President Roosevelt proposed a meeting of government representatives of all the countries of America and Europe except Germany. Recognising the tribulations of German and Austrian Jews the conference 'would manifest before the non-European world the urgency of emigrations, chiefly to Palestine'. The British did not like the sound of that. Roosevelt was asked to narrow the scope of the conference by avoiding the subject of Palestine, and at the same time to widen it by considering the problems of all refugees, not just German Jews. He agreed.

The representatives of thirty-one countries assembled in the Hotel Royal at Evian on 6 July 1938. To everyone's surprise Jewish delegates from Berlin and Vienna were allowed to attend. They were joined by representatives of at least a hundred distressed minorities who split into thirty groups, each to choose a spokesman to address the conference – which was soon to be dubbed the 'Modern Wailing Wall'.

That America seemed at last to be rediscovering her traditional friendship towards refugees inspired 'extravagant and almost Messianic hopes', according to Norman Bentwich who was at Evian for the CBF. But Bentwich went on to report that the hopes faded with the succession of vague resolutions – a decision to appeal to the German government to set fair conditions for evacuation; the appointment of a committee to work out plans for group settlement overseas; and a refusal by all governments to accept financial responsibility for emigration.

'The published outcome,' said Bentwich, 'seemed a little flat, like the mineral water of Evian.' Someone remarked that Evian spelt backwards gave 'naive'.

The only genuine encouragement was the American offer to cut the formalities on the entry of German refugees. By law, the upper limit on German immigrants was 30,000 a year, but throughout the 1930s this figure was never reached. So cumbersome was the bureaucracy (deliberately so) that only about half the quota got through. Now there was to be a genuine effort to achieve the maximum figure.

This much-heralded concession caused some worry in British government circles where the theory of appeasement held that any suggestion of a relaxation of the rules would simply encourage the

Germans to act more ruthlessly. As if to counterbalance American policy, the British government tightened up on immigration procedures. In April 1938, soon after the *Anschluss*, Central Europeans intending to come to Britain had to apply for visas, which meant a lengthy interrogation by a passport control officer attached to every embassy and consulate. This was thought to deter Austrians 'who were largely of the shopkeeper and small trader class and would therefore prove very much more difficult to emigrate than the average German'.

Thereafter, every obstacle was put in the way of extending the work of the refugee organisations. Official pressure could not be exerted on the Germans (for fear of making matters worse), old prisoner-of-war camps could not be made available for refugees and numbers admitted into Britain could not be increased. With money going out faster than it was coming in, Otto Schiff asked to be released from his undertaking that Jewish refugees would not become a public charge. He was told that any exceptions needed individual approval by the Home Office.

The softly softly approach to the Nazis was the preliminary to the 'peace in our time' Munich agreement and the tragic months of disillusionment when the German armies began the carve-up of Czechoslovakia. In October 1938 another wave of Jewish residents in Germany were deported back to Poland. Among them were the parents of seventeen-year-old Herschel Grynszpan, who was hiding out as an illegal immigrant in Paris. On 7 November, he entered the German embassy with the apparent intention of assassinating the ambassador. Instead, he shot the third secretary Ernst von Rath, who died two days later.

The Nazi leadership snapped at the opportunity to provoke another outbreak of anti-Semitism. A vicious tirade by propaganda minister Joseph Goebbels was the signal for party activists and stormtroopers throughout Germany to indulge in an orgy of destruction.

2

Kristallnacht

*'Late, late, my father came home – an old broken man –
because of what he had seen and could do nothing about.'*

At around midnight the fires started. By morning 267 synagogues
had been destroyed, thousands of Jewish shops and homes devastated, one hundred Jews murdered and many thousands arrested.
This was *Kristallnacht* – the night of broken glass.

A Quaker observer reported back to London:

In some towns every private house was entered, in others this attack
was partial. The usual procedure was to smash any articles of value
with axes, and often everything breakable, down to the last tea-cup,
was broken. The men were allowed to dress and were taken straight
away, carrying nothing with them. In a number of cases I heard
that the arrests were made courteously and with some expressions
of regret. But often the treatment was rough. In Erfurt the men
arrested were gathered in the hall of a school and there beaten before
being taken off to the camp. In Chemnitz one man was shot dead
in his own house and the rabbi was beaten and severely wounded
while trying to save his sacred books from the synagogue fire. A
number of men escaped arrest by flight or absence from home; these
were in hiding, in some cases in Christian homes . . . In some cases
in Dresden the wives were arrested and held as hostages until their
husbands gave themselves up.
   At both Buchenwald, where 10,000 Jews had been collected, and
at Dachau, where there were 12,000, conditions were very bad and
by the end of the month some had already died in these camps.
From Buchenwald some came out wounded, with torn clothing
. . . In Plauen I found only three men had come back and all were

in bed, seriously ill. I saw one, but he could hardly speak . . . Every day at Weimar station a group of Jewish women (led by the widow of a former rabbi of Erfurt) met the released men, with whatever supplies of clean socks, handkerchiefs, etc. they could get together, gave them coffee, and tried to clean them up a little before they proceeded by various trains to their homes. In the Erfurt area all the men released had to sign a paper undertaking to be out of Germany within three weeks, under penalty of reinternment.

Helga Kreiner, now Helga Samuel, was just eleven at the time of *Kristallnacht*:

One night is especially vivid in my memory – when we heard the Nazi boots tramping along the street, stopping at the main front door of the block of flats where we lived, banging on the door – and my mother hurriedly put out all the lights in our flat and hid with us in the corner of a bedroom, having to be quiet as mice . . . The boots tramped up the stairs, gruff voices, while our hearts beat faster and faster, the boots still tramping, halting for a moment's agonising silence outside our front door, and then going up the next flight to the flat above . . . We heard the next morning that the gentleman who lived there, also a Jew, had been arrested. This time, they had passed us by.

I remember being very frightened at having to hide and having to be so quiet, sensing my mother's fear. But really I was too young to appreciate the significance of the whole situation. This didn't really strike true, until the day my father was arrested on the street, on his way home from the barber around the corner, taken to police headquarters and from there to the concentration camp at Buchenwald. I had gone that day to play with a schoolfriend and had not accompanied my father, as was my usual custom, as I enjoyed sitting in the barber's looking at the magazines. My mother always said afterwards that I was my father's lucky mascot, his protection, until this terrible day. When my father did not return after a couple of hours my mother, fearing the worst, rang the police station and was told that he was being held in custody. For what?

This went on for several days, until she received a printed card signed by my father (address Buchenwald), asking for strong boots and warm underclothing. (These, we learned afterwards, he never received . . .) I did not see my father again until several months after I had arrived in England.

Lorraine Allard, then Sulzbacher, lived in Fürth in Bavaria, a town with a sizeable Jewish population. Her parents, both with solid roots in the prosperous middle class, thought of themselves as Germans first and Jews second. Until Hitler's arrival. On *Kirstallnacht*:

> I remember being woken up at 1 a.m. Two Brownshirts were running about in our flat. My mother was crying. We were told to dress. I remember walking to a square in the town and being assembled there with lots and lots of people we knew. Many were crying. People had come from the hospital, old people. It was pandemonium. It was very frightening. It was very cold and dark. They were beating the rabbi from our town and they made him jump on the Torahs which they fetched from the synagogue.
>
> We were there for what seemed like an awful long time and then we were taken to a theatre. We were told to sit down, men at the front by the stage and women and children at the back. We were there, I think, from daybreak. During all this time they called up men onto the stage and made them perform like animals. They had to jump over tables, over chairs. All kinds of things to make them feel silly, and if they couldn't do it they beat them. We were sitting there like at a performance. The women and children were sent home in the early afternoon. We hadn't had anything to eat or drink. My father came home long after supper, at about 9 o'clock. He was over sixty so they had released him. The men under sixty all went to Dachau. We were lucky because we were together again.

In every town, small or large, it was the same. Fourteen-year-old Ester Friedman lived in Vienna.

> My father had left early to go to the American embassy – one of many, many times – to see if there would be a possibility to get a visa to go to the States and leave Vienna. We were anxious, the atmosphere up and down the road was electric; we did not know why but a feeling of fear pervaded the air. I stood by the window – no sight of my father – but then it happened: a crowd of brown-clad SA men, with the fearful swastika arm band on their sleeves, marched down the road. I leant out further. They entered the old people's home of the Jewish community. The windows opened and out flew books. The doors opened and out came the old people, being pushed and pulled by their beards as they could not walk quickly enough for the hordes of brown youths. When they had congregated in a heap of old decrepit flesh, they were made to

watch their precious prayer books burn. And I watched. Buckets were brought and the ashes had to be shovelled by the old men and women. The youths and the crowds laughed at the sight. Water was brought and brushes and rags, and the old people were made to kneel and scrub the pavement. Beards were pulled until blood flowed, old women fainted – or died – I don't know. And I saw. I smelled smoke. I turned my head and looked up the road. Our synagogue was burning – bright and high the flames roared – but I heard no fire engines.

Late, late, my father came home – an old broken man, because of what he had seen and could do nothing about. He did not look Jewish and got away.

Once the most tolerant of cities, Berlin had its share of violence and wanton destruction. Leslie Brent, who was enjoying education of a sort in a Jewish orphanage, believed that he escaped lightly:

A mob stormed the orphanage and broke through the gates. There was a great *mêlée* with some of the older boys trying to keep the gate intact. Eventually it was broken into and the older boys just melted into the crowd and didn't come to any harm. A good friend of mine, Fred, and I were terrified and we rushed up into the highest part of the building, which was the loft under the roof, and hid amongst the rafters there until the whole thing was over. I learnt afterwards that the mob had ransacked the basement and the ground floor including the orphanage synagogue and were just moving up a rather grand staircase when a teacher (Heinz Nadel) met them with a small boy in his arms and said to them very calmly: 'This is an orphanage, we look after children here. Would you please leave the building.' And they did. One of those miracles.

After the crowd had gone we reassembled and had strawberries and cream in the garden, so strawberries and cream have always had a rather special significance for me, as you can imagine.

Even out-of-the-way places did not escape the attention of the stormtroopers, as Philip Urbach can testify:

When we came back that night from Leipzig, the police were waiting for us at home in the village and took us into what they called protective custody – the whole family – which meant in fact the local prison, in a cell – my first experience of prison. They kept us there just for twenty-four hours. Not very long. But on returning home, the police called again, this time accompanied by the Gestapo, or the SA or whatever, I forget now. And my father was taken away into a concentration camp.

After *Kristallnacht*, families were without a breadwinner. Youngsters had to make their own way, scraping a living as best they could. Clive Milton lived in Hanover:

My father was taken to a concentration camp and came out just before Christmas. The business I was working for was closed – the windows were smashed and I don't know what happened to the boss, whether he was picked up or went into hiding. I found a job in an electrical business – installing and maintaining radios and other appliances. A shop owned by a German guy. He knew I was Jewish. He apologised for wearing an LISDAP badge, but he had to. As far as he was concerned I was as good as he.

There was a young girl employed there too. One day she said: 'I have a terrible itch down here – could you scratch it for me?' In those days sex was sex, but played a lesser part in our lives. So I shrank back. Five or ten minutes later she said: 'It's just as well you didn't do that. My boyfriend is in the Gestapo and if you had done it I would have made sure he picked you up.'

Even for the youngest the chances of an education were remote. Many children shared the experience of Dorothy Sim who watched the destruction of her school in Hamburg:

Then came the morning I arrived at school to find men removing and destroying all they could lay their hands on. A lorry stood by to receive all the furniture that could be loaded on board. A man said to me: 'You'd better go home. It will be a long time before you're back here again.'

Reaction in Germany and abroad to *Kristallnacht* was not quite what the Nazis had hoped for. Incredulity that a supposedly civilised people could indulge in such atrocities was underscored by amazement that a political force which prided itself on economic efficiency should go in for so much wanton destruction of property. In the eyes of the world, the Nazis had proved to be savage and stupid, which was hardly the image they cultivated. The lesson was not lost on them. Henceforth, the vendetta against the Jews was carried out with greater discretion – behind closed doors and barbed wire fences.

The revulsion caused by *Kristallnacht* and the subsequent rounding up of 30,000 Jews for the concentration camps, the demonstrable failure of appeasement and the attack of conscience over the dismemberment of Czechoslovakia, all combined to swing public opinion in favour of giving more help to refugees though not to allow unrestricted immigration. Reporting on the rush of applications to the Home Office (over 1000 a day), the new Home Secretary, Sir Samuel Hoare, who was a Quaker and more sympathetic to refugees than his predecessors, told his cabinet colleagues that even Jewish representatives were 'averse to allowing very large numbers . . . to enter this country . . . since they were afraid of anti-Jewish agitation'.

For the same reason there was a reluctance to publish the number of Jews arriving since 'any number would be attacked from both sides as being too big or too little'.

But the trouble about doing good by stealth was that it failed to show the government in a creditable light at home or abroad. In particular, ministers were sensitive to criticism from the United States, where it was felt that Britain was trying to skirt round the problems that her faith in Nazi appeasement had helped to create.

So a grand gesture was called for, an act that was symbolic of Britain's resolve to be on the side of the righteous. A rescue plan for children in distress fitted the bill admirably. That such a plan was desperately needed was clear from the heartrending stories that filled the newspapers. From mid-1938 the *Jewish Chronicle* ran a whole section of small ads placed by British friends or relatives of distressed German and Austrian families.

> Please help me to bring out of Berlin two children (boy and girl – 10 years, best family) – very urgent case – RK, 96 Lordship Park, N16.

> Which family would like to take over Jewish boy, 15 years, from first-class orthodox Viennese family and give him the chance to be taught a trade? (Father was in the jewellery trade, now penniless). Very urgent. Pocket money and clothes will be provided. Communicate with J. U., 181 Commercial Road, London E1.

> Which family would give a home to two Viennese children, girls, aged 14, 10 years, very well educated, speak English and French?

Photographs and references willingly sent. Write to Ulman, 31 Dunstan Road, Golders Green, London NW11.

The lead for action at government level was taken in The Netherlands where, on 11 November, a deputation from the Dutch Refugees Committee called on the prime minister to allow temporary residence to an unlimited number of German and Austrian children. The idea was accepted in principle, on condition that the Committee deposited 100,000 guilders as evidence that the children could be supported. The money was lodged on 15 November, the day on which Jewish representatives of the CBF, led by Viscount Samuel, first raised the issue with the British government. Chamberlain was urged to allow into Britain an unspecified number of youngsters up to the age of seventeen. Samuel offered a collective guarantee that no public funds would be spent on these children and that all of them would eventually re-emigrate.

Doubtless anticipating that if he accepted too readily he would be storing up more trouble for Palestine – the only likely second stop for the young emigrants – Chamberlain adopted 'a rather negative tone' for his response. But the following day at a cabinet meeting he shifted his ground. When the Foreign Secretary, Lord Halifax, voiced his concern over the shift in American opinion and called for 'a lead which would force the United States in turn to take some positive action', Chamberlain suggested that Britain might act as a 'temporary refuge' for those fleeing Nazi oppression. The Home Secretary was asked to confer with his senior colleagues to draft a statement on government action 'to deal with the Jewish problem'.

It did not take long to decide on the impracticability of an open door policy, but there seemed to be room for compromise on an offer to make special provision for young people. On the morning of 21 November, just a few hours before a critical House of Commons debate on refugee policy, Hoare welcomed a deputation led by Sir Wyndham Deedes. Among the ideas discussed was the formation of a new organisation, working alongside the Children's Inter-Aid Committee, to cope with the rush of applications that would inevitably follow a relaxation of the immigration laws. This organisation was to be called the Movement for the Care of Children from Germany, soon to be abbreviated to the Refugee

Children's Movement. Its originators were Norman Bentwich and his wife Mami, a doughty campaigner for social reform and a leading light of the London County Council. Both were members of Deedes's deputation, along with representatives from the Society of Friends.

It is generally assumed that at this meeting a top limit was suggested for the number of children to be admitted. But there is no evidence for this and, indeed, in the parliamentary debate later in the day, Sir Samuel Hoare declared his opposition 'to anything in the nature of a quota'. Nonetheless, the government was now prepared 'to facilitate entry for all child refugees whose maintenance could be guaranteed either through their own funds or by other individuals'. To ease the bureaucratic process a special travel document, to be issued in London for each child, removed the need for passports or visas.

As to the magic figure of 10,000, it first crops up in an offer from the Jewish community in Palestine to adopt that number of German children, an offer which was rejected by the government who were now determined to restrict Jewish emigration to Palestine to 75,000 over five years. The 10,000 target was subsequently taken over by the CBF, and accepted by the government as the maximum which could be supported by voluntary effort. But outside this general understanding no upper limit was ever set, and it was unduly assumed that re-emigration to Commonwealth countries would hold down the total supported within Britain and allow for many more than 10,000 to be saved.

By way of a postscript, attempts in the United States to emulate the British with a bill to admit 20,000 European children did not get beyond a congressional committee. One of the arguments raised against the proposal held that accepting children without their parents was contrary to the laws of God.

3

The First Transports

'*My mother was very tearful but my father put on a stiff upper lip. To me it all seemed very bewildering. It is hard to describe my feelings. I was low but not utterly desolate because I realised that all this was being done for my good. I was aware of the fact that some great act of kindness had been extended to me. Certainly I had no idea that I would not go back again or that my family would die.*'

In late November 1938, less than a week after child refugees were given special status, Norman Bentwich was in Amsterdam talking with the Dutch Refugees Committee. It was a sensible move.

Of all the refugee bodies, the Dutch were best equipped to manage the first stage of the migration, the transfer to friendly territory. They were on the border closest to the heavily populated industrial Ruhr and there were extensive rail links between the two countries. In any case, hopes of establishing an alternative route through France had foundered on political vacillation (though a group led by the Rothschild and Gunzburg families were urging the French government to match the British commitment to child refugees), and the only other possibility, of sending children out from one of the German ports, was thought to depend too heavily on Nazi good will.

In the event, several *Kindertransporte*, including one of the earliest, did leave by boat from Hamburg, but the numbers were small, the children taking up spare berths in one or other of the trans-Atlantic liners calling at Southampton. Refugee ships were not a practical proposition. The Nazis were as keen as ever to get rid of their Jewish citizens but after *Kristallnacht* they were more sensitive to public awareness of how they went about it. A refugee ship could not easily disguise its function; a refugee ship crowded with children was liable to become a propaganda coup for the Jews. Far better that the refugees should go by rail. The time and place of departure could be more easily suited to the nefarious purposes of the German authorities.

If the Dutch offered the least troublesome route out of Germany, they also had the advantage of a competent welfare organisation used to dealing with young refugees, including those who took their chances by outrunning the border guards. The downside was the fear that even the most dedicated social workers were liable to be overwhelmed by the sheer magnitude of their task. There were reports of unaccompanied children of all ages massing at the border crossings. Just how many were waiting to come over was a matter of wild speculation, but in London 5000 was accepted as a not unrealistic estimate. Bentwich was not alone in believing that the first *Kindertransport* would consist of children lately arrived in the Netherlands but with nowhere to live.

In fact, the position was not as desperate as rumour suggested. Bentwich was told that over the previous month 600 child refugees had been admitted and, though another 800 were expected by the end of the year, there was hostel accommodation ready for all of these and more. Although the Dutch government had yet to pronounce on the limit of its hospitality, the refugee organisations assumed that at least 2000 could be accommodated without difficulty and up to 5000 with difficulty. For the moment, the only children the Dutch were keen to pass on were those who were either stateless or not of German nationality – about a dozen in all.

Bentwich returned to London with a promise of cooperation from his Dutch colleagues, the backing of Prime Minister Colijn for his country to act as a transit agency, and a polite request to the Foreign Office to give formal notification to the Dutch government of plans to help child refugees. So far, all they knew of the British initiative was what they had heard from Bentwich or read in reports circulated by the CBF. It was almost as if the Foreign Office was trying to distance itself from government policy.

Having decided on the main route for the *Kindertransport* – by train to the Hook of Holland and boat to Harwich – the next priority was to choose the passengers. Bentwich brought back with him from the Netherlands a list of urgent cases, including orphanages in Hamburg and Breslau which were threatened with closure, but their appeals would go unanswered until there was direct talk with the German authorities and with the Jewish organisations in Berlin and Vienna. The delegate chosen to negotiate the ground rules was Dennis Cohen, who divided his life between publishing and the Jewish Refugees Committee. He and his wife left for Berlin on 28 November.

They found that the capital retained a vestige of its once proud reputation for enlightenment. Jews still had some freedom of movement and the emigration section of the *Reichsvertretung* was able to make effective representation on behalf of Jews who wanted to leave the country. The same could be said of the *Paulusbund*, which spoke for Christians of Jewish extraction. It was expected that the Nazi authorities would approve of the *Kindertransporte* as long as the travel arrangements could be handled discreetly and at no cost to the state. There would be problems – lost documents, petty objections to this or that name on a list, last minute delays and cancellations – but the politics of hate were manageable; just about.

Inevitably, selection for the first *Kindertransport* was haphazard, often depending on knowing the right people or being in the right place at the right time. Half the 200 or so children were from a Berlin orphanage destroyed on *Kristallnacht*. Another forty were children of Polish descent who were threatened with deportation. The rest were mainly youngsters whose parents were in concentration camps or who were themselves liable to arrest and internment. All were urgent cases, but urgent cases were two a penny. Priority went to those in the know and in luck.

Within three days of Dennis Cohen arriving in Berlin, refugee children were gathering at the main station. The hours before departure were for deciding on the practicalities of travelling lightly – what to wear and what clothing to pack, what childhood treasures to take along (there was a warning that anything of resale value, like jewellery and cameras, were liable to be confiscated), what to eat on the train. Each child was allowed one suitcase and ten Reichsmarks. Luggage sent on ahead was invariably lost.

New clothing caused much vexation for parents who often had eccentric images of the well-dressed English. Tweeds were much in demand for boys who were togged up to look like young versions of Sherlock Holmes.

> 'My mother bought me an outfit which marked me as a complete foreigner as soon as I arrived in England,' Richard Grunberger recalls. 'I had a pleated jacket and tight-fitting trousers which I soon came to know as plus fours. But though I felt strange I didn't worry too much about it at the time. I was too concerned about the shop owner. He had a badge on his lapel which showed that he was a long serving Nazi. I was told that the shop had recently been Aryanised.'

The bolder parents set their imaginations to work on ways to get round the restrictions on taking out anything of value. A few boys carried new Leica cameras, which they hoped to sell in England, but others were more subtle. It was not entirely to support his musical talent that Leslie Brent's mother gave him a violin that had been bequeathed to her. Stringed instruments held their worth and could fetch good prices.

Yoash Kahn was nervous that someone would show an interest in the contents of his sponge bag:

> I had been given a medallion – the sort you wear on a chain round your neck. It had my initials on one side and some Hebrew letters on the other. My parents were determined that I should take it with me, so one of them got a tin of Nivea cream, peeled off the silver paper covering very carefully, buried the medallion in the cream and then resealed the tin. Of course, I was scared out of my wits the whole journey. I'm the sort of person who never takes anything through customs illegally because I just know that my face will give me away. But somehow I managed to get away with this. I remember, I couldn't quite believe it, and for days after arriving in London I kept the medallion in the Nivea, checking every now and then that it was still there.

Most parents played by the rules. The consequences of being found out were too grim to contemplate. Told not to take any money, Henry Toch left with three Pfennigs in his pocket: 'My first contact with the English was begging for a penny to send a card home.'

The constant admonition from parents was to be polite to the SS guards. Sometimes it paid off. When Felix Huttner was asked by a tight-lipped guard: 'Where are you going?' he replied, almost apologetically: 'To England.' The frown turned to a smile. 'Oh, you'll enjoy it there. I wish I was going.'

Other parents were all for braving it out. The parting words to Nina Liebermann were shouted by her mother across a crowded platform: 'And if they ask for your gold earrings at the frontier, just take them off and throw them out of the window!'

As the time came for leaving, parents and children suffered conflicting emotions – sadness, excitement, fear, relief. Dorothy Sim practised her English:

> All I succeeded in learning was 'I want to go to the WC,' which my parents and I in our ignorance pronounced 'VK' and 'I have a handkerchief in my pocket.' Among my clothes they packed a box full of precious family photographs, my own set of cutlery and a toilet case with cloth and soap. My father had taken the toilet case with him when he fought in the First World War. He had won the Iron Cross.
>
> I recall arriving at the railway station in Hamburg. There were two stone lions guarding the entrance. I was carrying my toy dog Droll and I had my leather shoulder bag on. I dropped Droll underneath the train and a man had to climb down and rescue him. I had a peach and a pear in my shoulder bag. We children boarded the train to get our places. Then I was sent off again to say farewell to my mother and father. I can see them to this day. They were standing in a corridor behind a barrier. I said my goodbyes and then walked back up the long corridor away from them and into the train.

Leslie Brent was seen off by his parents and his sister:

> My mother was very tearful but my father put on a stiff upper lip. To me it all seemed very bewildering. It is hard to describe my feelings. I was low but not utterly desolate because I realised that all this was being done for my good. I was aware of the fact that some great act of kindness had been extended to me. Certainly I had no idea that I would not go back again or that my family would die. That is something I couldn't have foreseen and I don't think anyone did.

It was the same feeling of perplexity for Hans Groschler, now Herbert Gale. With his younger brother, he travelled from his home town in Friesland to Berlin.

> Our father took us; Mother preferred not to come. I remember that I did not find it too distressing because I had been moving around the country for the past two or three years, from one Jewish school to another. Father dropped us off at the collecting point and he stayed in a hotel. The next morning when we went to the authorities to collect our papers, I was beginning to feel apprehensive and sad. On the second morning my father took us to the train. We said our goodbyes and promised to write often. I was very bewildered and I could not fully understand what was going on.

Celia Lee came from Hamburg to Britain. She was recovering from appendicitis when she was told she had been accepted for the first *Kindertransport*. Soon after the war, when she was still a teenager, she wrote about her experiences:

> For my twelve years I was hearing and learning too much lately. The hospital was a Jewish one. Half the male doctors had been sent to the concentration camp. Earlier Mummy had whispered to me that Daddy was in hiding. It did not make sense. Dad was no criminal.
>
> Nurse was helping me get dressed so that Daddy would not have to wait for me. When he came in I cried out and hugged him ever so tightly. Secretly I had been worried, but seeing him reassured me that things were not too bad. When I had finished telling him all the news I had been saving, he held me gently and said, 'How would you like to go to Holland or England, chatterbox?' I stared at him. 'Do you mean it? Is Max coming too? Why are we going? Are you and Mummy coming too?'
>
> My father looked at me gravely. 'You are old enough to understand. A lot has happened while you have been in hospital. Things aren't the same for Jewish people. It would be safer for you and Max to go to another country. Mummy and I will follow later, if we can.'
>
> 'Let's go to England, then.' I had made up my mind, thinking of the two years English I had learned at school. And my brother Max would be coming; that meant a lot to me.
>
> That was on the Sunday. On Thursday we left for England. The days between flowed by. There was shopping to be done and papers to be put in order. A big red 'J' was stamped on the front of my

passport. I was so excited, I did not notice the tired and strained expressions on my parents' faces.

When we said goodbye, I did not burst into tears. I was just so sure in my own mind that we would see one another again soon. Mummy gave me a golden necklace and Daddy gave me a lucky money piece to hang on the necklace. For the first time that week I came out of the haze I had been living in. I had a premonition that things were more serious than I had taken them to be.

The Berlin–Hamburg *Kindertransport* of 1 December was a masterstroke of improvisation. The entire exercise had been mounted in little more than a week and, though there were a huge number of disappointed families who failed to get places, there was the promise of more *Kindertransporte* to come.

★   ★   ★

The news from Vienna was less encouraging. Unlike in Berlin, the Jewish community was in total disarray. The German takeover of the country had brought the decimation of the *Kultusgemeinde*, with leading officials arrested, files impounded and buildings occupied. The Society of Friends had held on to its base, so too had *Youth Aliyah*, but no one working on behalf of refugees had direct contact with the senior members of the Nazi administration.

On 28 November 1938, Josef Loewenberg, leader of the Jewish community in Vienna, sent an urgent appeal to London. He reckoned there were some 35,000 young people who qualified for the British immigration scheme. Whether the Nazi authorities would cooperate was another matter. He asked for a representative to be sent to Vienna, 'to be of assistance to us in carrying through our plans'. This could be no ordinary ambassador. Whoever went had to have the strength of purpose to get through to Adolf Eichmann, not the easiest bureaucrat to pin down, particularly for a Jew.

Back in Amsterdam for more talks, Norman Bentwich met the ideal candidate. Gertrude Wijsmüller-Meijer was the wife of a banker, a determined and energetic lady who devoted all her formidable organising skills to the refugee movement. She was non-Jewish and spoke good German, but she knew little of Vienna and had no contacts who could help her scale the hierarchy of the

Austrian administration. Undeterred, she took an evening flight to Berlin on 2 December and flew on to Vienna the following day.

What happened next, she described in a testimony for the Eichmann trial in August 1960.

> I arrived in Vienna Saturday midday. I had a hotel reservation at the Ring, in the Hotel Bristol. I immediately made my way to the Jewish quarter to seek the *Kultusgemeinde*. This quarter was enclosed by ropes as the Jews were not allowed outside, not even to cross the street.
>
> On my way to the Palestine office, I was stopped and taken to a police station immediately next to the *Kultusgemeinde*, on the assumption that I was Jewish. I knocked on my cell door to explain that I was not Jewish. Eventually, when my cell door was opened, I declared that after my release I would inform all the newspapers in the world how Aryans were treated in Vienna. The mistake was greatly regretted and I was asked what could be done for me. I asked for an appointment with Eichmann. I was released with the assurance that I would receive notification as soon as arrangements had been made.

Mrs Wijsmüller saw Eichmann at his headquarters at 9.30 on 5 December.

> I was conducted into a huge room; there was a platform at the end of the room. Eichmann sat there. Next to him, a very bright lamp. I approached him with my hand outstretched. 'Doctor, I am Mrs Wijsmüller and I would like to speak to you.'
>
> Whereupon he yelled at me, 'We are not accustomed to speaking with women.'
>
> 'What a shame. As you know, I am married and my husband works, so you'll have to put up with me. May I sit down?'
>
> Eichmann was so astonished that I did not tremble before him, as he expected, that he allowed me to sit down. I then explained to him that the English government in London had given permission for 10,000 children to come to England. I had been requested to discuss with him how this could be arranged.
>
> 'Have you got a letter from the English government?'
>
> 'No.'
>
> 'I would like to see your hands. Now go a little further. Remove your shoes. Lift your skirt a bit higher.' Then he said: 'So purely Aryan and so mad.'
>
> I was permitted to sit down again. Then he rang the bell to bring

in the Jew Friedmann. He asked Mr Friedmann: 'Do you know Mrs Wijsmüller?'

'No.'

'Do you know Mr Friedmann?'

'No.'

Then Eichmann turned again to Mr Friedmann. 'Now we'll make the joke of a lifetime. This woman does not have a letter from the English government which confirms her claim that she is permitted to bring children into the country. We will put together a transport of 600 children and they must cross the frontier on Saturday (Shabbat!) midday, then Mrs Wijsmüller can show how she will bring the children into the country.'

I thanked him and told him I hoped I would see him again. Should he visit Amsterdam he should come to visit me as I would try and visit him, if I returned to Vienna.

Her next move was to telephone London, where the news that within the week 600 children would be on their way was received with some consternation. It was agreed that 100 of them would stay in Holland, the rest would be brought over in parties of 100–150.

In Vienna, the message quickly went out. One of those who picked up the signal was Fred Dunston, then Fritz Deutsch, a twenty-one-year-old former scout leader working with the *Youth Aliyah* organisation in Vienna:

At the beginning of December 1939 the *Palestina Amt* in Vienna received an official message from the *Kultusgemeinde*, who had received Eichmann's authority and permission to organise the children's transports. We were asked to nominate 100 children, who were eligible and able to travel on the first transport to England, which was to leave within a few days. Together with the names we were to supply within 24 hours a lengthy questionnaire, filled in and signed by a parent, a valid passport, 2 photos, and a medical certificate. If we could not manage this, the *Kultusgemeinde* would fill the places reserved for us from their own lists. What was to be done? At this moment my scouting experience proved invaluable and I set our well tried 'alarm system' into motion. I contacted two of my former Patrol leaders, who in turn got eight more of their former scouts and turned up with them and their bicycles very quickly. The office had in the meantime prepared lists of names and addresses sorted out by districts and the boys went on their way to contact the people concerned. Within an hour there was a long queue of children with their parents waiting to be interviewed. By working all through the night we managed to get everything ready and our allocation was fully taken up. It was a thrilling and exhilarating experience.

The first *Kindertransport* out of Vienna left on 11 December, just an hour or two ahead of the deadline set by Eichmann.

One of the few children to be eventually reunited with her family was Gerta Jassem, though by then, six years on, she was a married woman. She said her goodbyes in April 1938 at the Westbahnhof in Vienna.

> My father placed the single suitcase on to the overhead rack of the compartment and then as it was very crowded had to step down to the platform. We children crowded round the window to receive uncertain last-minute instructions. Nothing new or really important was said. The desperate hopelessness of the people left behind was not really grasped by us.

One of Gerta's last memories of parting was her mother asking her what food she wanted:

> I assumed she meant as a sort of farewell meal, so I chose my favourite dish, *Wiener Schnitzel*, and I was so disappointed when I opened a brown paper bag and found instead meat patties on a roll.

Another point of issue between Gerta and her mother was the bright idea of hollowing out the heels of her daughter's walking boots.

> She hid my watch, a gold bracelet and a few gold coins. This made me very conscious of my feet as I tried to walk nonchalantly in laced-up boots while feeling scared that someone would notice.

The Vienna *Kindertransport* stopped at Cologne to pick up a small group of boys in their mid-teens. Among them was Ernest Jacob:

> Most of us knew each other. There was an exception, a chap by the name of Meyer who none of us had ever heard of. He looked Jewish and about our age though he could have been older. He stayed with us for the whole journey and when we were in England,

but he never made friends and had nothing in common with us. Later he went to Canada and was caught spying. It turned out that he had been planted on our transport.

There was some comfort in journeying by train. It was a closed world in which the inhabitants, though unwilling companions, could take strength from knowing that they were all part of the same mad plot. Gerta Jassem shared a compartment with seven other girls and boys aged between six and thirteen, all strangers to each other.

We ate our sandwiches, exchanged stories, told jokes. The monotonous rhythm of the train made us sleepy. I remember putting my head on my arms and leaning forward on to the folded table in front of my seat. The next girl rested on my back and this started a sort of chain reaction of bodies. We woke up whenever the train stopped, and when we were at a station we got out for a while. Then there was lots of shouting from one track to another before we started again. We had no idea where we were, though we thought we had crossed from Austria into Germany. It was next morning before one of the supervisors came to tell us that we were near the Dutch border.

This was the moment when regrets at parting from family and friends were suppressed by the fear of being sent back.

Two uniformed, brown-booted Germans, one wearing the SS insignia, entered our compartment. They pointed at the suitcases they wanted opened. They never uttered a word and nor did we. We simply watched and tried to look unconcerned as they searched the cases. There was a rumour that if just one of the group was discovered smuggling money or jewellery the whole transport would be sent back. Finally, they left the train and we saw them standing in groups on the platform.

It was only when the train started moving that we began to relax. As we gathered speed, someone shouted: 'Look, we're in no-man's-land!' Somehow, the countryside did look different; less ordered, perhaps, or maybe there were just more houses. Anyway, what did it matter? We jumped about, cheered and sang. We opened the windows wide and held out our handkerchiefs, scarves, jackets to wave at the deserted fields.

Of those who had crossed the border a few days earlier on the Berlin–Hamburg *Kindertransport*, Nina Liebermann and her sister were made more nervous of the SS guards by the adult passengers who were sharing their compartment. Everyone was so much on edge, the girls were sure they were not alone in having something to hide.

> We stopped for customs inspection on the German side. I tried to look unconcerned as the cases were searched. I was certain I would lose my earrings. Jews were not allowed to take gold or silver in any form out of the country. But they left us alone. Suddenly the train started to move, first slowly, then gathering speed for a short way before stopping again. Two men in uniform appeared in our compartment. I was sure they had come back for my earrings. But how could that be? It dawned on me that they were Dutch border guards. They went over to a conservatively-dressed passenger in a corner seat and asked him to go with them. He did not come back. We heard later that a German spy had been caught.

Johnny Blunt was less fortunate in his encounter with German customs.

> I was very proud of my stamp collection which I kept in my rucksack. An SA man found it and put it on the seat beside me while he started searching someone else. When his back was turned I took the stamp album and sat on it. He must have realised because he turned and gave me a smack across the face. He took the stamp album and told me: 'You can start another collection when you're in England.'

The tension was increased by the sight of German troops massed along the Dutch frontier.

> I remember the train standing for a long, long time at the border,' remembers Kurt Weinburg. 'I watched from the window as German soldiers marched up and down. They were nothing to do with us; they were just drilling. But there was a tremendous sense of relief when we got into the Dutch station.

The contrast between the sullen dismissal by the Nazi guards and the welcome from the Dutch refugee workers could not have been greater. All along the platform were smiling women with trolleys loaded with food. They handed out cakes and sandwiches and chocolate ('which had a bitter flavour') and offered lemonade drinks ('the best lemonade any of us had ever tasted'). If there was time in hand or the train was held up, the children were treated to huge meals of meat and beans. ('It was as if we had never eaten before.') Presents and games added to the party atmosphere. Years on, many a *Kindertransport* girl would not be parted from the rag doll pressed into her arms by a total stranger on a Dutch railway station.

The older boys had their own way of celebrating. 'We lads from Cologne had a couple of bottles of egg flip,' admits Ernest Jacob. 'I can't tell you how drunk we were.'

The frantic activity in Berlin and Vienna and at the Dutch border to keep up the flow of child refugees was matched in London by efforts to make the journey worthwhile. Before much else was achieved, clearly there had to be some sort of accommodation between the newly-formed Movement for the Care of Children from Germany and the older established Children's Inter-Aid Committee. In principle, they had everything to gain by joining forces, but there was an underlying hostility at Inter-Aid to what some supporters regarded as a Jewish takeover of a non-denominational body. This was reflected in the lengthy discussions to find a name for the cooperative venture that accounted for all sensitivities. Eventually, a unanimous blessing was given The World Movement for the Rescue of Children from Germany; British Inter-Aid Committee, a forbidding and unmemorable title which was impossible to take seriously.

Even in its shortened form the Movement for the Care of Children from Germany failed to live up to the emotional impact of Save the Children, one of the original sponsors of the Movement, whose offices they shared in the early days. It was not until March 1939 that all previous attempts at a suitable epithet were cast aside in favour of the Refugee Children's Movement, or, more commonly, the RCM, the name we will now stick to even when referring to events preceding its inauguration.

On 29 November, the RCM moved to 69 Great Russell Street, where there was office space for the extra staff needed to handle the huge volume of correspondence.

Thousands of letters from all parts of Germany and Austria were received . . . letters begging for help, enclosing photographs and particulars. Many were so touchingly written that it required a hard heart to consign them to files and indexes; yet, how were we to know which children to choose since we could not take all? We obviously could not adopt the principle of 'first write, first come', and how were we to be sure that all the details in the letters were absolutely correct?

Thus the plea of mitigation contained in the RCM's first annual report for the piles of correspondence left unanswered or returned to Germany. But allowing for the bureaucratic nicety (did it really matter if all the details were not 'absolutely correct'?), the RCM was right in believing that operations had to be directed from Berlin and Vienna. However imperfect, the scheme depended on the authority of those in the front line. To have started an indiscriminate selection of children from London would have been fatal.

The ground rule was for lists of names with photographs and health certificates to be sent over to the RCM, who would then go to the Home Office for travel permits. In theory, nothing could have been simpler, but with the vagaries of the European airmail, the irresistible urge of the German police to demand last-minute changes, and the understandable dithering of families trying to come to terms with an indefinite parting, delays and mistakes were inevitable.

The Home Office signalled a willingness to cooperate, as far as circumstances would allow. On the credit side, the waiving of restrictions imposed on adult refugees enabled the Home Office to reduce the formalities of immigration to a relatively simple travel document. Not even passports were needed, though many did bring this last record of German citizenship. The hold-up came with the processing of the entry permits. The aliens department of the Home Office, the first stopping-off point for *Kindertransport* applications, was woefully understaffed. By the end of 1938 there were some 10,000 files waiting for attention, while those who were supposed to be clearing the backlog spent most of their time answering the telephone to callers pleading for immediate action to save friends and relatives. More civil servants were drafted in late January when the aliens department moved to larger offices, but this development barely kept pace with the increased demand for visas.

Even when applications had cleared the aliens department, they had to go to records for the issue of permits and from thence to passport control office for stamping before being posted back to Germany.

Colin Coote, a leader writer on *The Times*, who was soon to adopt a *Kindertransport* boy, wrote to Lord Winterton at the Foreign Office claiming that allegations of red tape were too numerous to overlook. Winterton replied unconvincingly that delays were all the fault of the Germans. But the refugee movement was not entirely free from blame. Reading between the lines of RCM reports suggests that Home Office tardiness was matched by RCM muddle.

Volunteer workers were strong on enthusiasm but weak on experience. This would not have mattered quite so much if there had been strong leadership. But those at the top like Norman Bentwich and Wyndham Deedes did not see themselves as executive officers, while Mami Bentwich who took on the role of organising secretary was easily diverted by competing responsibilities. Through to the spring of 1939 the chief authority seems to have rested with a Major Langdon, whose military style, deriving from the 'do as I tell you' school of management, was ill-suited to what was essentially a cooperative venture. Later problems with authoritarian, even anti-Semitic, wardens of hostels and training camps can be traced back to appointments made at this time.

A powerful compensating factor was the recruitment of two outstanding volunteer workers, both idiosyncratic personalities who were used to having things their own way. Lola Hahn-Warburg was the daughter of the Hamburg banker Max Warburg, wife to Berlin industrialist Rudo Hahn, and sister-in-law of the educationalist Kurt Hahn of Gordonstoun fame. With her husband and two children, she came to Britain in September 1938 after a tip-off that she was on a Nazi blacklist of outspoken Zionists. Two months later she was part of the Samuel delegation to the Home Office to urge government support for the *Kindertransporte*. It was not a role that she welcomed. Trying to make a home with what little her family had managed to bring out, and still struggling with a language which to her dying day she delivered with unmistakable Teutonic precision, she had much else to occupy her. But Norman Bentwich, who knew of her active participation in the emigration of young people from Germany, both on behalf of the *Reichsvertre-*

tung and of *Youth Aliyah*, pressed her to go along as a first-hand witness to the suffering of Jewish children under Nazi rule. After that it was a short step to the cramped office at the RCM, where Lola Hahn-Warburg became the reigning expert on children who were at odds with their foster parents or teachers or employers, or simply with themselves. Bearing in mind that at least one in ten of those who came over on the *Kindertransporte* ended up with psychological or physical disabilities, it was quite a responsibility to take on.

The second gifted amateur to strengthen the backbone of the RCM was Elaine Blond. The youngest daughter of Michael Marks of Marks and Spencer, she was wealthy, talented and frustrated by inactivity.

> It was at dinner with (brother) Simon and his wife Miriam when I first heard about the RCM. I knew of its existence, of course. Anyone who read the *Jewish Chronicle* had to be aware of the story. What came as a surprise was the evident lack of planning for such a mammoth enterprise. 'Someone ought to do something,' I said. 'You're right,' said Simon. 'Why don't *you* do something?'

And that was how Elaine Blond became involved, initially as a fund raiser but soon as treasurer of the RCM. She and Lola Hahn-Warburg made a strong partnership. Both were self-willed women, confident in their abilities and their right to lead, who could get things done by dint of perseverance, cajolery and a hint of retribution for those foolish enough to resist their demands.

With the gap between expenditure and income growing by the day, Elaine was an early advocate of a campaign to prise money out of the government. But whenever the subject was raised, in or out of Parliament, it was made clear to the RCM and to the other refugee bodies that they were on their own. However persuasive their arguments for a relaxation of the purse strings, they always came up against the irrefutable – the guarantee offered five years earlier by Otto Schiff that no Jewish refugee would become a charge on public funds. It was a handy get-out for Foreign Office ministers who argued that if Britain acted unilaterally in subsidising refugees, Germany would compel more Jews to emigrate. This proved to be a nonsense. The Germans needed no encouragement to tighten the screw, as even the Foreign Office had soon to admit. But by then, the Central British Fund, the chief provider for the *Kindertransporte*, was close to insolvency.

The strategy for dealing with the financial crisis was to call for volunteers who would be willing to act as foster parents at their own expense or with the help of a small allowance, and for guarantors who, linking up with relatives or friends in Germany, could nominate particular children for short-term adoption. The campaign was to get underway on 25 November, when Lord Samuel delivered an emotional radio appeal to the British public to open their homes to refugee children. The response was encouraging. Of the offers that came in, at least 500 were worth following up. But it took time to inspect accommodation and to assess evidence of a good character. By early December the work had hardly begun.

In any case, there were few offers of help which extended to the older children. Most potential foster parents were fixed on the idea of starting at the nursery level, but the early transports contained a high proportion of teenagers up to the age of sixteen who had been threatened with imprisonment, or who had actually been detained and released only on condition that they left the country.

Desperately searching for temporary homes for their young guests, the RCM hit on the idea of taking over two holiday camps: one at Dovercourt, a small seaside resort just along the coast from Harwich, the other further away at Pakefield, near Lowestoft. It must have seemed an ideal solution. Out of season the camps were unoccupied and cheap to rent.

The chalets, made to look like miniature bungalows, were purpose-built to keep a respectable distance between teenage boys and girls; all the essentials of mass catering were on hand; and the owners had allowed plenty of space for recreation. There was just one problem. The camps were designed for summer living. The RCM proposed reopening them in December, at the beginning of what was proving to be one of the coldest winters on record.

Preparations were still a long way from completion when the first *Kindertransport* was filing on board the *De Praag*, docked at the Hook of Holland. For those brought up in central Germany it was likely to be their first encounter with the sea. The experience was not encouraging. The crossing from the Hook to Harwich can be rough at any time of year, but in the winter of 1938 it was like riding a roller coaster.

Nina Liebermann was lucky enough to be a good sailor. Not so her younger sister, Ella:

> She became violently seasick and for the next couple of hours I had to hold her head over the railing, all the while bathing her face with eau de cologne. (To this day, the very smell of it makes my sister feel ill.) When, at last, her bouts of seasickness subsided, I sank down exhausted onto our luggage in the cabin hold of the boat. The next thing I knew was someone pinching my cheeks and saying: 'Don't worry. She can't be dead with rosy cheeks like that.' When I opened my eyes, my sister was staring at me, her lips quivering. I don't think I have ever slept so soundly. But it was my first rest in more than twenty-four hours.

Coming from Hamburg, thirteen-year-old Gerd Nathan was not entirely unfamiliar with the North Sea. But his advantage was slight:

> On the boat we were two to a cabin and I occupied the top bunk. It must have been one of the roughest nights, it was terrible, and it was the one-and-only time I have been seasick. The chap below me was sick and that of course triggered me off. But I do recall after being sick I was very hungry, and I had my favourite sandwiches in my coat pocket (sardine sandwiches – sandwiches in oil!) and I wanted them. But I was so weak I couldn't get off the bunk to get them and the boy below was too weak as well.
>
> The first thing I did on arriving in England was to have my sardine sandwiches – I was very hungry.

There was more to concern Ruth Michaelis than the rolling waves, even though she was one of the lucky few whose mothers travelled with them:

> I can remember the boat very clearly – how enormous it seemed. Everyone was putting their cases into a big pile as they went on the boat. We were hustled down into the bunks and put to sleep and I can remember being terribly worried because I couldn't imagine how this huge boat could possibly float on the water; I imagined that once it was unhooked from the side it would just sink like a stone. Nobody was concerned and I remember asking and being told to shut up. Then I was very, very seasick. I remember being in the upper bunk, calling for my mother and leaning over and being sick all over her as she looked up from the lower bunk. The

cabin was tiny. My brother was very calm and quiet. I didn't see the open sea and all my worries about the boat sinking were forgotten about.

For those who could face up to a meal there was a first hint that English people and English ways might be, well, somehow different. Milk in tea was thought to be a curious habit and there was some consternation at the sight of square, thin slices of white bread. Alfred Cooper assumed he was being offered cake but thought how crazy it was to eat it with butter. Up to then he had been used to thick slices of rye bread.

Those who understood some English were puzzled by the crew's frequent use of certain adjectives which did not appear in any dictionaries. Practising these new words in front of supervisors they soon found out why.

The *De Praag* berthed at Parkeston Quay at 5.30 a.m. on Friday 2 December 1938. By 6 o'clock the children were ready for their first encounter with their British benefactors. A reporter from the *Eastern Daily Press* observed the scene:

> As each child filed through the ship's lounge, which had been turned into a temporary office by Major Langdon, who was in charge of the landing arrangements, and his little band of helpers, an official 'labelled' him or her. 'Hans Jacobus', somebody called out. A youth stepped forward, took off his cap, and a woman tied around his neck an ordinary luggage label, on which was scratched his number and name. 'Manfred Landau . . . Hella Richter . . . ' and so the disembarkation went on.
>
> It was not until more than four hours after the *De Praag* had drawn alongside Parkeston Quay that the refugees had left the ship.
>
> Never has a sadder boatload of passengers filed through the customs barriers at Harwich. As the officers patted their pockets, trying to put the children at their ease with smiles and words of broken German, some of them timorously emptied their pockets and there was laid out on the long table an odd assortment of fountain pens, propelling pencils, cheap flash lamps and schoolboy odds and ends – their only possessions apart from the clothes they wore and the few garments stuffed in the rucksacks.

Another reporter, this one from *The Evening Standard*, detected a more cheerful mood.

Full of excitement at visiting a strange land the children showed little effect of their long journey and rough crossing, or indeed of the modern tragedy in which they have been involved.

It was more likely that the bland smiles were a thin disguise for total bewilderment. Few had any English; they could only guess as what was being said to them. Helga Samuel was not alone in fearing the worst.

> Perhaps because I looked more lost and sad than the other children, I was picked out by a photographer who came over to me and said something which of course I did not understand. I began to cry so he put his arm round my shoulder and gave me a coin (I later found out it was half-a-crown). Then he called over one of the helpers, and with her looking at the label round my neck he took our picture.

The friendly policeman who appears in other photographs was a comforting influence. There was much interest in the shape of his helmet and even more interest in the fact that he did not carry a gun.

Other first impressions crowded in: small houses in different colours, front gardens, buses but no trams, pennies and half-crowns, lattice windows, open fires and smoking chimneys. A double-decker bus took the children to Dovercourt Camp in groups of sixty. Driving through Harwich, a girl on the lower deck found herself looking out at a bookshop window. She recognised just one title amongst the books on display – *Mein Kampf*. My God, she thought, what have I come to?

4

Essex by the Sea

> '*If you go down Harwich way*
> *Any evening, any day,*
> *You'll find them all*
> Lachend den Harwich Skandal.'

Dovercourt in the thirties was an Essex coastal village favoured as a retirement home for those who enjoyed stiff breezes and bracing walks. From the seafront up to a mile inland was an uninterrupted expanse of tall grass and fern, the delight of ramblers. In the wet months it could turn into a quagmire.

Billy Butlin was not much interested in winter conditions. What he wanted was wide open spaces that could be converted to one of his new-style holiday camps, offering bargain, trouble-free holidays for the whole family.

At Butlin's everything was laid on. Mum and Dad could relax knowing that the children were being looked after, that someone else was cooking the meals and that every evening would bring some form of entertainment. And all for a price that at an ordinary hotel would barely cover the cost of bed and breakfast.

Butlin knew that the leisure industry was about to be revolutionised by a law forcing employers to give their workers holiday with pay. The millions who would soon be looking for somewhere to spend their hard-earned break were his natural customers. He set about looking for new sites.

Dovercourt was ideal. The land was cheap and there was plenty of it, room for an amusement centre and communal dining hall, children's play areas between the fir trees and lines of tiny chalets fronted by pebble-dash walls and mock Tudor porches, copies of the latest fashion in middle-class suburbia. The hint of quality did not allow for heating and surface drainage, but neither were strictly essential in the summer months.

Dovercourt had just one season as a holiday camp before it was taken over by the RCM as short-term accommodation for refugee children. With Harwich and the docks at Parkeston Quay not more than two miles away, and a direct rail line to London, it would have been hard to think of anywhere more convenient for the RCM to set up a distribution centre.

When the first *Kindertransport* arrived at Dovercourt, it was cold but dry. The children's immediate reaction was a sense of relief at having arrived somewhere. Then there was the excitement of finding out about this strange miniature town with its open view of the North Sea over the mud flats.

Celia Lee's first impression of Dovercourt was roses. 'I couldn't believe it: roses in wintertime! It made a strong impact on me. What a beautiful country.' Others remember the green of the countryside. 'The first question they asked,' reported a voluntary worker, 'was, "May we go on the grass?" They were astonished when we said "Yes".' Everyone remembers the holiday chalets – 'our little houses' as they were soon to be called.

In the way children have of promoting the incidental to matters of vital importance, settling in was a flurry of inconsequential activity. When Johnny Blunt was given his pocket money, he immediately went off and bought a tin of pineapple.

> That was my first purchase in England. But how to open it? One of the other boys had a penknife and it took us about half an hour to get at the pineapple. But it was worth it.

There was curiosity and wonderment at those features of life that went unremarked by the natives but to foreigners were so eccentric, and so quintessentially British, like porridge and kippers for breakfast, 'a peculiar liquid which looked like coffee, tasted like poison and was said to be tea', and bottles of HP Sauce and vinegar on the dining table. Outside, men in wellingtons excited comment, though it was not long before everyone appreciated the value of waterproof boots. Those from middle-class homes, the great majority, were puzzled by the lack of double glazing and by the custom of shooting loads of coal into iron stoves which sent most of the heat up the chimney.

In the chalets, stone hot-water bottles were a puzzle; so too were blankets ('I had always associated them with picnics, holidays and Wild West stories'), and English toilet paper, 'hard and shiny'.

The new experience everyone enjoyed was eating bananas and it was a great disappointment when the supply stopped short at the beginning of the war. The greatest deprivation was German sausage, made more intense for one boy who had brought a whole salami all the way from Vienna only to have it thrown away by a Dovercourt helper 'because it didn't smell right'.

A reporter from the *Jewish Chronicle* visiting Dovercourt a week after the arrival of the first *Kindertransport* had nothing but praise for the RCM.

> Everybody I saw was dressed in the warmest clothes . . . and all the children are given plenty of blankets to keep them warm at night . . . Some were playing table tennis, some darts (it was amusing to watch their efforts at this game, which was entirely new to them) . . . In a side room there were several surrounding a piano which was being played by a youngster of about ten.'

But it did not take a sharp journalistic instinct to realise that for refugees – particularly young refugees – life could never be that simple.

> Closer observation revealed here a group of three little girls, one with a doll clutched to her, seated quite silently in a corner, and there a boy rubbing his eyes furtively.

In the weeks ahead the loneliness would intensify, but in the early days there was too much happening to keep homesickness at bay. A stream of visitors turned up at the camp. J. S. Homes, the National Liberal MP for Harwich, made an early visit, closely followed by the mayor who arranged for the town band to give a concert. The chief rabbi made two visits, the first to distribute his *Book of Jewish Thought*, the second to plant a commemorative tree.

For Celia Lee the excitement of meeting new people soon wore off. She recorded her impressions of Dovercourt in 1941 when she was still only fourteen.

All day long we had no peace. At first it was fun but afterwards we
got tired of standing, jumping, dancing and sitting, of talking to
and shaking hands with more or less important people from the
district.

For the first time in its history, Dovercourt was news. Though
some newspapers like the *Mail* and the *Express* harped on the theme
of 'charity begins at home', the general line was to stress the
potential benefits of taking in such 'lively, sturdily-built and intelligent' children. *Picture Post* thought the young refugees would be
a credit to Britain:

> They will be trained . . . to become farmers and farm-workers,
> artisans, plumbers, builders, electricians. Many of the girls will
> become nurses, maids or farm assistants.

What their parents would have made of this is another matter.

Of all the journalists who made the pilgrimage to Dovercourt,
the team from the BBC caused the greatest excitement. Radio
was still something special and the idea of putting out a half-hour
programme on the young refugees – to be called *Children in Flight*
– was a great public relations coup for the RCM. The word from
Woburn House was that everybody should cooperate with all the
enthusiasm they could muster.

For a week, producer Robert Kemp had free run of the camp,
interviewing whoever he chose for as long as he chose. The result
is the single most comprehensive account of the early days at
Dovercourt.

This is not to say that it was wholly accurate. The style of BBC
Radio was to report but not to offend. The editing of the draft
script reveals an overwhelming urge to remove any hint of criticism
of the administration and to avoid other possibly contentious
errors, like education and employment.

Where the programme is most revealing is in its assumption that
the proper way of handling young refugees was to treat them as if
they were entrants to a minor public school. The doctor set the tone:

> '*Kommen Sie hier, bitte!* Do you speak English? Well, just take your
> shirt off; I want to listen to your heart. Breathe please. Open your
> mouth wide. Let me see your eyes, please. Rightho, you're healthy.
> *Alles gut.*'

The contributions from the children suggest cheerful acquiescence in a slightly dotty game, though doubtless this mood was created largely by careful rehearsal. Their chief spokesman was Leslie Brent, who was chosen for his grasp of English. The words came over clearly but cautiously:

> A bell rings at eight o'clock and we have to get up. Some boys get up earlier to make a run to the sea which is near the camp. At 8.30 we have a good English breakfast, which we enjoy. First we did not eat porridge but now we like it. When we finish the breakfast we get the letters or cards from our parents, and then we are all very happy. After that we clear and tidy our rooms, then we have two hours lessons in English. When the lessons are over we take our lunch and then we can make what we like. After tea we can go to the sea, which is wonderful, or we play English games of football. In the evening we learn a lot of English songs till we go to bed. I sleep with two other boys in a nice little house. Now it is very cold and we cannot stay in our house. We like to sit around the stove in a very large hall, and we read or write to our parents. The people are very kind to us. A gentleman invited me to go with him in a car; then we drove to his house and there we had tea. Oh, it was very nice. Sometimes we go to a picture house in Dovercourt. We have seen the good film *Snow White and the Seven Dwarfs*. We were all delighted. Now I will go to school, then I can speak English good and then I would like to become a cook. We are all very happy to be in England.

Leslie Brent was denied his ambition to be a cook. Instead, he became a professor of immunology but says that he still enjoys cooking. One line of his broadcast – 'Now it is very cold and we cannot stay in our house' – hints at a crisis that nearly closed Dovercourt and did result in the evacuation of Pakefield, the overspill camp near Lowestoft.

Around Christmas the cold became so intense that children slept in their sweaters or coats. 'Four of us shared a double bed,' recalls Margot Barnes. 'When one said "turn" we all turned.' There were nights when stone hot-water bottles left out on the floor froze solid. Top blankets were nearly always damp.

In the early morning, waking up to a fierce easterly wind and a leaden sea, the children gathered in the dining room to find snow fluttering through the rafters and piling up over the breakfast plates. It was too much for the older boys, who had the bright idea of purloining some old electric heaters from the stores. But when they were switched on they blew the main fuses, which deprived them of lighting for the day and taught them why they had to rely on coal fires.

Erich Duchinsky, a *Youth Aliyah* worker at Pakefield and Dovercourt, encouraged his youngsters to keep on the move. 'You could not stand still for a moment. Running about and trying to organise energetic games was my total preoccupation.' Those who were too tired to move and still felt cold took themselves off for a hot bath.

In the last weeks of December, Pakefield had to be evacuated. Two hundred and fifty children were moved to St Felix's Girls School in Southwold, where the staff gave up their holiday to help look after their guests. The luxury of single cubicles and warm beds lasted until the end of the first week in January when the regular boarders returned. Then it was back to Lowestoft and a new set of problems.

After the snow came the rain. One night the water in the gullies flooded over into the chalets. Children were carried shoulder-high to the road, where a bus took them to a seafront hotel. They spent the night sleeping on the ballroom floor. After that it was boys only at Pakefield. The girls went to Dovercourt. Not that conditions there were very much better. The chalets on the lower ground nearest the beach were liable to flood and more than once young children had to be lifted from their beds in the middle of the night. On these occasions a dormitory was improvised in the dining room.

Early in the New Year, Anna Essinger, the doughty headmistress of Bunce Court, was asked by Norman Bentwich to take charge of the welfare and education of all children at Dovercourt and Pakefield. Having emigrated from Germany with most of her school some five years earlier, she and her team of staff and older children knew a thing or two about the traumas of young people settling in a strange country.

It was impossible not to notice Anna Essinger. She was tall and imposing, but in a rather distant way; her formidable look was emphasised by dark glasses. But the personality belied the appearance. She got on with children and dedicated herself to their wellbeing. Anna Essinger did not like what she found at Dovercourt. She thought the domestic arrangements were too primitive and the facilities for education, particularly language training, at best inadequate. One of her immediate problems was overcrowding. Dovercourt was designed for at most 500 residents but was providing for up to twice as many. Those children leaving the camp to go to foster parents (about one hundred in December) were vastly outnumbered by new arrivals.

The sheer volume of young people clamouring for attention frustrated Anna Essinger in her ambition, which was to recreate the spirit of Bunce Court by the sea. But she did try. From her own school she enlisted five teachers she could ill afford and ten senior boys and girls. Then the call went out for teaching assistants. Train fares and free board and lodging were offered, plus pocket money 'where necessary', but this was never more than a pound a week. Undergraduates on Christmas vacation were the biggest group of helpers, but their colleagues were attracted from a wide catchment of background and experience.

Vera Tann's husband Fred was a railway shipping clerk at Parkeston Quay continental office. When he told her about the children at Dovercourt she and a friend went along to help in teaching English.

> We put everyday articles on a table, sat round and taught them to ask 'What is this?' – a spoon, fork, knife, sugar, milk and, later, because they watched the workmen, a saw, hammer, screws, nails. It was all a game but they learned very fast.

A volunteer who had lately returned from China where she had seen another aspect of the refugee problem spent her first evening at Dovercourt simply observing the children.

> . . . hundreds of them, ranging in age from six years old to sixteen. Watching a small, fair-haired girl with a cross hanging from a silver chain round her neck, the visitor wonders whether the little non-Aryan Christians in these strange surroundings are not even more to be pitied than their Jewish playfellows, who already take persecution for granted as the burden of their race. Some of the older children are talking round one of the stoves, a few of the younger ones have toys to play with, and there are always groups round the ping pong tables. Very few are reading, partly because it is difficult for these children to concentrate after all the excitement of their journey and arrival in a strange country, and partly because

the books which have been presented to the camp are nearly all English. But there is one occupation which is unfailingly popular among them all, no matter what their age, and that is writing letters.

She forgot to mention the noise. Everybody else remembers the uproar in what was known grandly as the Palm Court, the former bar and dance hall where during the day several lessons were held simultaneously, including at least one assault on the piano. Classes gathered round the pipe stoves which gave out a strong smell of soot.

There was great fun learning English songs: 'Tipperary'; 'Underneath the Spreading Chestnut Tree'; 'Daisy, Daisy' and the 'Lambeth Walk' – simple, rousing tunes to which new and more appropriate lyrics would be added.

> *If you go down Harwich way*
> *Any evening, any day,*
> *You find them all*
> Lachend den Harwich Skandal.

But singing songs and letter writing, though powerful antidotes to homesickness, did not amount to a decent education, as Anna Essinger was well aware. Writing in 1941, Walter Friedmann, who taught at Dovercourt, regretted

> . . . that the staff for these transit camps had to be assembled at very short notice. Many had no proper qualifications or training to deal with young people and were not really good organisers either. As it was most important to move the children away from the camps as quickly as possible to enable others to come over from the continent, there was really no chance for a proper selection and many a gifted child . . . was sent to places where all the qualities they had were useless, whilst sheer luck led others to places which offered splendid opportunities for which they were not qualified to take advantage.

That luck played a big part in the distribution of favours at Dovercourt is confirmed by Anna Saville.

> One day a violin teacher, who had come over to England with Anna Essinger, told me that an English family was prepared to give a home to a musical boy or girl and give him/her musical training.

Would I like to go? Before I could say 'Yes please' she added: 'I would advise you not to go. You can't make a living with art or music in England.' Do you know who went in my place? The late Peter Schidlof of the Amadeus Quartet! I have never stopped kicking myself from that day to this, regretting the only opportunity I had and lost.

Children in Flight was broadcast on the evening of 3 January 1939. Gladys Rushbrook heard the programme at her home in Leigh-on-Sea. Her husband had just finished the day's work at his butcher's shop and they were settling down to supper.

It was so terribly sad, we felt surely there was something we could do. So we decided that at the weekend we would go to Dovercourt to see the children and find out if we could help in any way.

We were introduced to four boys, all of about seventeen. Each Sunday we used to go to Dovercourt and take them for a ride in the country and then to Clacton, where we had tea before bringing them back to the camp. This was our first contact with the Jewish world.

One of the boys was Ernest Jacob.

At that time I was in hospital but my best friend mentioned my name to them and they came to see me. I was on the danger list for two or three days and Mr Rushbrook contacted my parents in Cologne. The result was that the Germans permitted my father to come over and one morning, at about seven o'clock, my father stood at my bedside. He was given permission to be in England for a fortnight, and during that time Mr Rushbrook went with my father to Bloomsbury House where their application to come over to England had been registered. But my parents' file couldn't be found. Mr Rushbrook told the man in charge that if he couldn't find the file by the time Bloomsbury House closed at 5.30 he would go to the Home Office first thing the next day. Mr Rushbrook and my father returned at 5.30, by which time the file had been found. It was now of course time for my father to go back. I was so desperate that he shouldn't go, but the Rushbrooks said that if he didn't go there wouldn't be any chance for my mother ever to come out. I drove the matron at the hospital so mad that she got hold of my father at Croydon airport and I was able to talk to him there. But he said 'No, I must go back.'

There was a happy ending. Ernest Jacob's parents did get out of Germany, just four weeks before the outbreak of war. But if the Rushbrooks had not encouraged a father to visit a sick son, it would have turned out differently.

Another of the boys was Herbert Rothschild. Mrs Rushbrook resumes the story:

> I will always remember Herbert saying to me one day when we were out in the garden: 'I wonder if you could do me a great favour? I have a cousin on my mother's side who would like to come to England and it would be helpful to her parents.' That we found very amusing. Her name was Margaret. She settled in with us beautifully, so thoughtful for our comfort and all the help she could give us. It was a very sad day for us when she had to leave for America, but we have been in touch ever since and regularly I hear from her and she always phones me on my birthday, Christmas, New Year and the anniversary of my husband's death. She was on holiday in Italy when he died and she made a point of coming over for two days for his funeral. Ernest and Paul (Sonnaberg) also came. You couldn't ask for more respect than that.

After *Children in Flight*, parcels of food and clothing started arriving at Dovercourt. There were shoes and coats from Marks and Spencer, the National Sporting Club sent a pair of boxing gloves and an Essex butcher provided beef sausages for all, once a week. Free tickets at the Harwich Electric Cinema provided a welcome diversion from camp routine, not to mention a painless method of learning English. News of Dovercourt travelled abroad. One day a trunk-load of winter woollens turned up, a gift from Johannesburg where a news item in the local paper had inspired a ladies' circle to start knitting.

But however welcome, such generosity did not help solve the central problem which was to find suitable homes for the children. Every Sunday, prospective foster parents gathered at Dovercourt to view the inmates. It was a ritual that distressed Anna Essinger and her staff but, given the pressure to move the children out of the camp so that others could take their places, nobody was able to come up with a better alternative to what was known as 'the market'.

Sunday was the day for looking smart. For three hours in the morning the dining room became a barber's shop, with a queue of youngsters waiting for their short back and sides. Baths were mandatory and not just a lazy soaking but a good scrubbing with carbolic soap. Then the best clothes were chosen, none of them the height of fashion nor even necessarily a good fit, but neat, tidy and clean.

The adults were told to arrive when the children were having lunch. That way, by walking between the long tables as if on a tour of inspection, they could view the prospects without embarrassment. Anyway, that was the theory. In reality, adults and children usually ended up furtively edging round each other, anxiously trying to detect matching personalities.

Leslie Brent was in Dovercourt for three weeks before going to Bunce Court, a happy chance which put him into the most favoured category of child refugees.

> The selection process was not always done altruistically because some of the families wanted, for example, a blonde girl with blue eyes and of a particular age – hoping perhaps that she would be useful in the house. Fortunately, I was never involved in that. Couples sometimes had a rather clear idea of the kind of child they were looking for, and naturally the more attractive children 'went' more quickly than the less attractive, and those with difficult emotional histories probably would have been the most difficult to place. I don't think one can be too critical of the way this was organised because it was all done in a terrific hurry, and the pressures were intense.

In the evening, the names of those who had been picked from the line-up were read out over the camp tannoy. The children were apprehensive, none more so than the newcomers who were still struggling with their English and were generally mystified by events. When Zita Hirschhorn heard her name, so little acquainted was she with all that was going on, she cried out: *'Ich bin verkauft'* ('I am sold').

The greatest sadness was the children who felt unwanted. These were not necessarily the shy or reserved ones, who were quite likely to be snapped up by 'parents' who were looking for a quiet life. But a child who was unusual in some way – a thin, undernourished-looking boy, for example, or a large, overnourished-looking girl – were liable to feel the pain of rejection.

As a group, the older ones were the most difficult to place – because, inevitably, they were the most difficult to manage. It was said that these teenagers were easily offended. But who could blame them? Exiled from their own country for no reason, they developed keen antennae for any insult, actual or implied. They resented stern reminders not to speak German, to be polite and always, always to be grateful. Stuck in Dovercourt with little prospect of continuing their education or of fulfilling their parents' ambitions, they did not see what they had to be grateful for.

Perhaps it would have been better for them if they had gone straight to hostels or agricultural training camps. This was certainly the view of *Youth Aliyah* workers like Erich Duchinsky. He argued that teenagers were wasting their opportunities at Dovercourt, keeping the futile hope alive that they would be adopted by rich families and lead a fine life, when they could have been using their time to constructive purpose.

Why then did the RCM insist on fostering as the only way of emptying Dovercourt and Pakefield? A report circulated in the spring of 1939 admitted that the camps 'became slave markets where people with the best intentions in the world went to help one child, yet unconsciously did harm to many by looking them over and rejecting them'. But the report concluded: 'There was good reason for the Movement not to follow the example of the continent (where hostels were the rule) for France and Germany are definitely clearing stations. It would not profit the children there greatly to learn the culture of those countries when in a few months they would have to go overseas. Yet the case is different with the children in England, for when they emigrate, the vast majority will go to English-speaking countries, and they will have profited from the intimate contact they had with the English life and language.'

As it happened, re-emigration was a non-starter, but it remained government policy and, until the war, it was seen as the only long-term solution to the refugee problem. The other question that needs answering is why the RCM did not take more care in choosing foster parents. As many children were soon to discover, being taken into a family was no guarantee of happiness. But the RCM was working against the clock with little in the way of professional back-up. As one organiser put it:

In an ideal world we would have checked the needs of the children and matched them with carefully compiled family profiles. But in an ideal world, refugee children would not have existed.

The longer the older teenagers remained at Dovercourt, the more dissatisfied they became and the more difficult to control. Anna Essinger tried to keep discipline by appointing group leaders, but responsibility did not rest easily on youngsters who were preoccupied by their own future, or apparent lack of it. Formal discipline gave way to the survival of the strongest. Not surprisingly, the younger ones associated the bullies with the violence they had encountered at home:

> There were rumours that some of the older boys were members of the Nazi party. I was certain that two boys were members of the Hitler Youth Movement planted there as spies.

There was no evidence of this, but it is clear that old rivalries were used as an excuse for fights.

> I remember being amazed at the enmity between the Austrian boys and the boys from Berlin – they hated each others' guts! There was evidently some enmity between Austria and Germany and the Jewish boys were part and parcel of this; they had accepted this. There were some knife fights in the camp between sixteen- and seventeen-year-old boys. I was quite shocked about that – it had never occurred to me that one might hate someone merely because he came from a different city. So Viennese and Berlin boys – boys who had just escaped from Nazi Germany – were kept apart in separate chalets.

As one who did get into quite a few scrapes, Henry Schwartz admits that the Viennese and Berliners divided into rival camps, but thinks that the seriousness of the fighting was overstated.

> The Germans still thought of themselves as Germans and the Austrians still thought of themselves as Austrians; they didn't think of themselves as Jews primarily. When you think back on it there was no justification. One of the Germans said: 'You shut up. You have only come to Greater Germany; we were there before,' and I said: 'Why the hell don't you keep it? We didn't want to come.' He was proud of the fact that he was part of the German empire, so

we had fights over these things. Of course, boys will have fights, but they were not that serious. There were tensions which were a bit stupid. We just didn't mix with them. It seems a bit silly in retrospect.

At the time, it was anything but silly. Fears of serious outbreaks of violence were real enough, as too were the risks of public reaction against the *Kindertransporte* if stories of indiscipline got out. Those who had to keep order had no power of retribution, except the withdrawal of minor privileges. All they could do was plead for commonsense or, in desperation, threaten a stern lecture from Anna Essinger, a device which usually succeeded when all else had failed.

Youngsters falling out was one thing, but just as worrying were reports that some of the more mature boys and girls were getting on with each other just a little too well. Like other teachers at Dovercourt, Howard Franks was under orders to curb the romantic inclinations of their wards.

> I remember patrolling chalets, loos, shower rooms for this kind of thing, and I actually discovered and separated youngsters who had had intercourse!

The nearest Dovercourt came to real scandal was when some of the boys discovered the red light district of Harwich. Ironically, it happened when a party was staying at the Salvation Army Sailors' Hostel for a fortnight before going on to Dovercourt, at the kind invitation of Major and Mrs Parker. In the evening, some of Major and Mrs Parker's guests wandered off into town.

> 'The boys had a few shillings,' recalls Erich Duchinsky, who had to find the miscreants and return them to camp. 'I don't know where they got the money, but it was a nightmare. I tried talking to them. I don't know how successful I was but I don't think it happened any more.'

The incident came at an awkward time, preceding by a few days a visit by the Chief Rabbi. Fortunately, he was diverted from any inquiry into the sexual morals of the camp by a report that boys were playing football on the Sabbath. A reasonable defence might have been that field sports were preferable to roaming the docks but, instead, the chief rabbi was assured that the boys needed the exercise. He was not convinced:

> As these children have had little exercise before, one day of rest, after six days given over to sport, might do their constitutions more good than any additional exercise on the Sabbath.
>
> If, however, there are reasons why such additional exercise is advisable, I am of the opinion that something less strenuous than football should be selected.

Rabbi Hertz had his way.

Dovercourt ended its days as a refugee centre in March 1939 when there were less than a hundred, mostly older boys, still in occupation. The orthodox boys went to a hostel at Westgate (closed at the end of 1939) and the non-orthodox to Barham House, just outside Ipswich, which soon became an agricultural training centre.

For a short time, Dovercourt was restored to its original function, but in 1942 it was requisitioned as a prisoner-of-war camp. It was another five years before the holiday-makers returned. Today, a few of the ticky tacky chalets occupied by the refugee children can still be seen. Until recently they were the location for the television series *Hi Di Hi*. But the days of Dovercourt holiday camp are numbered. There is a plan to clear the site to make way for a spanking new conference centre. No doubt every comfort will be laid on, though, in winter, there will always be the sharp east wind to remind occupants of tougher days at Dovercourt.

5

The Price of Humanity

*'So one morning the day of our departure had come – I
remember crying bitterly and saying – "Please Mummy, please
don't send me away." I saw the heartbreak that was going
on around me. I was eleven years old.'*

By Christmas 1938 the RCM was in desperate straits, though the
staff were working too hard to realise it. At the root of the crisis
was a shortage of hard cash. While demand for places on the
Kindertransporte showed no signs of letting up – indeed, was beginning to increase at an alarming rate – the resources to meet the
challenge were simply not to hand.

On 8 December, the former prime minister, Stanley Baldwin
(Lord Baldwin), had made a successful radio appeal on behalf of
refugees, 'the victims . . . of an explosion of man's inhumanity to
man'. The broadcast was subsequently distributed on record at
eight shillings a disk. Christie's held a charity auction, and up and
down the country the rotaries and women's institutes geared
themselves for yet another season of money-raising fetes and flower
shows.

The Baldwin Fund brought in some £500,000, but not all of this
was for child refugees. In fact, it was not until April 1939 that the
RCM was given its allocation of £200,000. By then, the critical
decision had been taken to restrict the flow of refugee children into
Britain. Forced back on a policy of self help, the RCM soon
discovered that the public responded best when appeals were made
on behalf of specific projects – £40 to support one boy in a course
of agricultural training, say, or £60 for a year's schooling. The
next step was to call for volunteers to act as foster parents, either

at their own expense or with the help of a small grant. The campaign was got under way on 25 November when Lord Samuel delivered an emotional appeal to the British public to open their homes to refugee children. The response was encouraging; over 500 offers came in, and though the inevitable, lengthy process of inspection deprived those on the early *Kindertransporte* of any immediate benefit, the principle of recruiting guarantors to act as foster parents was well and truly established.

Faith in the government as the banker of last resort was consistently misplaced. Chamberlain's cabinet was obsessed by the fear that if taxpayers' money was used to shore up the refugee organisations, other countries, not least Germany, would be encouraged to hand on to Britain yet more of their unwanted citizens. Accusations of defeatism were countered by the naive assumption that Sir Herbert Emerson, the League of Nation's high commissioner for refugees, who was based in London, had a trick or two up his sleeve.

The fact was that Sir Herbert was a desperately unhappy man. He spent his time looking for a Jewish homeland that was not Palestine. It was a hopeless task. Ever more fanciful proposals were raised, discussed at enormous length and consigned to the reject file. There was talk of setting up a Jewish state in Abyssinia, the Russians offered the Amur basin, as long as the population of the new republic was limited to 100,000 and several Latin American countries declared an interest in farmers who had a start capital of at least £500. (Few European refugees qualified either by occupation or savings.) Mexico welcomed single, able-bodied men, but they had to promise to marry local girls. Much praised at the Evian conference for a bold offer to absorb up to 100,000 refugees, the Dominican Republic had closed its application list at 2000. By November 1938 it had shortened to just twenty.

The best hope, decided Emerson, was British Guiana, which offered sub-tropical wide open spaces. The trouble was it offered little else except tropical wide open spaces. Essential services like housing and transport were not even on the drawing board. Emerson was not deterred. 'The prospects have been greatly improved,' he reported breathlessly, 'by the promise of the British government to provide the main roads if the stage of mass settlement is reached.'

If this was the likeliest prospect for a major resettlement, what chance was there for the re-emigration of the *Kindertransporte*? As it happened, of the 5381 children who arrived in the first six months of 1939, only 113 re-emigrated, and most of those went to join their parents who had escaped Germany by other routes. Yet, throughout, re-emigration remained the official policy. Its place at the centre of government thinking was re-emphasised in April 1939 when the RCM was told that, henceforth, each guarantor would have to put up a deposit of £50 to support the cost of a child's re-emigration. The order was supported, a trifle ingenuously, by a claim that the government was trying to broaden the scope of the RCM to take in more of the not so urgent cases. But, of course, the £50 deposit, at a time when the annual wage was less than £500, was a powerful deterrent to all but the wealthiest families and remained so until the Baldwin Fund agreed to put up the money for children without guarantors or for foster parents who could not afford to pay.

The government was on stronger ground with the proposal to set up a coordinating committee to act as a channel of communication, mainly to the Home Office, for up to thirty organisations involved with refugees. Lord Hanley, a bluff, no-nonsense administrator who had learned his trade as governor of the Punjab, was appointed chairman. He had the unenviable task of trying to reconcile the disparate interests of, say, the RCM and the International Solidarity Fund, whose interpretation of their grand title was to resist all efforts to open up the labour market to non-nationals.

Still, there was some virtue for the RCM in having the chance to compare notes with like-minded bodies such as the Society of Friends and the Christian Council for Refugees, the latter a long-sought-after but, at times, bitterly contested amalgam of the Catholic Committee for Refugees from Germany and the Church of England Committee for non-Aryan Christians.

Between them, the Quakers and the Christian Council looked after about twenty per cent of those who came over on the *Kindertransporte*. Often these children had no idea why they had been sent away. They knew nothing of Judaism, did not feel Jewish, and yet had enough Jewish blood in them to make them somehow different from their former friends, if not quite enough for them to be welcomed unreservedly into the Jewish community. They were to figure prominently among the more tragic case histories.

The experience of the coordinating committee, with its balance weighted towards non-Jewish affairs, undoubtedly persuaded the RCM to adopt more of a non-denominational role in its refugee work. Leading figures in the RCM like the Marchioness of Reading, who had been born into a Jewish family, converted to Christianity and had now converted back to Judaism; Elaine Blond, Sigmund Gestetner and Lola Hahn-Warburg quickly caught on to the message that the best chance of currying public favour was to play down the religious factor.

Malcolm Muggeridge was one of many observers of the political scene to note the 'unmistakable tang' of anti-Semitism in the air. British Fascists were a small and divided minority, but not, it seems, without their influence.

> Sir John Simon found it necessary to issue a statement that, despite a biblical name, he was of Welsh extraction; Lord Camrose, proprietor of the *Daily Telegraph*, brought a successful libel action against an organ of the British Union of Fascists for having falsely implied that he was a Jew; in one of his articles, Dean Inge suggested that Jews were using 'their not inconsiderable influence in the Press and in Parliament to embroil us with Germany'.
>
> (Malcom Muggeridge, *The Thirties*, p. 263)

Moreover, there was a powerful lobby of Jewish opinion in favour of putting adopted nationality before race and religion; indeed, this had been the keynote of Jewish immigration to Britain since the 1880s. Assimilation implied a working partnership with the religious and social establishment.

For this reason there was no resistance when Lord Hailey urged the RCM to take on Sir Charles Stead, another old India hand, as executive director. It was a post for which he was singularly unsuited and from which he removed himself or was gently pushed in September 1939, but, though he failed to hit it off with the central committee, he did bring to the organisation the stamp of institutional legitimacy.

After Stead's appointment, the RCM deliberately set out to become broad church. A religious triumvirate was formed with a Catholic, Canon George Craven, and a Protestant, the Reverend William Simpson, elected to the central committee to join Rabbi Maurice Swift.

The next move was to find a chairman from the ranks of the

great and the good, someone of acknowledged independence who combined the qualities of Solomon and Job. The choice fell on Lord Gorell, the son of an eminent judge who had inherited his title from his elder brother. At 55 he could claim a distinguished record of philanthropic and public service which included setting up the Royal Army Education Corps. As a cross-bencher in the House of Lords he had steered clear of party politics, but his writing and speeches put him firmly on the side of the underdog. That he was not Jewish was seen as another point in his favour.

Endorsed by the central committee, the invitation to Gorell to head the RCM was sent by a roundabout but significant route:

> On 23 February 1939, the Archbishop of Canterbury, then Dr Lang, wrote to me to ask me to take on the Chairmanship of the Refugee Children's Movement, as a duality with Lord Samuel. With that diplomatic disingenuousness for which he was distinguished he added that he understood that 'the duties would not be very exacting' – a humorous prelude to ten years of continuous, responsible, very difficult but also very rewarding work. I accepted, but almost at once, after a conference with Lord Samuel and Lord Hailey, it was agreed that I should carry on alone. I was therefore sole chairman until the Movement, having done its work, wound up ten years later.
>
> (Lord Gorell: *One Man, Many Parts*, p. 303)

A second, critical appointment was that of a professional to take charge of the administration. Dorothy Hardisty did not actually take over from Sir Charles Stead as executive director until the outbreak of war, but by then she had already made her presence felt as an able and energetic deputy. A widow of fifty-eight, Dorothy Hardisty had the great quality of adoring children, though her generosity of spirit did not extend to all adults. For her, there was never any question of suffering fools gladly. Her capacity for work can be judged by her later career. When she retired from the RCM in 1948 she went on to run the Violet Melchet Infant Welfare Centre near Sloane Square, a job she held for the next twenty years. One of her joys was taking the bus along the King's Road when that thoroughfare was the epitome of the swinging sixties. At eighty-two, Dorothy Hardisty took her grandchildren to Battersea Fun Fair. When they showed an interest in the water chute, she decided it was too dangerous for them to go on it alone. So she went with them and thought it was great fun.

The religious and cultural mix that was now characteristic of the RCM at national level showed too in the provincial committees which sprang up to recruit foster parents and organise hostel accommodation.

The first of these committees were in Manchester, Birmingham, Bristol, Cambridge and in South London (Battersea). All of these began work in the same week as the first *Kindertransporte* were given the go-ahead. That they managed to start up so speedily was largely thanks to local representatives of the Jewish Refugees Committee who simply doubled up for the RCM. Cambridge-shire was the exception in that a child refugee group, led by Greta Burkill, had been active since 1933. By September 1939, there were twelve regional committees and sixty-five area committees, the latter increasing to 175 by the end of the war.

In the early days, the chief burden of committee routine was inspecting likely homes for refugee children. A list of suggested lines of enquiry was circulated by head office – What is the husband's, or breadwinner's work? Is German spoken by anyone? General views on bringing up child. Is a maid kept?, and so on.

If the home was judged to be satisfactory, the prospective foster parent, or 'befriender' as the RCM preferred to call them, was given some reading matter to prepare for the day. A pamphlet which achieved wide circulation was called *Helpful Information and Guidance for Every Refugee*. Though intended primarily for adults, the advice held good for young refugees. They were urged to learn English, to refrain from speaking or reading German, not to make themselves conspicuous by manners or dress, and to accept, without criticism, the way things were done in Britain. 'The Englishman,' they were told, 'attaches very great importance to modesty, understatement in speech rather than overstatement . . . He values good manners far more than he values the evidence of wealth.'

If the proposition is doubtful it is yet more evidence of the all-pervading influence of the public school ethic in refugee work. The ideal counted for more than the reality.

The responsibilities of the regional and area committees increased in line with the numbers of refugee children needing care. By mid-1939, in addition to finding places to live for children who arrived without guarantors, the committees had delegated to them the twice-yearly inspection of homes, arrangements for schooling and vocational training, and the task of sorting out any difficulties over religious education.

Along with the spread of the RCM organisation across the country, the head office was put on a firmer footing with the purchase of Bloomsbury House, the former Palace Hotel just off London's Bedford Square. The deal was put through by Lord Hailey on behalf of all the major refugee bodies. At about the same time the aliens department of the Home Office took on extra staff and moved to Cleveland House on Thorney Street. Bloomsbury House was Hailey's finest achievement. At last there was room for a central bureau of information, which went a long way to reducing the confusion caused by overlapping responsibilities. The offices were cramped and without essentials like typewriters which had to be shared. Still, they were better than everything that had gone before.

In the first six months of 1939, the staff of the RCM at Bloomsbury House, mostly volunteers, fluctuated between sixty and seventy. They dealt with something like 5000 letters a week and interviewed up to 500 petitioners on behalf of children still in Germany. The visitors were herded into two large halls, which were once the hotel ballroom and dining room. There they had to wait, often for hours at a stretch. Tempers frayed with time.

'If some of our visitors are somewhat lacking in restraint,' noted an RCM report euphemistically, 'it must be remembered that many are overwrought with anxiety.'

Perhaps this was an example of the famous English preference for 'understatement in speech rather than overstatement . . . ' The same talent came into play whenever the religious issue surfaced. It was inevitable that the RCM commitment to accepting help from wherever it was offered would be seen by orthodox Jews as a betrayal and a challenge. A counter-attack was only a matter of time. It came in February 1939, when Harry Goodman, a dyspeptic character who worked alongside Rabbi Solomon Schonfeld on the Chief Rabbi's Religious Emergency Council (CRREC), launched a bitter diatribe against the faint hearts of Bloomsbury House. Goodman contended that the RCM was putting at risk the interests of the Jewish faith by its readiness to enlist help from the Christian community. That gentile foster parents were liable to imbue youngsters with their own values, however hard they tried to take a neutral line, was undeniable, but the alternative, to turn away children because there were not enough Jewish homes for them to go to, was rejected out of hand by the RCM's ruling council.

It was the beginning of a long-running feud which rumbled on throughout the war and beyond. The RCM tried hard to play down the issue, arguing that all those working for refugees would achieve most if they cooperated. But, uncompromising in their beliefs, the leaders of the CRREC chose to go their own way, negotiating directly with the Home Office for permits to bring over the children of strictly orthodox families. These were fostered by other strictly orthodox families or sent to hostels in north London – the girls to Stamford Hill, the boys to Amhurst Park.

A happier relationship was forged between the RCM and *Youth Aliyah*, though here again there was a clash of ideals. For *Youth Aliyah*, Zionism came before all, an article of faith expressed with terrifying force by David Ben-Gurion, Jewish leader in Palestine when the flow of refugee children was at its height.

> If I knew that it would be possible to save all the children in Germany by bringing them over to England and only half of them by transporting them to Palestine, then I would choose the second alternative. Against the lives of these children we must weigh the history of the people of Israel.

Here spoke the man of destiny whose singleness of purpose over-rode all other considerations. The RCM had its Zionist sympathisers and there were those like Lola Hahn-Warburg who had a foot in both camps. But at Bloomsbury House, the interest of the children took priority over any political cause, a philosophy which supported the family environment over other forms of upbringing. For *Youth Aliyah*, who were now sending over more children on transit visas, foster homes, even orthodox foster homes, could not inspire the full-blooded commitment to a pioneering life in Palestine. While cooperating closely with the RCM, children brought over from Germany under *Youth Aliyah* auspices surrendered home comforts for the spartan discipline of the barrack room in agricultural training camps like Whittingham House near Edinburgh and Great Engham Farm and Pine Trees in Kent.

Youth Aliyah had a knack of bringing in the money. What with Becky Sieff crusading the country and a succession of charity dinners and film and theatre premieres, close on £300,000 was raised in the first half of 1939. A third of this came from a sixteen-day British tour by the Broadway singer and comedian Eddie Cantor. Himself the child of Jewish refugees, Cantor insisted that all proceeds from his tour should go to a special fund to support the re-emigration of young Jewish refugees to Palestine.

But whatever money was raised, it was never enough. In March 1939 Norman Bentwich, who more than most realised the desperate straits of the Austrian Jews, wrote to Josef Löwenherz in Vienna:

> I regret, too, that there can be no question of our taking into the refugee transit camp additional numbers from Vienna, until some of the 1100 for whom the lists have already been prepared have emigrated from England. It may be possible to consider a list of a few individuals in addition to those that have been chosen, but no more. The Movement for the Transport of Children, again, cannot bring over more unguaranteed children until those already here have been placed. I regret that it is no use to continue to ask for more help than we are giving, because it is not in our power to grant it.

As competition for places on the *Kindertransporte* mounted to panic proportions, the chances of success turned increasingly on knowing the right people – an official who could hurry through an application or, more critically, someone in Britain who was willing to take on the financial responsibility of acting as a guarantor.

Having a close relative in Britain, even a recent arrival, was a huge advantage. For example, an older sister found a sponsor for Gerta Jassem just two months after arriving in London to take up a job as a chambermaid.

> She had never before boiled an egg or made a bed. Her only preparation for her new life was a few intensive lessons in English and much good will. She found my guarantor by putting an advertisement in *The Times*. An elderly couple whose grown-up children were no longer at home agreed to take me on. The reason I think Lily took a fancy to them was the goldfish pond in their garden. She had always been a dreamer.

For Nina Liebermann, solution was a chance acquaintance with a wealthy businessman.

> Mr C was taking the cure in Bad Gastein, a spa in the county of Salzburg. At the approach of the Jewish High Holidays, he sought a congenial place to attend services and so met my father, who was a rabbi, my mother and us two girls. He took a fancy to my sister who reminded him of his own youngest daughter. He joked with my mother. 'I'd like to educate this girl in England.' She laughed. 'I don't give up my daughter as easily as that.' But eighteen months later she wrote to him pleading for refuge for her children. That's how we came to be on a children's transport.

With a mother who was active in *B'nai B'rith*, Anne Barth was offered a place on one of the early *Kindertransporte*, but her parents decided to hold back in the faint hope that conditions would improve. By February 1939 they were reconciled to the inevitable. The parting was less traumatic than some, however. Anne left Germany in the expectation of seeing her family again before very long. It was simply a matter of waiting for their visas to be approved. Their patience was ill-rewarded. When the visas did come through they were dated 5 September. Just two days too late.

Much effort went into tracing remote family connections abroad on the off chance of identifying a benefactor. Johnny Blunt's father worked his way through the sporting calendar:

> My mother's maiden name was Levinski and there was a boxing champion in Ohio called Kingfish Levinski. My father wrote to him without realising that Levinski was his ring name. I found out later that he was called Kingfish by his wife who divorced him because he used to eat fish in bed and the bones stuck into her!

Young mothers who had kept their looks had an obvious advantage when it came to extracting vital documents from unhelpful bureaucrats. The more blatantly they were prepared to use their charm, the smoother was the way of escape.

Sometimes it was the children who forced the pace, pleading in all innocence to join their brothers, sisters, or friends who had somehow won this great distinction of a place on a *Kindertransport*.

My parents put my brother's name down for the *Kindertransporte*. Children are jealous of everything – and I remember crying: 'I want to go . . . ' My best friend's father was one of the organisers. My mother went to him – I don't know whether it was because I cried – it must have been a terrible thing to send children away – and somehow or other I got onto the transport. It must have been very last minute, because when I got to Holland my papers weren't finished and I had to wait for a week.

My mother packed one little suitcase for me. We were lucky to have one change of clothes and a *shabbat* dress. That's what I had. My mother took me to the station . . . I didn't realise I would never see her again. They must have had such courage to send us away. I don't think I could have done it.

There were a few friends sitting together in the carriage, laughing and joking. We can't have realised the seriousness. A boy lit a Hannukah light. I remember that some children had to travel on *Shabbat* and some of the orthodox children cried bitterly. It was explained that these were not normal times. It was to save our lives and it was all in order.

But for all those like Thea Rudzinski who managed to blank out the significance of the journey there were more who shared with Helga Samuel the anticipation of worse to come.

So one morning, the day of our departure had come. I remember crying bitterly and saying 'Please Mummy, please don't send me away' – again I saw the heartbreak that was going on around me. I was eleven years old.

All the children from the different towns met in Berlin, each with a small suitcase, ten marks and a label around our necks giving our name and number. There was much confusion and many tears were shed . . .

I was told to go into a compartment with several other children of my own age, my sister in the adjoining one. I recall vividly our arrival at the German–Dutch frontier, when the Nazis boarded the train for the last inspection before the train crossed into a 'free' country. One Nazi per compartment . . . The one in our compartment pulled down the blind, made us stand erect in the gangway, pulled down all the suitcases from the racks, opened them, whereupon he threw everything on the floor, taking one or two small items (really of no value – except a sentimental one) such as a gold necklace, watches, rings and even a camera. He also asked each one of us to hand over our money, taking nine marks from each child. And so we left the Fatherland with one mark in our pocket . . .

Fear was in all of us, until the moment the Nazis disembarked, the whistle blew and the train slowly moved out of the station and crossed the frontier into Holland. At this moment, we opened the windows and started shouting abuse . . . It was terrible that we were learning to hate so early in our lives.

In the early part of 1939 the *Kindertransporte* were nearly all from Vienna, where pressure on the Jews was at its most severe. Then in February, attention switched back to Berlin. Jewish sources attributed the sudden rush for places to the arrival in the city of Adolf Eichmann. His orders were to apply the methods that had proved so successful in Vienna to mop up the surviving Jewish influence at the heart of the *Reich*. Accordingly, leaders of the Jewish community were packed off to Vienna to receive first-hand information on organising mass emigration, though how anyone could think of forcing thousands of destitutes over the border – with a passage on a leaky tramp steamer to Shanghai or Trinidad as their only hope of salvation – as 'organised emigration' defied the imagination.

In any event, this latest tightening of the screw brought about a sharp increase in the number of *Kindertransporte* from Berlin and a change in the composition of the *Kindertransporte* from Berlin and Vienna. The average age of child refugees fell dramatically. As Wilfrid Israel noted, 'Babies in their cradles and small children of the tenderest ages were handed over by their parents.' But handed over to whom? The few adults who were allowed to accompany the children had too many demands on them to act as full-time baby minders. That role was assigned to older children, not always with their approval. A despairing mother, spotting a thirteen-year-old boy seated by an open window, thrust her infant into his arms. The train pulled out. He looked after the little girl throughout the journey, everyone, including the Gestapo guards, assuming that it was his sister nestling in his lap. He held on to his charge until he came off the boat at Harwich. To this day, he wonders how she made out.

The Nazi-imposed rules for managing the *Kindertransporte* were made more restrictive in early 1939, presumably as an attempt to disguise from decent citizens what was being perpetrated in their name.

Lorraine Allard had only had four days' warning before leaving from Berlin:

> I had to fight to take the family photo album. My mother didn't want to part with it and what a blessing it is that I did because that's all I have. I had a stamp collection, which was just a child's stamp collection, but I wasn't allowed to bring it. You weren't allowed to take anything of value. I played the accordion at that particular time and I carried that and on the train the SA made me play it to prove that I wasn't taking it to sell. I was shaking as I tried to play it.

Greater use was made of quiet suburban stations or of quieter platforms on the main stations; trains left at night and the number of family wellwishers come to say goodbye was restricted to one parent for each child. The new rules were self-defeating. To load up a *Kindertransport* in lonely isolation was to attract more, not less attention. As for the limit on the number of adults allowed near the train, this merely served to intensify the emotional pressure and to cause more breakdowns.

Vera Coppard left Berlin in May 1939 when she was thirteen.

> Mother couldn't bear to come to the station. I went with my father. There was a terrible scene when they were shouting out the names of the children. There was one woman who was very agitated and when her children were not on the list she became hysterical. The guards hit her with clubs and knocked her to the ground. Then we were handed on to the platform. I just had time to say goodbye to father. My former nanny, who had married one of father's patients, managed to get on to the platform, I don't know how. She threw oranges through the carriage window.
>
> The journey was terrible. At stations all along the way, parents had gathered to catch a last glimpse of their children. I'm glad my family didn't do that.

Vera went to a Quaker school in Cornwall and a short time later to school in Letchworth. Meanwhile, her mother was arrested in Berlin:

> She was a very attractive woman and the senior Nazi officer who interrogated her took a liking to her and said that he would have her released if she would go to bed with him. She said that if he

could get tickets to England for herself and her husband she would do what he wanted. But when the tickets came through she sent a message saying that she was ill and that she was going to the mountains to convalesce. Instead, she went straight to the airport and flew to England.

She was followed by Vera's father who arrived on 1 September.

He wasn't allowed to practise as a doctor so he had to work as a cleaner at the Cumberland Hotel. Then he was allowed to work as a medical orderly in Newquay Hospital looking after soldiers who were injured in the First World War.

The support given to Vera Coppard and her family by the Quakers came at a point when the Jewish organisations in Berlin and Vienna were reduced almost to the point of impotence. Many others had reason to be grateful to the Quakers for refusing to give up their mission to help refugees.

With her mother in prison, ten-year-old Angela Carpos was adrift in Vienna.

I was handed on to the Quakers, probably because I was half-Jewish. They tried to get me out but I had no passport. I missed two or three *Transporte*. Then I heard about a transport on a particular night. I was told that the only way I could get out was to have a Jewish passport, with Angela Sara Pfeffer, with a 'J' on it. I said I didn't care what passport I had, so I was issued with a Jewish passport.

Somehow, I was conscious of what was happening. I had a little bit of money and I took myself on a tram round the city. I knew this was the last time I would be seeing Vienna.

I packed a small suitcase. We were not allowed to take anything with us. I was very conscious of that . . .

All I knew was that I was going to London. That meant nothing to me. I was in a trance. When I got to the station I was given a label to put round my neck. The station was a nightmare, with the wailing, screaming and crying. I was slightly removed because my parents weren't there. It was like a battlefield. I was impressed but was not part of it.

The train was absolutely packed. A couple of small children were bedded down in luggage racks. There were kids in corridors, standing, sitting, lying.

I don't remember Nazis overseeing it – but we must have gone through Germany. There seemed to be an electric fear that some of us would be pulled off the train. I don't know where the rumour came from but it buzzed through the train. Some of the children cried. A little boy was told he was going to London to see his Daddy. Halfway through he decided he wanted to go back to his Mummy. I was in the middle range of years – I tried to comfort the little ones. The older ones seemed to know where we were going but most of us hadn't a clue . . .

When we got out of Germany, there was a sense of relief. We were through. There wasn't any singing. I think there was a shortage of food, which didn't worry me because I was a very bad eater. But other children were hungry. They cried for food and drink.

The boat was heaven. The crew were wonderful. We got into the dining room and the children were overwhelmed with food. The children started to relax. I remember laughter coming through and relief. We hadn't seen such food for months or years.

The ferry crews on regular service between Harwich and the Hook evidently took to their unexpected role as child minders. David Mann was a steward on the SS *Amsterdam*:

I was working in second class . . . We gave up our own cabins so the children could have somewhere to sleep. We also made bunks in the restaurant, just blankets and pillows, but it was a bit more comfortable than standing around on deck.

There was no panic; the children were very well-ordered.

When we landed at Parkstone Quay I had charge of a big wicker basket, like a fisherman's basket, which I hung over the side of the boat. From it I handed out to each child a paper bag with an orange, an apple and a bread-and-butter sandwich.

To the children, uniformed crew represented the menace of state authority. They could hardly bring themselves to believe that such people could behave politely. Herbert Rothman still experiences a sense of wonder that 'they apologised if they bumped into you'.

Harwich, too, is a source of happy memories, a favourite being the policeman who actually smiled. 'It was then that I made up my mind that I would never leave England,' declares Lotte Bray (Lowenstein). 'A country where a policeman smiled had to be a good place to settle.'

There were the inevitable difficulties with English. Johnny Blunt could say 'Yes; no; door; window', but he did better than Harold

Waterman (Hans Wasserman) who knew a complete sentence: 'The gardener's in the garden.' He waited thirty years to use it in conversation.

Equally inevitable were the moments of sadness, made more painful by their sheer incongruity. 'I wrote a postcard to my parents,' recalls Margaret Olmer; 'I can't remember if I addressed it to both. It still makes me feel guilty.'

6

Boat Train

'Someone on the platform screamed hysterically: "Rosi! Rosi!" and there was a rush towards a jolly little girl in a plaid coat who was leaning out waving from a carriage door. "Please stay right where you are!" shouted a lady in a sable jacket, "In two minutes a whistle will blow and you will all march over to the gymnasium." Rosi looked a bit bewildered but she seemed to get the idea.'

The scene shifts to Liverpool Street. Those from the *Kindertransporte* with homes to go to – belonging to relatives, friends or sponsors – or to hostels, did not pause at Dovercourt but went straight to London, to a central distribution point set up by the RCM to the rear of the station concourse.

Liverpool Street has changed enormously in recent years, but those who remember the taxi ramp leading into the station from the old Broad Street side will recognise immediately where the RCM set up shop. It was in the large, dimly-lit room below and to the left of the ramp, one of those cheerless spaces which Victorian architects (or their clients) felt bound to utilise, as with the arches of urban railway viaducts which were originally blocked off to make cheap classrooms for council schools and are now occupied by small garages and furniture makers.

The Liverpool Street dungeon was known, incongruously, as the gymnasium, presumably in memory of its intended purpose, though it had long been used for general storage. In preparation for the *Kindertransporte*, the room was cleared of boxes and other flotsam. Close to the door, rows of slatted chairs were set out behind a rope barrier. At the far end was hung a large tarpaulin.

A large handwritten notice was propped up by the door – *Bürge bleibt hier* (guarantors' seats here) – with an arrow pointing that way. Behind the tarpaulin there were tables and chairs for the RCM workers, mostly, as an American journalist noticed, elegantly turned-out young ladies who looked 'a good deal more like a junior league committee getting together to discuss a costume ball than officials waiting to sort out a trainload of Jewish refugee children'.

One of these smart socialites who belied her appearance was Elaine Blond (then Elaine Laski) who often went to Harwich to escort parties of children to London.

> When the train pulled in to Liverpool Street, there was always a line of people waiting on the platform. In front were the guarantors, families who had offered to take in a child and who were eager to catch a first glimpse of their boy or girl. They were inevitably anxious, wondering perhaps, at this critical moment, if they had been too reckless with their hospitality or simply worried about getting over the awkwardness of introductions. One mother told me she was so nervous that when it came to the point she could not remember the name of the boy she was meeting. I am sure that many of the children suffered the same problem in reverse.
>
> However well meaning, there were guarantors who could behave with dreadful insensitivity – by letting the disappointment show when the flaxen-haired beauty of their dreams turned out to be a tiny tub with pimples, say, or, conversely, by building up to such a pitch of enthusiasm for their chosen one that other children in the group felt neglected and inferior. This second group was just as likely to snatch up little Josef or Annette and make for home without telling an organizer. Many an hour was wasted searching the station for a child, presumed lost, but who in fact was already well on the way towards Ruislip. Experience quickly taught us that for the first hour after our arrival, it was the adults more than the children who were likely to misbehave. They had to be watched like hawks.

This impression was confirmed by a reporter from the *New Yorker*, one of the many journalists who turned up regularly at Liverpool Street in search of a heart-warming story.

> There were children jammed in the corridors, flattening their noses against the glass, hanging pigtails out of the open window. Someone on the platform screamed hysterically: 'Rosi! Rosi!', and there was

a rush toward a jolly little girl in a plaid coat who was leaning out waving from a carriage door. 'Please stay right where you are,' shouted a lady in a sable jacket. 'In two minutes a whistle will blow and you will all march over to the gymnasium.' Rosi looked a bit bewildered but she seemed to get the idea.

Once into the reception hall where the children were ushered to seats, the process of identification began against a medley of shouted greetings and grievances.

'I don't see why I can't take her now. I'm her auntie, aren't I? Look, here are the papers, Schmitt is the name. I am Mrs Schmitt and Elsa Schmitt is my own husband's brother Max's only child!'

'Yes, yes. I understand. But please, would you mind waiting just a little while!'

Eventually the RCM lady with the loudest voice had to climb on a chair and appeal for order. 'Will the guarantors please remain behind the barrier until they are called. I will now read the list of names. When you hear your name, please come forward to the table where you can sign the papers and take your child.'

Only the children with a smattering of English had any idea what was going on. Pacified by what was now a familiar hand-out of a packet of sandwiches, some chocolate and an orange, many, like ten-year-old Angela Carpos, were bewildered.

The room was awesome; cold and grey. And I had a problem. I wanted to go to the loo but I didn't dare ask. My name was called and I was given to Mr Littlejohn, who couldn't speak a word of German. I couldn't speak a word of English. He proceeded to take me round London. He wanted to buy things at shops. I said no. I was well brought-up and didn't accept presents. All I wanted was to go to the loo. Eventually he took me to a Lyons Corner House. He put two pennies into my hand (I had never seen a penny) and sent me upstairs. I went into the washroom but couldn't work out how to open the door to the toilet. I went to an attendant, and, trying to be polite, said '*Hände waschen*' and mimed washing my hands. The stupid woman took my penny, gave me a towel and put me in front of a basin.

When the claimant was a relative or friend, the first reaction after the hugs and kisses was to take hold of the label round the child's neck, tear it off and throw it to the ground. The gesture was entirely understandable.

With strangers the preliminaries were taken at a more gingerly pace. Dorli and Lieserl Oppenheimer were met by the Lerskys, friends of their parents, a Palestinian photographer and his wife who appreciated the traumas the children were suffering. Mrs Lersky reported back to Vienna on the day's events:

> On Thursday at three o'clock we were all at the station with thumping hearts. Punctually at three o'clock the train drew in and it was very moving how all the small and big children streamed out; there were surely none on that platform who didn't have tears in their eyes. I worked my way through all the scenes of greeting and then quickly found both of ours, waiting very nicely, hand in hand.
>
> Of course there was a frightful commotion and it was a bit difficult to get to the processing point. Dorli naturally comported herself very well but the little one was still very tired. We stowed them in a taxi and at home they were quickly refreshed and the little one was immediately put to bed where she soon dropped off to sleep peacefully. At this time, as always, your 'big' daughter showed such touching selflessness and such motherliness to the little one, one could only be amazed. When Lieserl was already in bed, Dorli was still in her coat and could not be moved to think of herself. I have never seen such a thing in a ten-year-old. Everyone was full of praise for her. Both of them then slept well all night, had a good bath the next morning to be rid of travel grime, and when my husband and I collected them at 11 o'clock both were cheerful and lively.

The last stage of the journey was the train north. The Lerskys were soon to return to Palestine. The arrangement was for Dorli and Lieserl to be looked after by a young Leeds couple, Theo and Tilly Hall, who had offered to take in refugee children. It all seemed straightforward, but Mrs Lersky was up against a dilemma:

> . . . whether I should travel with them to Leeds or whether I could allow these little ones to travel on their own. The fare is incredibly expensive and Dorli assured me that they could undoubtedly travel alone. I was still debating it when we arrived at the station. In the meantime I had discovered that a third child from the transport was also travelling to Leeds and I had arranged that she would depart at

the same time. She was a delightful, tall girl of about eleven years, and Dorli, who knew her from the transport, was pleased to have her company.

Third class on the trains here is really so wonderfully comfortable, like first class elsewhere, with wide express train carriages, large windows, upholstered seats and big tables in between. We chose the best possible seats for our two, and Lieserl, with her back to the window and her little arms on the big table, felt really grand. She was sliding two and fro on her big seat with delight!

Then I saw a Salvation Army officer getting in; a respectable-looking man with glasses who was stowing away his luggage opposite the children. I asked if he was also travelling to Leeds and whether I might put the little ones in his care. At first he was somewhat surprised but then he smiled kindly and agreed. Then I was quite relieved. I watched him in the next few minutes; he just sat and smiled and didn't take his eyes off the children. I am convinced he sat like that for the next four hours!

The memory that would always stay with the Lerskys was of the tiny Lieserl waddling along the platform.

How many pairs of pants was the little one really wearing? It was very sensible to do it like that. But there was a dumpling ambling along the station platform, and afterwards, when all the layers were shed, there was a very graceful and slim little girl. Fantastic!

Even when relatives were on hand, the first critical days could be horribly disorganised, as Kurt Weinburg can confirm:

At Liverpool Street Station my aunt collected me. The plan was for me to go to a hostel but for some reason it wasn't ready. Suddenly there was a panic and accommodation had to be found. My aunt knew a family who had come to England a few months before, from Düsseldorf, who were planning to open an old folks' home for German refugees near Lewisham. She asked them if they could give me shelter until the hostel was ready. That's how I came to spend my first night in an empty house on a camp bed. I arrived on a Thursday and on the Sunday I wanted to visit my uncle and aunt in Putney. I went on a train via Waterloo. I had written out everything I had to say in English – I was very nervous.

Real fear came on those who thought they were abandoned. Barely able to speak English, adrift in a strange country, Nina

Liebermann could find no trace of Mrs Landers, from the West London Synagogue, who was supposed to be at the station.

> None of the women I approached answered to that name. My sister could not walk any more. Looking back, I saw her fall asleep on top of the luggage. All the other children had, by then, been met and spirited away. Desperately, I made another sweep of the now almost empty platform. I spotted a comfortable-looking woman, who seemed also to be on a search operation. I went up to her. 'Yes, I'm Mrs Landers. Where have you been? I've been looking for you for at least two hours. You should have arrived at 9 o'clock.'
>
> A full session at Liverpool Street gymnasium took from two to three hours. At the end of it there were always some children left over – those who had come on the wrong day or, more frequently, whose sponsors had muddled the date.
>
> At half past three, all but four of the children had been sorted out. They sat quite stoically, glancing up when anyone came in, but their eyes were a little anxious. Presently, they were rounded up by a brisk young woman who took them to a hostel for the night.

This left the adults without children ('possibly they had been taken off at the Dutch border; the SS guards liked to give a lasting impression of their authority') and a few veterans of earlier *Kindertransporte* who returned to Liverpool Street – sometimes, like Martha Levy, three or four times a week, on the off chance of spotting friends from home. It was invariably a wasted journey, though in her loneliness Martha always found some comfort in the sight of Jewish taxi drivers. In Germany, they were not allowed access to the main stations.

*   *   *

In late October 1938, some 15,000 Jews of Polish extraction were taken from their homes in Germany and dumped across the Polish border. Among them was ten-year-old Harry Katz.

> The Poles didn't want us in and we couldn't go back, so we had to wait. In the end they let us go through. We had to walk and walk and walk until we got to a deserted army camp and they told us we could stay in the old barracks. Each family was given a mattress cover and we had to fill it up with straw. Five people to one

mattress. The next morning, lorries came and gave each person half a loaf of bread and a boiled egg. We managed until they organised a communal kitchen and we then got better food. They told us later that the Polish Jews donated it to help us. We were in the barracks for several weeks but because my mother had a baby girl we were allowed a tiny room. I don't know who paid for it; we didn't because we had no money. My parents, my little sister and I all slept there. My brother went to a hostel for boys because he was thirteen. It was not comfortable but it was better than the barracks of course.

Later, I too went to the children's camp. There were no lessons; we just mucked around. After a few months my mother told me that my brother and I were going to England. My little sister couldn't come as she was only three years old, but my parents wanted my brother and me to go. I was in one of the later groups; it was four weeks before the war. My brother came about one week before the war so he was really lucky. We were taken by train to Gdynia (Danzig), where we had all our hair shaved off. Then they put us in a shower that was boiling hot and you couldn't leave it because the doors were locked. It was a terrible experience but they were probably right because we were very dirty and goodness knows what vermin we were carrying. When we were cleaned up we were put on the boat for London. What I remember about the boat is that we had boiled eggs for breakfast, lunch and dinner.

We docked just by Tower Bridge. We must have looked pretty weird: children about ten years old, with no hair and in tattered clothes. I remember British dockers chucking us pennies. They probably realised who we were.

This was one of the last *Kindertransporte* from Poland. The first, carrying thirty-four boys and twenty girls, docked on 15 February. It had started in Zbonszyn, a small town on the Polish border where 7000 deported Jews found refuge in stables and barns. Marga Goren-Gothelf was one of the survivors.

We left Zbonszyn on 15 January 1939 on our way to Warsaw where we spent about a week resting (Zbonszyn was no picnic!). From there on to Gdynia to board the Polish 'Flagship' *Warszawa* and through the Kiel Canal to London. Both the Baltic and the North Sea were as rough as only they know how to be and most of us were so seasick that we found it difficult to believe we'd ever stand on solid ground again. When the German officials boarded the ship at the entrance of the Kiel Canal we were scared stiff as we thought this was the end. Nobody had told us that this would happen and that it was normal procedure. I was thirteen years old at the time and the whole situation was frightening. We arrived at the London docks on 15 February 1939. When we saw the Tower Bridge, which we recognised from pictures in our schoolbooks, we felt relieved and knew that we were out of danger.

The money for three *Kindertransporte* from Zbonszyn (154 children in all) came from the Polish Refugee Fund in Britain which raised £5000. The RCM was not involved either as sponsor or as provider of accommodation. Nearly all the children went to orthodox hostels run independently of the Movement. The last group of Zbonszyn children arrived on 29 August, three days before the outbreak of war.

Apart from the Society of Friends, there was no established organisation ready to come to the help of children under threat in Czechoslovakia. The RCM held aloof for the same reason that it kept out of Poland – the resources did not stretch to additional responsibilities, or so it was argued. Those who rejected the conventional view and took up the cause of Czechoslovakian children were largely outside the mainstream of refugee aid. One such was Nicholas Winton, a young stockbroker set apart from his colleagues by his radical views.

> I went to Prague because my great friend Martin Blake, who was a master at Westminster School, rang me up one Friday and asked me to cancel my holiday. He said he was on to something he knew I would be interested in.

Abandoning winter sports for the refugee camps, Nicholas Winton was quickly convinced that a German invasion of Czechoslovakia was imminent. This made the plight of the refugees more desperate than anyone in London could imagine. Winton duly threw himself into the muddled affairs of the British Committee for Refugees from Czechoslovakia, a group of diverse personalities whose good intentions far outstretched their capacity to offer constructive help. He soon discovered that the Czechs were no better organised.

> We had to deal with at least five committees looking after special groups such as the Jews, the Communists, the writers and so on. I

met a lot of people and I had to keep explaining that I wasn't empowered by my government or anything like that; it was just me. In the end I got together a list of children and then went back to London to raise help.

By this time, the British Committee had a boxroom office in Prague run by Quaker ladies and other volunteers from the British community. As the queue of would-be emigrants handed in their names, Nicholas Winton spent every spare hour collecting guarantors and publicising his cause. His principal allies were the Society of Friends, the Unitarian Church and *Picture Post*, the popular weekly magazine which published a series of articles on the Czech crisis.

> Thank God I was in a business which closed for the day at 3.30. It took me half an hour to get home, then I ran the refugee office until ten at night. To some it must all have seemed very strange. In fact, the police came round and asked me why I had this enormous correspondence with Czechoslovakia.

When all that was lacking was someone to chaperone the *Kindertransporte*, Trevor Chadwick, a Latin teacher from Swanage, made a timely appearance.

> I was teaching at [Forres] our family prep school. Rumours of the many distressed children in Central Europe reached us and it was decided to adopt two . . . Another master at the school and I set off to Prague to select our pair . . . We got a clear impression of the enormity of the task. We so often saw halls of confused refugees and batches of lost children, mostly Jewish, and we saw only the fringe of it all.

Before his return to England, Chadwick made contact with Nicholas Winton. He then went back to Prague to recruit the first *Kindertransport* to take to the air. Twenty children were flown to Croydon, and 'They were all cheerfully sick, enticed by the little paper bags, except a baby of one who slept peacefully in my lap the whole time.'

In March 1939, the German army marched into Prague. Air lifts were now out of the question, but trains were still a practical proposition – as Chadwick discovered when he came to deal with the Nazi official in charge of emigration.

Kriminalrat Boemmelburg was an elderly, smiling gentleman, far from sinister, who eventually proved to be a great help, sometimes unwittingly. He was really interested in my project and his only Nazi-ish remark was a polite query why England wanted so many Jewish children.

He happily gave his stamp to the first train transport, even though I had included half a dozen adult 'leaders' on it. I went to the station accompanied by a Gestapo clerk and all the children were there, with labels tied round their necks.

There was trouble over the adults and Chadwick had to grovel to earn approval for his second train transport. Shulamith Amir was one of the passengers.

The scene at the railway station in Prague before our departure will forever remain in my memory. Most of the children were crying at the prospect of being parted from their parents, who themselves were trying to put on a brave face. My mother assured me that our parting would only be temporary and that she would follow me very soon to London, which I tried very hard to believe. Presumably most of these parents were fated, as was my mother, never to see their children again.

Our group consisted of over 120 children, accompanied by perhaps half a dozen adults. I was just twelve and among the oldest. I was entrusted with two toddlers of less than two years of age, for whom I was totally responsible throughout the three-day trip. Our train stopped frequently, sometimes for hours, at small stations where we were given food. At times, when the train travelled at a slow pace, German peasants would throw us sweets. Those of us with small charges used the overhead luggage racks to bed down these babies during the long nights whilst we ourselves sat up and tried to keep warm.

Finally our train arrived at the Hook of Holland where we were transferred to a Channel ferry. The crossing was rough and we were all very sick. A very miserable and bedraggled group arrived in London, to spend most of the night in an enormous bleak room lined with benches.

I was among the lucky few who had a parent waiting. My father collected me, and he and I spent the next eight years together in London.

The arrival of this transport took refugee workers by surprise since none of the children had proper documentation. When essential papers had failed to come through to Prague, Chadwick had decided to cut corners by manufacturing a few of his own. Convincing enough to persuade the Germans that London had kept to the bureaucratic niceties, the stamp of approval was secured and away went the train. Chadwick anticipated a row but the Home Office telegram, threatening to send the children back, he refused to take seriously. 'I figured the mob of legally accepted guarantors would stop that one.'

The British Committee was divided on the issue of cooperating with the Gestapo. There were those who felt that Chadwick was too friendly with *Kriminalrat* Boemmelburg and his cohorts but, as Nicholas Winton points out, there were no advantages in antagonising the Germans.

> The one thing the Germans didn't want at that time, I am absolutely certain, was a row with the British. So, in a curious way, they cooperated with us. But there was always the risk of being caught up in their propaganda.

Trevor Chadwick's unauthorised transport from Prague was not the only one to catch reception workers on the hop. With weeks, sometimes months between the issue of travel documents and their actual use, frequent changes in timetabling and the inevitable delays on overworked railways and sea routes, predicting when and where a transport would arrive was about as reliable as betting on a roulette wheel.

In the spring of 1939 clashes between Germans and Poles in the so-called 'free city' of Danzig added another starting point to the already confused map of *Kindertransporte* routes. Four transports carrying a total of 124 children came from Danzig, travelling by train via Berlin to the Hook where they joined up with other groups waiting to be ferried across to Harwich. The muddle was such that the welcoming committee threw away their lists of expected arrivals and started from scratch.

There was less of a problem when individual benefactors like Lord Sainsbury, Jean Hoare (a cousin of Sir Samuel Hoare) and the Reverend Alan Bateman, provost of Coventry Cathedral, set up their own lines of communication, dealing directly with families who wanted to send their children over to Britain, as well as arranging travel and acting as guarantors. Jean Hoare virtually handed over her Bloomsbury flat to young refugees. When Czechoslovakia was in terminal crisis she raised money from the Royal Institute of British Architects to bring back a planeload of children from Prague.

Towards the end, as the German hold on Prague tightened, the *Kindertransporte* were beset by bureaucratic delays. Nicholas Winton identified the state travel agency as the source of the trouble.

> They made more and more difficulties as time went on. One girl was asked why she hadn't brought her dog licence and she said it was because she didn't have a dog. They told her to go away and come back with proof that she didn't have a dog.

On the outbreak of war, a transport of 180 children was left stranded in Prague. They were commemorated by a note in the RCM annual report:

> What these children must feel like, having packed all their clothes, having sold everything that could not be removed, having said goodbye to their friends, can readily be understood.

*   *   *

Cast in the unenviable role of responding to the ever more frequent appeals for help from Vienna, Norman Bentwich decided to see for himself what needed to be done. He travelled in the second week of August 1939. His report offered not a vestige of comfort.

> The poverty and destitution of the remnant of a great community are heartrending. Well over half of the 67,000 are fed daily through the communal soup kitchens, most of them collecting for their families their one square meal of the day . . . They have no meat; and a large number are glaringly undernourished . . . Every single Jewish shop or business has been aryanised, destroyed or shut.

The only hope was emigration. But the quotas imposed by the United States and Britain – a thousand to each country – fell a long way short of Eichmann's target of clearing another 45,000 Jews from Vienna, at least a third of them children, within six months. The interview with Eichmann, which the Jewish community had struggled to arrange, failed to yield results. Bentwich was told to go home and persuade his own government to do more.

On the Vienna and Berlin routes every transport had its smattering of adult supervisors, who had to sign a pledge to return immediately they had handed over their charges to the RCM. Failure to do so would have put at risk all future *Kindertransporte* and, though in the last weeks of the peace the temptation to stay on in Britain must have been great, the escorts always did their best to get back. They were mostly recruited from one of the youth movements, or were teachers or social workers with a readiness to handle any problem thrown at them. A common experience was suffering the unwelcome attention of Gestapo guards who were inclined to lift items of value (sentimental as much as practical) or to vandalise luggage. When the intimidation became unbearable, as at Bentheim on the German–Dutch border, the route was abandoned in favour of a Belgian crossing at Herbesthal, but usually there was little that could be done except to comfort the children and to urge calm.

Lotte Freedman's husband Freddie accompanied several *Transport*.

> He went back and forth. He took hundreds of children. I used to help him. I'll never forget a little boy with a label round his neck, standing at the carriage window. As the train pulled out his mother ran down the platform, ran with the train crying, 'My child, my child'. It was awful.

Newly married, the Freedmans were able to obtain exit visas for themselves. They spent much of the war running a hostel in North Kensington. 'We had forty boys aged fourteen to eighteen. I could barely boil an egg. But I learned.'

The principle of learning by doing was familiar to all supervisors, not least Käthe Fischel from Prague, one of the youngsters who was sufficiently self-possessed to be recruited for nursery chores.

> We left from Prague by train. I don't remember the date – but it was spring, a few months before war broke out. The journey was unpleasant. There were very few people to look after the children and they gave me four or six little ones to take care of. I had never

looked after small children and these were very distressed. They kept wetting themselves and being sick and I had absolutely no idea what to do with them. Now with a daughter and grandchildren I can understand what it must have meant to a five-year-old to be stuck on that train – no wonder many of the children had breakdowns later on.

Another young helper holds a particular memory of a little girl with brown eyes.

I had to put her to bed in my cabin. We said prayers and she went to sleep. I wanted to go upstairs to join the other helpers but I had a little trouble because they said I was too young.

Twenty-two years on, a social worker was on duty with a new colleague. 'There was something vaguely familiar about her; she had lovely brown eyes . . .'

The adult supervisors really came into their own in negotiations with British customs. Everyone knew that the rules were being stretched, but it took a skilled operator to persuade an official to ignore evidence that was blatantly paraded before him. Norbert Wollheim was a master of the craft.

I was questioned about a boy who was carrying a valuable violin. Why had he brought it? I knew that his parents had given it to him as security, something to sell if the money ran short. But I couldn't say this. So I bluffed. 'The boy is a gifted musician; he must practise on his violin.' The customs officer was not convinced. 'If he's so clever, let me hear him play.' I turned to the boy and said in German, 'Can you play anything?' He nodded, took up his violin and started playing 'God Save the King'. After three stanzas the customs officer had had enough. 'All right. I believe you', he said, which was fortunate for us because, as I found out afterwards, the boy only knew three tunes and 'God Save the King' happened to be one of them.

On another flying visit, Norbert Wollheim found that one of his charges was over the age limit.

He had just been released from Dachau and his head was shaven. I asked him when he was born and sure enough he was over eighteen. He looked it; he was tall and broad. There was no way he could have been much younger. But I told him that whatever happened he had to say that he was born in 1924, three years on from his real birthday. At Harwich the immigration officer called me over. The boy was standing there, shaking. 'Ask him how old he is', said the immigration officer. The boy was word perfect. 'He says he was born in 1924', I translated. The officer looked at me, he looked at the boy. There was a long silence. Then he said to me, 'If there is an error, do you take responsibility?' Of course, I agreed. We were in.

On rare occasions a parent would act as chaperone. Ruth Michaelis and her brother were taken by their mother 'all the way to our first foster family, a rector and his wife in Kent, and then she went back to Germany'. There was some jewellery in their luggage and, to put the Gestapo off the scent, Ruth aged four years one month, was urged to carry a large, overdressed doll.

> As my mother expected, the doll got all the attention. They insisted in taking off every bit of its clothing. I protested and made an enormous fuss, which frightened my mother, especially when I demanded that the guards should dress the doll again. But they just walked off. I'm sure my screaming drove them away.

The only complete family to come over on a *Kindertransport* was the Alperns – Leo and Adele and their children Heinrich, Anita, Sonja and Irena. They came from Freiburg, where Leo was a credit draper. Like other Polish Jews, he was arrested in October 1938, but Adele and the four children ended up at Zbonszyn. Three months later the three older children were told they could go to Britain. A week after they left to join a transport at Warsaw, permission came through for their parents to follow them 'for domestic service'. By sheer coincidence the family was reunited on the boat train and sailed together, on the *Warszawa*, which docked at Cotton Wharf near London Bridge on 15 February 1939. Having made it, that family was split up for more than a year, but was reunited after the Blitz and eventually settled in Torquay.

In the last month before war was declared, families who were still on the waiting list for places on the *Kindertransporte*, but knew they had little chance of moving up the queue, took to waiting at the main rail stations, watching and hoping.

Seven-year-old Sonia Altman had a guarantor in Middlesbrough but, having missed one transport date because she had to have her tonsils out, there seemed little prospect of an early escape from Vienna.

> My mother was getting desperate. So every day, she packed my case and we haunted the station. I was getting quite used to these trips, me in my best clothes with a little label saying who I was and where I was going. Then, on 13 June, we were standing by a crowded train when we saw a mother who was in a dreadful state. She just couldn't bear to part with her child and at the last moment held her back. My mother took her chance and literally threw me on to the train. The doors were slammed and off I went. I remember holding my doll and crying all the time. I wanted my mother but of course she wasn't there any more.

At Leipzig, Betty Israel saw a baby handed up through a carriage window. 'The thoughts and feelings of that poor mother, giving over that tiny tot to a complete stranger, still haunt me today.'

The responsibility every *Kindertransporte* worker wanted to avoid was a last-minute decision on numbers. With the demand for places on the *Kindertransporte* shooting far ahead of the capacity of the RCM to provide guarantors, disappointments were inevitable. But that did not make it any easier to break the news. Philip Urbach was on a transport that was supposed to leave in mid-August.

> But then there was a message from England to say that instead of 180, only sixty could come. Rudolf Melitz, a fund raiser for *Youth Aliyah* who organised several transports, was given the job of reducing the list. It was a dreadful thing to have to do, as you can imagine. He worked on the principle that those who were isolated in the small towns and villages were in more urgent need than those in the cities where Jews had each other for support.

It was the second last transport to leave Berlin. Rudolf Melitz was on board. When they walked off the boat at Harwich, they saw a news hoarding with 'ultimatum' in large letters. Philip Urbach was encouraged by a German-sounding word ('Maybe English wasn't so difficult after all'), without realising that it meant war over Poland.

> In London, Melitz left us. He was booked to fly back to Berlin, but when he went to the Lufthansa office in Bond Street they told him

all planes had been cancelled because of the emergency. He said 'I must go. I have my mother there', but all they could offer was to hire him a private aircraft. Of course, he hadn't the money so he had to stay, which was his good luck though he didn't think so at the time.

The last of the pre-war *Kindertransporte* left Berlin on 31 August. It was a close-run thing. Just hours before the train was scheduled to depart a call came through to the *Youth Aliyah* office in London, warning that the transport was about to be cancelled. The imminence of war had compelled the Dutch to close the border, which meant that the train would be stuck in Germany. It was pointless even to start the journey.

Intense lobbying of the Dutch authorities forced a concession. The train would be allowed to cross the border if there was an absolute assurance that the children would be taken on to Britain. The promise was delivered and the train left on time, though with fewer children than expected. There were places for sixty-six passengers, thirty-one with *Youth Aliyah* and thirty-five with the RCM, but as the train was boarding the total was cut to sixty. The youngest were left behind.

Waiting at the border was the irrepressible Gertrude Wijsmüller with a bus she had managed to commandeer. She had been less fortunate with the driver, who was not at all sure of the route to the Hook and had to rely on friendly passers-by to give directions. But they made it to the boat, which sailed in the early hours of 1 September, two days before war was declared.

Any lingering hopes of bringing more children out of Germany were finally stifled by a Home Office ruling that refugees from enemy territories would no longer be allowed entry under any circumstances. This left open the possibility of further *Kindertransporte* from countries threatened by Germany, but in the first months of the war no one was willing to engage in such defeatist speculation. In fact, it was not until the German army invaded Holland on 10 May 1940, that any action was taken on behalf of the 26,000 non-Dutch Jews who were sheltering in and around Amsterdam. On 11 May, an order went out for German refugees to remain in their houses. Three days later, the head of the Jewish community was told that a boat was docked at Yjmuiden, ready to take any Jews who wanted to go to England. It was a case of first come, first served. The office of the Jewish Refugee Committee was soon overflowing with eager claimants for places on the boat. One of the more persuasive was Gertrude Wijsmüller, not on her own behalf, but for the Burger-Weeshuis, a hostel which accommodated some seventy-five children. She promised to make all the arrangements, including the hiring of as many buses as she could find. One o'clock was agreed as the deadline when Mrs Wijsmüller and another refugee worker, Gertrud van Tijn, were to meet at the American Hotel to decide on their next move. When the time came there was not much doubt as to what they should do.

Mrs Wijsmüller had not only hired four buses,' wrote Gertrud van Tijn, 'but had also asked for and received a sort of written permit from the Chief of Police of the aliens department for the buses to proceed to Yjmuiden . . . I then told Mrs Wijsmüller to fill the buses as far as possible with refugee children and then with families who did not have private cars . . .

When I wanted to leave the hotel, there was passport control. The Dutch police kept me forty minutes because they thought my [Dutch] passport made out in Johannesburg – renewed in Mombasa with Palestine, Egyptian, many English, German and French visas – suspicious. I was so frantic because every minute was valuable, but there was nothing to be done about it.

While I waited the radio announced that the Queen and the government had left Holland. The large restaurant was crowded. There was no sound and no comment. The shock was indescribable. People realised the war was lost. When I finally left the hotel it was nearly a quarter to three o'clock.

I went to the Lijnbaansgracht first to see how things were proceeding there. The scene was indescribable. The buses were there and there was practically a free fight to get in. We arranged as much as possible to take people with children and those who had special 'Jewish' claims on us.

When the buses were well on their way, Gertrude van Tijn followed in her car.

The road was thronged with cars and bicycles – most of them coming back; many called out to me that it was no use to proceed as the police did not allow any but military authorities to get through to Yjmuiden. I proceeded and every time I was stopped by the police I somehow hypnotised them to let me pass. They had allowed the buses to pass because of the special permit they held. I told them that I had the nurse in the car who was to look after the children on the boat. Somehow I got through to Yjmuiden. About a quarter of an hour's drive from the quay where the large boat was anchored there were hundreds of cars with Dutch and German Jews who were not allowed to proceed. I knew many of them; some returned, discouraged; some waited and eventually got away – I do not yet know how. There was plenty of room on the boat; up to this day I do not know how it was possible that the Dutch civil authorities who had informed us of the chance to leave had not also seen to it that the military authorities were informed and the road was given free for the people to pass.

One of Mrs Wijsmüller's passengers was Ilse Wertheimer. She related her experiences to a BBC radio reporter in September 1940.

On the first day of the German invasion, at about five o'clock in the morning, we heard dull explosions and from then onwards we had continual air raids. As we had no shelters, we just had to lie flat on the ground. On the fourth day, just as the sirens started to howl at midday, we were told to put on our best dresses quickly and go to the waiting bus and we were then driven to the port. There, in front of us, we saw a sinking ship with many screaming people on it and behind it a big cloud of smoke.

We then went on board another ship (the SS *Bodegraven*) that was in the harbour and sailed at 8.30 p.m. When it got dark we heard the sound of aeroplanes overhead, everyone thought our last hour had come. We threw ourselves on the decks and after a few minutes the planes flew away again, without having done any damage.

The SS *Bodegraven* was an elderly steam freighter, serviceable for short hauls but not built for military action. Fortunately for the young refugees, there was much to divert them from the risk they were taking. Ya'acov Friedler recalls the scene:

As we walked towards the vessel we noticed the arrival of two small warships – they must have been torpedo boats – from which soldiers wearing dark blue uniforms and British-style steel helmets were disembarking. The dozen or so men, Royal Marines I guess they must have been, were staggering under the weight of their kitbags and the heavy machine-guns they were bringing ashore. We crossed paths as they walked off the pier and we walked on to it. They smiled and gave us the thumbs-up sign, shouting words of encouragement at us. We did not understand their language, but there was no mistaking the tone.

By now the two Gertrudes, Wijsmüller and van Tijn, were on their way back to Amsterdam.

The boat left at eight o'clock exactly. We had to run hard because the English warned us that before leaving they would blow up the pier. We heard the detonation immediately behind us. We drove back to Amsterdam, passing the burning oil tanks of the *Royal Dutch*. The road was deserted. The Dutch military authorities who had stopped us every few hundred yards on our way to Yjmuiden had left. The Germans had not yet arrived. Then we neared Amsterdam and saw the town blazing with lights. We knew then that Holland had capitulated. There was a terrible irony in the fact that this one night – at the blackest hour of its history – Amsterdam was ablaze with lights. (The next day the Germans re-enforced the blackout regulations.) We went to the houses of several of our friends who had all come back from Yjmuiden discouraged. We told them that the road was now free and that we believed they still had a chance to get away. They were all too disheartened. That night many Jews (particularly Dutch Jews) tried to commit suicide.

Meanwhile, the *Bodegraven* was having a hard time trying to clear Dutch waters.

We sat watching the shore recede when two German planes appeared in the sky and started bombing the harbour. We could see them making their run and diving to release their bombs, which dropped slowly to explode below. It was like watching some spectacular fireworks. Then, suddenly the two bombers turned towards the sea and made straight for our ship. They swooped low as they approached and we could see their Luftwaffe markings. The planes started sweeping the ship with machine-gun fire and we instinctively threw ourselves face down. The captain issued rifles to the crew who took ineffective pot shots at the planes.

This continued for a few moments. Then the captain announced that Holland had surrendered and ordered his crew to cease fire. The men lowered their rifles and pressed against the side of the superstructure for cover – a bizarre scene.

All this time the children were crowded on deck. It had been assumed that, because the journey would only take a few hours, it was better to be in the open air than in the dark and unventilated cargo holds. But when at last the planes turned away and headed for land, the order was given for all passengers to get below.

> There were no ladders on board the freighter so the crew put planks down into the holds for us to descend. We found it quite difficult to negotiate the steep planks in the gathering darkness, but the sailors gathered us up in their arms and slid down the planks with us, depositing us safely at the bottom. We simply lay down on the hard floor and went to sleep.

There was one more attack to come, not from German planes but from British gunners. Thrown off course in dense fog, the *Bodegraven* drifted south towards the Kent coast, where it was spotted by a local defence unit. At the sound of gunfire the refugee ship turned away and made off round the southern counties and up towards Liverpool, where it was finally recognised as a friendly vessel. The *Bodegraven* docked to a hero's welcome. When asked how they had managed to escape, the younger children chanted 'Mrs Wijsmüller, Mrs Wijsmüller'. There was not much else they could say that was understandable in English. Immigration formalities were waived and the passengers from the very last *Kindertransport* were taken in by the Manchester branch of the RCM. Two hostels were opened for the group henceforth known as the 'Amsterdam children'.

Between December 1938 and September 1939, the RCM brought over 9354 refugee children. Of these 7482 were Jewish. Adding to these the 431 children sponsored by Inter-Aid in the months before *Kristallnacht*, the 700 or so who came to Britain under the auspices of *Youth Aliyah*, the 100 orthodox children rescued by Rabbi Schonfeld and the Union of Orthodox Hebrew Congregations, and the Polish and Czech refugees saved by Nicholas Winton and his friends, brings the total to well over 10,000. By the end of 1939 only 331 of these children had re-emigrated, either to join their parents or relatives mostly in Palestine or the United States. More would have gone if there had been money to pay for their fares. But the RCM could barely cover its existing commitments while American refugee groups, though ready in principle to advance funds, were prevented by immigration law from subsidising transportation costs. The best that was on offer from the National Refugee Service in New York was cooperation to 'get in touch with American relatives and affiants and attempting to secure the steamship fare, or as much of it as possible, from them'. So small was the number of beneficiaries, they were outnumbered in the war years by those children who joined the RCM ranks having turned up in Britain by long and roundabout escape routes.

In 1943, there were several arrivals from Scandinavia including Wilhelm Flehner, born in Vienna, who had escaped from Norway over into neutral Sweden. His parents had sent him to Oslo immediately after Hitler's annexation of Austria, when he was only nine. Soon afterwards his mother and sister came to Britain. Five years on, with the Nazis extending their anti-Semitic reach, Willi's guardian, a Russian Jewess who looked after several refugee children, decided it was time for a mountain trek to more hospitable territory. They did it in winter through deep snow. A few weeks later, when the link had been made between Willi and his mother, who lived in Rochdale, the Movement collected money for the rest of his journey.

Also from Sweden, but after a more convoluted adventure, was Rudi Neumark. He and a friend had fled from Vienna over the border into Czechoslovakia. When the German army followed them, they kept on the move, taking on odd jobs along the way, until they ended up in Warsaw. There they split up, Rudi going by train to Gdynia where he managed to work his passage on a Polish boat to Stockholm. This brief experience as a merchant seaman qualified him for another voyage, this time on an American cargo vessel bound for London. This was when his troubles really started. Having been on the run for nearly four years, Rudi had grown from an early teenager into a young adult. So instead of a hero's welcome, he was put in charge as an enemy alien to spend his eighteenth year in an internment camp.

7

Home from Home

*'Our first day in Birmingham was hell. It suddenly hit me
that we were in a foreign country without knowing the
language, without relatives or friends, and I was trying
desperately to be brave as a thirteen-year-old boy was expected
to behave. I spent most of that day in and out of the toilet
so that no one could see the tears rolling down my cheeks.'*

To qualify as a model foster parent you had to be at the wealthier
level of the middle class, with an already established family; it
helped if you lived in the country (away from urban enticements),
spoke a little German, and could tolerate moody children who
suffered bouts of depression and were inclined to long silences.
And you had to be Jewish.

The typical foster parent was not at all like this. Recruited from
the lower-middle or working class, the representative benefactor
lived in a small house in a town or city, had no children or had
children who were grown up, spoke not a word of German,
knew nothing of Germany beyond the front-page news of the
Express or *Mirror*, and did not begin to understand the trauma
of being a young refugee. And the typical foster parent was not
Jewish.

This last discrepancy between the ideal and the typical foster
parent was the cause of much anguish within the Jewish community and much criticism from without. Why were there no
more Jewish families willing to take in refugee children? The
Union of Orthodox Hebrew Congregations (ADATH) suspected
a dastardly plot by the RCM to subvert orthodox Judaism by
favouring Christian hospitality. The ADATH policy of rejecting

all non-Jewish offers to help assumed that if the RCM took an equally hard line, the faithful would rise to the challenge.

But the argument did not stand up.

The Jews of Britain were a tiny minority, less than one per cent of the population. For six years up to the war, they had raised millions to help their German cousins and had absorbed over 60,000 refugees, not all of them living off charity by any means, but with the great majority owing thanks to Jewish organisations for giving them a new start.

The dismissive view – 'They can afford it' – derived from the anti-Semitic assumption that all Jews were well off. It was propagated by otherwise intelligent people like the eminent bishop who greeted a party of refugee children, kitted out in their ill-fitting hand-me-downs, with the cheerful observation: 'I didn't know there were any poor Jews.'

Anyone who was familiar with the less fashionable districts of London, Manchester and Leeds knew otherwise. The average Jew was the average Englishman, living off a weekly pay packet of four pounds a week or less at a time when, in the worst-hit areas for unemployment, up to twenty per cent of the population was below the poverty line. Allowing for those who were too selfish to want to help even when they were well qualified to do so, and those who were manifestly unsuitable to act as foster parents, because they were too young, too old or too inexperienced – a third, say, of the total, it was unrealistic to expect the Jewish community to absorb 10,000 refugee children.

In fact, the community was near the end of its financial tether. The warnings had been clear for some time. In early 1939, Lord Hailey had voiced fears that 'the problem would frankly become unmanageable', but his appeals to the government to support the refugee cause with public funds had met with blank refusal. The risks of establishing an expensive precedent were considered too great to countenance.

As the pressure of numbers built up, Sir Samuel Hoare, the Quaker Home Secretary, began taking his lead from Hailey, telling the cabinet that the funds of the refugee organisations 'have been strained to the utmost'. By July, Hoare was forecasting that before long refugees will 'have to be supported from British public funds if scandal is to be avoided'.

The rest of the cabinet was still reluctant to commit the taxpayer, but it was ready to take seriously a scheme put up by Lionel Rothschild for an international trust fund. The idea was that the leading countries on the Evian Committee would join in promoting a public subscription of £20 million, of which £5 million was to be raised in London. Revealing a touching faith in the stability of money, Rothschild suggested that no interest would be due on the loan but that the capital would be repaid after forty years. To start the ball rolling, the government was asked to contribute £1 million.

Opposition came from the Treasury ministers who objected to a handout of a cool million as a near sacrilegious attack on the principle of sound finance, and from the Foreign Secretary who had no faith at all in the capacity of the Evian Committee to agree on joint action. Decisively outvoted, Hoare went away to think up an alternative plan. But by then it was too late.

The only concession forced through before the critical days in September was on the tax allowance to foster parents who were now able to claim for any child in their care under the age of sixteen or in full-time education.

On 30 August, the RCM announced that it could not accept any more refugee children. Two days later, war was declared. On 3 September, Hoare was replaced as Home Secretary by Sir John Anderson, who promptly declared a banning order on immigrants from territories controlled by the Third *Reich*.

Cutting off the flow of refugees did not solve the financial problem, though for a time the government acted on the assumption that the refugee organisations could now look after themselves. When the evidence proved otherwise, the Home Office held out the prospect of a sizeable loan to be repaid on an unspecified date. The Jewish bodies turned the offer down flat, arguing that it was immoral for them to accept a loan which they had no reason to believe they would be able to repay. They were, however, ready to accept an outright grant and on 1 December they warned the Home Office that, if the money was not forthcoming within a week, the refugee organisations would close down, leaving their charges to be maintained on the local rates.

At this point, the Home Office negotiating team, led by Sir Alexander Maxwell, promised to think again. The next offer was more attractive. Maxwell suggested that the government might be prepared to make a grant equal to the amount collected by the refugee organisations. After some discussion on back-dating, the formula was accepted though it had only six months to live. By the summer of 1940, the Central Council for Jewish Refugees was again feeling the pinch, with the result that the government accepted, in principle, the responsibility for the whole cost of maintaining refugees at scales to be agreed and seventy-five per cent of the cost of administration. Since the scales were minimal by any standards, the refugee organisations were still in need of help, none more so than the RCM which, for some curious reason, was not immediately included in the government's grant scheme. It was not until 1942, after a lengthy investigation into the efficiency of the RCM, that state support was forthcoming for child refugees, to the limit of eighteen shillings a week for each child. One of the conditions held that 'where a youth or girl was being adequately cared for by foster parents or was satisfactorily settled in life with sound views and reliable character . . . then the Movement might and should reduce, or in some cases discontinue, its welfare work.'

In these restrictive circumstances, the quality of foster parents was all-important.

The RCM understood this as well as they understood the realities of keeping up the supply of foster parents. They were less well-informed when it came to knowing the sort of people who were likely to volunteer as foster parents. RCM activists were drawn largely from wealthy and privileged families. Early on, they imagined that all foster parents would be like them – not so rich perhaps, but sharing the same basic standards. It came as a shock to find that the Englishman's home did not necessarily have a spare bedroom or a bath or inside lavatory. Another revelation: enthusiastic volunteers were not necessarily best-suited to be foster parents, either by temperament or circumstances. But since the RCM staff were not trained social workers, many undesirables slipped through the inspection net, including quite a few whose only interest was in acquiring cheap household labour.

Ursula Hutton, nee Cohn, did not even get a good night's sleep before plunging into the realities of her new life with her foster family in Willesden:

Unfortunately, they did not look after me very well. On the day I arrived they gave me a hot drink and after an hour I did the

ironing – the ironing for the whole family, having just arrived in
England . . .

Ursula was expected to do all the housework, look after the baby
of the family and was paid 2/6d a week.

> They would not let me go out – they were afraid I would go to
> Bloomsbury House. They were very religious Jews and they spoke
> Yiddish to me because I did not speak English. I thought I had to
> do all this work to earn my keep.

Split up from her brother, Diane Garner had no complaints
about her foster mother – 'She was a very loving woman.' Her
brother was less fortunate:

> His foster parents were, what I would call, professional do-gooders.
> I found out some time later that they were paid for having him.
> My foster parents weren't because they never knew they were
> entitled to it. My brother's foster parents would never say he was
> German. She used to say he was a Polish refugee. I think he had a
> far superior home to me – he used to get taken away on holidays
> and things like that – but after about four years they said they
> couldn't cope with him. He was expelled from school at the age of
> seven and they said he was destructive when in fact he just tried to
> find out how things worked. He'd take a watch to pieces and then
> couldn't put it together again. They put him in a national children's
> home and told my mother he was in boarding school. They washed
> their hands of him and my brother had terrible hang-ups for the
> rest of his life.

Parents naturally worried about their children, how they were
settling in, how they were behaving with their new families. Tom
Berman, now in Israel, still has the first letter his mother wrote
from Czechoslovakia to the Millers in Glasgow on 14 June 1939.
Described as 'kind-hearted, yet . . . a lively and obstinate boy',
Tom was brought up in a prosperous house (his father was a
manager of a textile firm) and was used to a well-stocked meal
table.

> He is mostly fond of soups and I give them first after meat and
> vegetable dishes . . . he likes chocolate tart without cream . . . and
> is very fond of fruit, especially bananas . . . He eats all sorts of
> meat, poultry as well, but only cut to very small pieces.

With the nervous worry comes the loneliness: 'The house is quiet as the grave', and the fear of the future: 'Though we have registered we are told at the American consulate it may last [take] years until we get the possibility of emigrating, the quota being overcharged.'

And the worry again:

> Please let me know whether he cries sometimes and about whether he annoys you and refuses to obey, as I know well that the child has bad points which will be polished by time.

Tom stayed with the Millers, who were a childless couple, until 1952. His parents did not escape.

Manfred Drake (formerly Manfred Drechsler) remembers how much he missed his mother at first:

> My mother and I were very close. I so loved her. She mollycoddled me. I cut her out of my mind. I can remember my father's face without looking at a photo, but without a photo I can't remember my mother's face. When I came to England I couldn't breathe, I was so longing for my mother. I missed her terribly.

For those children going straight to foster families, without even the support of the friends they had made on the journey, natural feelings had to be forced down as adjustments to a new environment and a new language were made. Herbert Hobden (Holzinger) tried hard to keep a stiff upper lip as he was introduced, with his ten-year-old sister, to his new home:

> Our first day in Birmingham was hell. It suddenly hit me that we were in a foreign country without knowing the language, without relatives or friends, and I was trying desperately to be brave as a thirteen-year-old boy was expected to behave. I spent most of that day in and out of the toilet so that no one could see the tears rolling down my cheeks.

Martha Blend had her first sight of a new foster mother in the cavernous waiting room at Liverpool Street Station:

> I found myself being taken charge of by a small plump woman who spoke to me in the nearest she could get to German which was Yiddish. She took me home to a little Victorian terraced house in Bow, East London. Her husband was an out-of-work London

cabbie. As they had no children of their own they had decided to take me on. When she asked me what I wanted to do I replied with one word, *schlafen* [sleep], and was glad to sink into the bed she had prepared for me in a little room on the first floor of the house.

Next morning, waking up in a strange room in a strange house, the reality of the separation hit me with full force . . .

Then there were those who were favoured by the luck of the draw. One girl remembers her first impression of her foster father: 'He had Sephardi eyes, like my mother. I felt at home at once . . .' And Helga Samuel was given every support and care by her well-off foster parents. She describes the first meeting at Liverpool Street:

An extremely kind-looking couple stood there and a welcoming arm was placed around my shoulder . . . I was driven 'home' in a large car, complete with chauffeur – past St Paul's Cathedral, Buckingham Palace and other places of interest (although not to me that day, as my heart was filled with such uncertainty it is hard to describe and I had a lump in my throat), and I sat in the back of the car, still with that comforting arm around my shoulder . . .'

On arrival at my new 'home', the maid opened the door, I saw a lovely open coal fire burning in the grate – the first thing – a cup of tea and something to eat and more kind words to help me to bear it all. I remember crying all that first day – the strangeness of it all – the sadness of having first to part with my mother – then with my sister – now being all on my own – in a strange country – a strange house – strange people – but with wonderfully kind faces.

So the days passed, difficult at first, mostly sign language, as I had only learned a few English words by this time . . . gradually getting used to my new environment. I had acquired a new 'sister' and 'brother' – everyone was doing their utmost to make me feel happy . . . children adapt and learn quickly and learn to forget even more quickly the sad things . . .

For those who did not reach a secure environment as quickly as Helga, lack of basic English could lead to weird experiences. One boy thought that 'To let' signs indicated a toilet. Another, on his first bus journey, noted down the name of a shop as a landmark for the return trip. It took a little time for him to realise that 'Bovril' was not a local retailer.

Herta Stanton stayed two days in London before travelling to her new home:

> That was the worst experience for me – it was terrible but funny in retrospect. It was in Crawley. I had an address and in England you write the road first and the town last, whereas on the continent you did the opposite – the town first, then the street. It had the name of a house called Kingscourt and I asked for a ticket to Kingscourt and they gave me one. I arrived at a little halt in the country, somewhere near East Grinstead. And there was nothing there. One man was station master, porter, the lot. I showed him the address and he laughed. He realised what had happened. I remember there was a woman there who gave me a lovely red apple to eat because I was in such distress. They put me on a bus and the bus driver was told where to put me off. And that was my first impression of England. Terrible.

After arriving at Liverpool Street and spending the night in London, Angela Carpos was sent off to Edinburgh with another girl.

> Nobody told us it would take all night to get there. We sat up, waiting for the station called Edinburgh . . . We were told a lady would pick us up. When we arrived, in a right state, not having slept a wink and having nothing to eat, the platform emptied and there was no lady. A young man came and picked up our cases. We were very suspicious children and we started to scream. Nobody came to help. He jabbered in English and, before we knew where we were, we were in a car.
>
> My friend said: 'I've got a penknife – you scream *Hilfe*! (Help! – which would have done a lot of good in Edinburgh) and I will stick the knife in his back.'

Luckily the driver had some idea of what was going on – and managed to escape assassination.

Letters from home contained frequent reminders to show appreciation. As Marietta's mother and father wrote to her in Birmingham on 1 July 1939:

> It is very lucky that such a nice family have enabled you to come over. Thank God for that. Continue to be good, grateful for everything, nice and decent to everyone . . .

But it was hard to express gratitude for what was bound to be seen as a harsh deprivation – the loss of natural family. Inge Joseph, then twelve-year-old Inge Polloch, kept a diary from June to September 1939. She promised to tell everything but added: 'I hope you won't be too shocked if I complain too much . . .'

Inge stayed with the Robins family in Falmouth in a large house and had the benefits of a private tutor but she was homesick for Vienna. 'I feel I shall die of misery . . . when I die I want written on my tombstone: "Here Lies a Child Who Perished Miserably From Homesickness".' Mrs Robins comes over as a cold, strict woman who was for ever giving orders. Great upset was caused when she forbade Inge to speak German with her sister Lieselotte. For Mr Robins, Inge felt the beginnings of a schoolgirl crush and hated him when he did not take her side. Often she hated everyone and spent a lot of time crying, which the Robinses evidently decided not to see. It is easy enough to put another interpretation on the behaviour of the Robinses, to argue that they were doing their best in trying circumstances (to forbid German was not a bad way of teaching English), and that they had their work cut out dealing with precocious children.

Gratitude, perhaps, comes more easily with hindsight. Miss Harder was a spinster in her early fifties who ran a small tobacconist's shop in London's Archway. She had continuously offered her services to the RCM committee as a foster parent, but they had never found a suitable child and perhaps also felt that she was too poor to cope. But when she heard about Lore Selo and her two sisters, whose mother did not want them to be parted, Miss Harder promptly offered to take all three and the committee were shocked into acceptance. Miss Harder even refused the offer of financial assistance, in case it led to another child losing his chance of coming to Britain.

Lore will never forget her first meeting with Miss Harder:

> A lady dressed rather shabbily in old-fashioned clothes came towards us and into my hands she put a card on which the words 'Mother Love' were written. I knew a little English, just enough to understand what she meant to convey, but at the time my sisters and I were rather bewildered and, quite frankly, disappointed. We were young and frightened and I suppose we really had no idea what to expect, but we certainly never thought that our new foster

mother would look so unattractive. We had even more of a shock when we saw her dingy home. It was a two-room flat in an old mansion block. She had given up her bedroom to the three of us and she slept in the sitting room on the sofa. It all seemed very cramped and poor and the flat was dark.

Those early weeks when we were miserable – we missed our mother and often cried – must have been very difficult for Miss Harder. She had to spend a good deal of her time in the shop and rush back to cook meals and care for us. Three tearful children who spoke very little of her own language cannot have been easy to love. But she was patient and understanding and even treated us to a holiday on the Isle of Wight, which, we found later, she could barely afford. She was helped to pay for it by friends and customers.

After a few months the three girls began to settle down. When a message came from a friend in Prague that their mother had disappeared, Miss Harder did everything she could to console them and they became very close. With the outbreak of war, the shop fell on harder times. When Miss Harder had to do without her assistant, Lore helped out:

> We were too young to realise that it must have been a most worrying time for Miss Harder. Sometimes we were naughty, as children inevitably are.

Six months after the sisters arrived in England, Miss Harder died of consumption. The sisters were separated, Lore working as a maid and the others going to foster parents. Twenty years later, in a talk which was later broadcast on Woman's Hour, Lore looked back:

> I think it is only now, after all these years, that I quite understand what a truly kind, wonderful and courageous woman Miss Harder was. She was my second mother for those few months. My sisters and I owe our lives to her but we can never repay her for her kindness, for having taken three unknown children into her home, given them love and understanding and compassion.

Clearly, concern for children in what appeared to be less than propitious circumstances could be misplaced. Martha Levy, too, was happy in what many would have found an unenviable situation. She had a room in Exmouth Street in London's East End, with a family of five adults:

At that time the East End was not a particularly nice place but luckily there were a lot of Jews there. I worked extremely hard. The first morning the lady had to get up at six o'clock to show me how to make a fire; I had never seen an English fire. I was very lucky because although I had to help in the house, I was able to go every Sabbath morning to *Schule*. The family were extremely sympathetic and very, very nice to me.

The reason I had to leave was a friend of mine came over from Germany to bring me a present from my stepmother. Because he came early he saw me on my hands and knees scrubbing the floor. He got very upset and went to Bloomsbury House and told them that it was not for this that the children had been brought over. Believe it or not, they took me away a week later to a girls' hostel in Ladbroke Grove. And I had been very happy with that family.

Ya'acov Friedler experienced two very different, but both very English, foster homes, adapting with ease and enthusiasm to both ways of life. Staying first of all with the Maggses – 'the first parents I had in four years and I have good reason for not putting parents in inverted commas' – in a small country town, he learned the respectable, middle-class way to do things:

Mealtimes were the real lessons for me. Mrs Maggs instructed me how a young Englishman should use his knife and fork, drink his soup without making a noise, and never leave the table without permission from the head of the family. The slices of bread for tea were cut razor-thin, a habit that has stayed with me.

One day, when I refused the slice of dried fruit cake (oddly enough called English cake in Israel) because I had already eaten all I could, Mr Maggs pointed out to me that a well-mannered young man leaves enough room for the cake because it is always an integral part of tea. It might have been frivolous to worry about tea and cakes while the war for the very survival of Britain was raging, but I felt that these apparent trivialities were at the heart of what we were fighting for . . .

Once, when a classmate invited me to tea with his foster parents, Mrs Maggs made enquiries and informed me that she did not think it advisable for me to visit that family, because they would add little if anything to my education or culture. I was sorry to have missed a day out but happy that she cared enough not to allow it. My own mother couldn't have done more . . .

Every Wednesday, at eight-thirty in the evening, the whole family listened to *ITMA* (one of the most popular wartime comedy shows). We assembled in Mr Maggs's bedroom, where he retired early due to frail health, and arranged our chairs round the fireplace to listen to the big radio . . .

Happy though he was, Ya'acov wanted very much to be together with Solly, his brother, and the Maggses were not able to accommodate the two of them. They found a new billet in a working-class household. The Crooks, middle-aged and childless, made them welcome. There was just one problem:

> They treated us with much love in the year we spent with them and it pains me still that we were forced to live a lie with them.
>
> When it was first suggested that they take in two Jewish refugee boys from the continent, they made it plain that they would not have any German boys under their roof. It was impossible to explain to them the difference between German Nazis who were trying to destroy Britain and Jewish refugees from Germany. We had to pretend we were Dutch and kept up the pretence to the end.
>
> The Crooks' old cottage had neither electricity nor a bathroom. The parlour and kitchen were lit by gas light, and if anybody tells you that electric light is better than the pure white light of the gas mantle they have probably never experienced it. Moreover, it was possible to turn the light up or down, depending on the brightness you wanted, which at the time was an advantage over electric light that could only be switched on or off. The radio worked on a liquid acid battery that had to be recharged every few months. Upstairs there were two bedrooms with no lights at all, and when we went up to bed we would take a candle in a china holder and snuff it out the moment we were between the sheets.

Margaret Olmer found her working-class foster parents in the Midlands very anxious to learn as much as possible about her background:

> He worked in the local shoe factory and she worked in a clothing factory. They had no children and lived in a terraced house. She fretted when I went to grammar school – because I was getting opportunities that she never had . . . but they were quite cultured. She had wanted to be a teacher. They weren't Jewish but let me go to Jewish classes. They said I must have some sort of moral education and they didn't send me to church, which is consecrated ground, but to chapel, which is unconsecrated. From the pulpit you got morality, so I grew up with the religious morality but not

Jewish dogma. This was at Raunds, near Wellingborough. Their niece looked like my cousin. That was very nice for me. At one time I was the only Jew there. I joined the Brownies and my friends' parents were always very nice to me.

The family who took in Lorraine Allard had a long-term relationship in mind:

Their only son had a girlfriend who was not Jewish. By bringing me into the house, they hoped he would switch his affections. That I was only fourteen never entered their minds. In fact, their son did marry his girlfriend who converted. They had an extremely happy marriage with four children.

In any case, Lorraine was far too preoccupied to think about romance. As the prospects of war increased, many children became obsessed with getting their parents out of Germany. For Lorraine it was her one and only thought:

I could not get across to my foster parents how bad things were in Germany. I set out in Lincoln knocking on people's doors. I found expensive areas and knocked on the doors of big houses and asked if they needed a cook or a gardener because that was the only way you could get people over without money being involved. Most of the time I knocked on doors and burst into tears; sometimes, although I barely spoke any English, I could get some words out. I spent every spare moment doing this and I think if the war had waited a little I would have found someone to help. I did find homes for three other children but it was hard to get my elderly parents out. My first boyfriend in Germany came to Lincoln but the two girl cousins I found homes for didn't make it. Nor, unfortunately, did my parents.

Children who made a successful adjustment and settled in happily with a foster family were devastated when they were subjected to another round of upheaval and insecurity. This was Peter Prager's experience:

I thought that I would stay with my foster parents for good but that wasn't what they thought. They had their down periods, and their business suffered with the war. They wrote to the Jewish Refugee Committee saying they couldn't keep up the guarantee and what they did was just push me out at Christmas – it was overnight. They told me, 'Wouldn't you like to see your father?' and because I had not seen him since he came to England I said I would love to. So they told me to stay in London for a week and tell them exactly how much I spent so they could pay me back. I did that (I spent 17/6d) and they said, 'That's good. You stay in London always and we will give you £1 a week.' I said: 'So I stay there and come back at weekends . . .' but they said: 'Oh no, we don't want you to come back at weekends.' Then I suddenly realised they wanted to get rid of me. They said I could stay with my father or brother, but my father lived in a furnished room and my brother just had two rooms and now a child . . . It was a very traumatic experience for me because, although I felt they were a bit peculiar (they couldn't understand why I was so sad all the time), I thought it was my home and I suddenly realised I didn't have a home.

Michael Brown's sister stayed with a family where her brother was able to visit. She was seven years old and he was ten:

. . . they put us in the same bed and we would weep and weep, both of us. She was absolutely distraught and missed her mother desperately. Later on, unfortunately, the mother of the house where my sister stayed died . . . it was hard for my sister because the father was a miser, heartless and couldn't deal with a youngster in the house.

Ruth Michaelis felt betrayed from the time her mother brought her over to England and left her with the Reverend Stead and his family.

The only clear memory I have that gives any sort of insight into my feelings about my parents has to do with the big doll's house at the rectory. I was allowed to play with it for a while and I remember getting all the little dolls out of the doll's house and putting them into the rubbish bin, and when somebody had put them all back I did it again. I can remember being smacked for it but I did it again. It was quite compulsive. I think my feelings about people were that they were rubbish. I can remember being astonished at myself for doing it, having been told not to.

She was constantly promised that there was not going to be a war and that she would soon go back to her family. A sixth sense told her otherwise.

The total darkness of night without any street lights made me feel unsure if there was anything there. I remember an awful feeling of there being nothing and scratching myself to test out if I was still alive because I was uncertain of whether I still existed.

Unhappy with the Steads, where she was beaten with a leather strap for wetting the bed, Ruth found a happier relationship with another family, but she could not rid herself of the insecurity.

I mistrusted people because they ditched you sooner or later, and important things they said could not be relied upon.

The job of inspecting foster homes, which was supposed to be carried out at frequent intervals, was shared between the national office, regional committees and the provincial committees. The quality of inspection varied enormously and was dependent not just on the inspectors' powers of observation but also on their view of how young refugees should be treated. There were those who, almost despite themselves, equated refugees with second-class citizens. Not for them the comfortable life; they might get ideas above their station, which was to devote themselves to hard labour and be grateful for small mercies. This attitude was not entirely absent from the ruling council of the RCM where, among others, the Marchioness of Reading, wife of the former Viceroy of India, judged every problem within narrow class conventions. Refugees were seen as deserving sympathy and help, but they were not to be pampered. She even turned down a government offer of extra clothing coupons on the grounds that hand-me-downs were quite good enough for her refugees.

Class prejudices were just as strong, perhaps even stronger, at regional level. When a mild complaint was made against the Tunbridge Wells paid secretary and she was invited to Bloomsbury House to discuss the matter with Lola Hahn-Warburg, her reaction was hostile, to put it mildly.

I should like to make it quite clear that if the English paid staff of the Movement is to be asked to be interviewed by an alien, however friendly, of whatever position she holds on your Executive Committee, I should rather as a British woman accept the unemployment benefit of the British government. I consider your request that I should meet Mrs Hahn-Warburg further abuse of the hospitality that England is giving to refugees from Nazi oppression. I am not aware that she is a naturalised British subject and even if she were, where personal matters are concerned, she is still a German.

Against such examples of blatant petty mindedness must be set the tone of sympathetic understanding adopted by Lord Gorell and those closest to him in the RCM. The letter he sent out to regional chairmen and secretaries in December 1942, is a fair indication of his philosophy:

> There is a matter of some difficulty and delicacy about which I feel I should write to ask for your cooperation. You will have seen the many accounts of the fearful, indeed the unprecedented, mass-murder of the Jewish population of Poland and elsewhere being carried out systematically today by the Nazis. So large a proportion of the children for whom the Movement is responsible are Jewish that this terrible persecution cannot but affect our work.
>
> What goes on in the mind of a child is always difficult for an adult, even the most experienced and sympathetic, to know; but there can be little doubt that many of the Jewish children, especially the older ones, are aware of the calamity afflicting their race and in a state of great suspense and anxiety about their parents or relatives.
>
> Certain it is that no children have ever been in greater need of loving care than ours are today. I feel that this aspect of our work should be brought as delicately and tactfully as possible to the thoughts and hearts of the foster parents, who will in most cases know best how far it is practicable by talking to the children to help them through their mental distress.
>
> I do not feel that I can do more than bring this to your notice, assured that you will do all that is possible to alleviate the suffering, probably the secret and unshared suffering, of many of the children under our care.

What notice was taken it is impossible to say. But the records suggest that the hard school of child rearing prevailed, at least to the extent that there was not too much sympathy for youngsters who were not entirely happy with their foster parents. There was still less appreciation of the problems encountered by youngsters old enough to go into lodgings.

Aside from the psychological strain of settling in, some had to face considerable physical hardship. Brought up in Vienna when anti-semitism was rife, Peter Hugh Granby (Peter Hugo Guens-burger) knew what it was to be self-reliant:

> I was thirteen when we had to go and live with my grandmother. I slept in the hall (there were only two other rooms) with a bayonet in my hand, and my father slept with a gun because we said we would never be taken alive. And for years afterwards, if anyone came near me and woke me I used to go at them – I even attacked my wife twice, when we were first married and she woke me. That is something that stays with you.

But as a child refugee, he needed all his resources to cope. One of his group's first lodgings was in a boarding house in Southend on Sea:

> It was also a day nursery. We found in the kitchen they had piled the bread onto a table and nappies were hanging up, and to our horror we discovered they weren't washed nappies, they were just hanging there and dripping on the bread. The cat sitting on it did not seem to mind.
>
> We found a brown patch under the wallpaper and the patch began to move. It was bed bugs. Vienna was riddled with bed bugs, so we all knew what to do. Immediately all the mattresses were stripped off the beds and the beds were pushed into the middle of the room. Then we filled bowls of water and stood the bed legs in the water. All our belongings were packed and put on the beds and covered with sheets. We refused to sleep there.

It was the bugs that drove Philip Urbach from his first lodgings:

> . . . I found myself a room in Drummond Street for ten shillings a week, but as soon as I got into bed I was attacked by an army of bugs. I had known some rough living but I could not sleep in that bed. I sat up all night watching the bugs with a candle because the landlady had switched off the main light and there was no electricity . . .

Philip had to enlist the aid of the police to get his ten shillings back before moving to another room in Victoria:

> I found a room for eleven shillings a week, but this included an evening meal . . . I had an Irish landlady. When she got to know

me better, she even did my washing for me. I had a wonderful time there . . .

Philip was working long hours for Charles (now Lord) Forte and was so tired one night that he slept through the air raid warning and the attempts of his landlady to rouse him. The house was hit by a landmine and collapsed. Philip was so tightly wedged that when he was pulled out he left his pyjamas behind and emerged stark naked, although not seriously harmed.

Landladies were among the more frequent visitors to Bloomsbury House as the records indicate:

> Mrs Landau in the main complains that Ernst is taking advantage of her in the way of burning three bulbs in his room, as well as having a wireless and an electric heating apparatus on, thereby causing frequent short circuits in the house. She has told him frequently to stop this. She is quite willing to keep him for 35/- per week if he cannot pay more. I assured her that he really could not pay more but he must stop the misuse of electricity.

Often, lodging and employment went together. Families who were used to servants, but were now finding domestic staff hard to come by, took immediately to the idea of having a young refugee about the house. Herta Stanton was taken in by a naval widow:

> . . . very well-to-do, very rich, who just wanted a little skivvy and wanted to show off that she did something for refugees. I was given an attic room and a little paraffin lamp to take up with me – that was the only light I had. It was the middle of winter. I had a bowl and a water jug on a stand and the water was frozen solid. I piled all my clothes on top of me and in the end I crawled under the mattress – it was so heavy! I stayed four months before I could tell the woman I didn't leave Germany to come into another concentration camp.

Regina, younger and less assertive than Herta, was visited at her foster home by an RCM worker:

> I visited Mrs de Gray accompanied by Mrs Joseph, Chairman of the Children's Section, Birmingham Council for Refugees. Mrs de Gray is one of the Birmingham City foster mothers. She lives in a

very small municipal house on Stirchley estate. We found her in a front room where one small baby was in bed recovering from pneumonia and her young boy was on a couch recuperating from an illness which had left him with heart trouble. The house seemed clean but terribly cramped.

Regina seemed very ill at ease when she saw us and one felt that she had been carefully prompted for our visit. She is very undersized, slightly hunchbacked and abnormal in her figure. Her face seems old for her years. Mrs de Gray complained that Regina is very unresponsive and difficult to get on with, but she felt she could 'manage' her. Regina is very unhappy at school and has no interest in anything whatsoever. Mrs de Gray had kept her home from school for the past two weeks in order that she could help her with the two invalids . . . we informed Mrs de Gray that Regina must finish the term which had been paid for by the Movement.

Regina was eventually moved and found work – but it was still hard to communicate with her:

> . . . the girl is very shut up within herself and does not make friends. She either sits at home reading or visits the cinema on her own. Her sole interest is her dog Rover of whom she is overfond . . .

Fortunately, someone at Bloomsbury House realised that getting through to Regina depended on making friends with her closest companion.

> . . . invited her to bring her dog and call and see me in my office on Saturday . . . Regina called with Rover. She seemed more happy and friendly and ready to talk.

Visits by RCM workers were liable to be resented by foster parents – not necessarily because they had anything to hide, but because they felt their housekeeping and parental capabilities were being questioned. Sometimes that attitude rubbed off on the children:

> Ruth visited the office. She was delighted to have news about her brother. We discussed her previous impolite letters in reply to our communications. She was very embarrassed but admitted she had been in the wrong. When she first heard from us she had the feeling

that her foster parents had no wish for her to visit the office, but since that time she has grown up and developed her own ideas and outlook . . . Now she has got to know us she will try to attend any functions we hold.

It was easy to offend middle-class pride. Reporting back to Bloomsbury House on a visit to the Jacobs' residence where Ilse, a probationary nurse, was staying, Miss Smith recorded Ilse's hospital treatment for flat feet. A few days later, an irate Mrs Jacobs was in touch: 'She stated that neither she nor her husband saw our representative and she is annoyed that "some person" should have questioned her servants about their private affairs.'

Bloomsbury House made soothing noises which seem to have done the trick. After several weeks, Miss Smith visited again:

> A very good home. Mr and Mrs Jacobs seem very fond of the girl. The mother lives quite near and is in constant touch with her. Mrs Jacobs gives the girl one pound a month, in addition to money she earns, and buys all her clothes. Her illness was not 'flat feet' but swollen legs, due perhaps to a disorder of the blood. Nursing may therefore not suit her and if this is so, Mr Jacobs will pay for a business training for her and she can then enter Mr Jacobs' factory.

Ilse passed her State Final Exams in nursing in 1945.

★　★　★

With the large number of children spread out over the country, it was inevitable that visits were infrequent. Many former refugee children report never having seen a Bloomsbury House representative. Where problems do crop up in the records they are often of the type that are familiar to all families with teenagers. Complaints from young adults about being treated like children come thick and fast:

> Brigitte called. She explained the personal relationship between her and Mrs Kreeger. She said they were not antagonistic towards each other, but that Mrs Kreeger persisted in treating her like a child of fourteen or fifteen [she was in fact seventeen] and seemed to resent her having a life of her own.

Brigitte and Mrs Kreeger were able to settle their differences. In other cases there were stronger emotions at work:

> Eva called to see whether we could give permission for her to leave Mrs Payne . . . Since August she does not seem to be able to do anything right . . . She could not give any reason for these sudden difficulties, but says it started when Mrs Payne wanted her to go swimming with Frieda (Mrs Payne's fifteen-year-old daughter) and Eva did not want to go. Since then, the atmosphere seems to have been strained and unhappy. There was another disagreement last Sunday about a lunch appointment Eva made and to which Mr Payne disagreed. Eva complained that she was not allowed her own choice of clothing and that her correspondence was supervised . . .

Without disclosing the actual reason for the call, Mrs Payne was visited. She said she was finding Eva difficult and that she was telling lies. Eva had pretended she would have to do office work until after lunch on the Sunday, when in fact she had wanted to have lunch out at a cafe with a girlfriend. Mr Payne had forbidden this because Eva had not been straightforward. Eva had been very upset. Shortly afterwards, Eva called again at Bloomsbury House to register her feelings about her foster family:

> She is in a very nervous and agitated state of mind, looking worn out and depressed. She is quite determined that she cannot stay with Mrs Payne any longer – the main difficulty seems to be a certain kind of jealousy between her and Frieda. Eva says Mrs Payne always takes Frieda's side, especially if Eva does better than Frieda, and Eva feels treated very unjustly.

There was no prospect of a reconciliation. Eva moved out and went to a hostel.

A different sort of jealousy was at work in the Baran household:

> When I called . . . only Mr Baran was in. He is about fifty years old. The house and the shop are very clean. He told me his wife would not keep Franziska any longer. There had been difficulties between them for some time. but she had definitely made up her mind that Franziska must go . . . He told me that his wife, who is twenty years older than he is, was easily excitable at present . . . She was suffering from blood pressure . . . When Mrs Baran arrived she seemed a very kind and motherly, though easily excitable,

woman and she wouldn't tell me what is at the root of the trouble. She complained about Franziska being difficult with her food and about her lack of cleanliness, but she definitely gave me the impression that these things alone would not have brought matters to a head. She would prefer not to say anything more.

It did not take long to realise that what really worried Mrs Baran was Franziska's relationship with her husband, although: '. . . from the way in which Mr Baran talked about Franzi I did not at all get the impression that there is any reason for Mrs Baran to be jealous'.

The flow of complaints was by no means one way. Foster parents were as likely as their wards to find a justifiable cause for bellyache.

Mrs Coles phoned to ask if it would be possible for us to place Mary in a hostel, as her own child was on the verge of a breakdown and she could not cope with both children. Mary was getting rather difficult and was also bedwetting.

Shortly afterwards:

Mrs Coles phoned to say that Mary had thrown a bottle of gripewater over the baby and she wanted her removed as soon as possible.

Perhaps such behaviour was more easily endured if the children were one's own. Mrs Coles expressed great regret when she parted with Mary, continued to provide her clothes and had her back to stay for the Christmas holidays.

Lutz, who at twelve was three years older than Mary, was even more of a handful:

Letter from Mr Speakman complaining about Lutz's behaviour, bad manners and disobedience. Mrs Speakman had been ill and found it impossible to cope with the difficult boy . . . Mrs Speakman had had to undergo a serious operation and her husband explained to the two children that they must be helpful and prevent her having extra work and trouble. This had no effect whatsoever on Lutz's behaviour. It seems apparent that the boy realises he can do what he likes with her and 'plays her up'.

The Speakmans decided to keep Lutz with them but he continued to have problems. Four years later in Birmingham, he was arrested for breaking and entering.

Only about fifty children actually had to be removed from their foster homes. Friederike was one of the most serious cases. From the age of thirteen in 1939, 'Fritzi' lodged with Mr Argles, a former refugee worker in his sixties, and his wife in Staffordshire. In October 1944, Mr Argles telephoned the Birmingham office and said that his wife was severely indisposed. He asked that Fritzi and her brother Mickey be removed from his house at once. The Argleses were closing up their house and leaving the district on the advice of their doctor. Later, the doctor himself telephoned to explain what had happened. Owing to an 'indiscretion', Fritzi must be removed from the household immediately.

Gradually the unpleasant truth emerged. Fritzi had been forbidden by Mrs Argles to reveal what had happened but, once she had left the family, she spoke:

> She admitted having had intimate association with Mr Argles for the past three and a half years, the first time occurring shortly after she joined the family. The intimacies have taken place early in the morning when Mr Argles called her to get up, on several occasions at night when Mrs Argles was away, and also in the grounds of the house. She denies that such relationships have occurred with any other men but, after I left her for a few moments, she was in tears when I returned and told me that she did not give a truthful answer and that the first time actual sexual intercourse had taken place was when she was alone in the house with Mrs Argles's son, nineteen years of age, who forced her to acquiesce to his will. She had been extremely frightened and had screamed but no one had heard her. She told Mrs Argles when she came home, who promised to deal with the matter, but Fritzi never heard anything further about it except that she was never allowed to be alone in the house with the boy.

It would have been hard for an outside eye to have detected anything wrong, although Fritzi's brother Mickey had provided a clue. For some time, he had suffered psychological problems which were attributed to his experiences in Germany. It was later revealed that Mr Argles had employed a boy who had been convicted of offences against young children. Doubtless this was the source of Mickey's difficulties.

Fritzi's file ended on a positive note:

> I do feel that given the right start and real friendship and guidance from a strong-minded and broad-minded woman, she will live down this episode . . .

Missing the affection of friends and relatives, and short of material goods and luxuries, the young refugees were open to temptations which were liable to shock the ladies at Bloomsbury House. But they were quickly on to Mr Schwartz, who had paid young Freddy large sums of money for running errands for his shoeshine business.

> FJW saw Mr Schwartz. He is a Czech refugee and helps Freddy out of the goodness of his heart. FJW explained the legal position of the Movement regarding Freddy and got Mr Schwartz to appreciate that we were responsible for Freddy and like to know what kind of friends he had. He told him we are suspicious of people who give away one pound notes.

Mr Schwartz promised to tell if he gave Freddy any further money or clothes. Soon, Freddy was asking if Mr Schwartz might buy him a suit. His RCM contact tactfully pointed out that, unless he started to buy his own clothes out of his savings, he would not learn to be self-reliant. Some months later, came the denouement.

> FJW learned that Mr Schwartz of the Shoe Shine is a homosexual. Freddy called in to see FJW, who had a long and open talk with the boy. Freddy confirms that Mr Schwartz is homosexual and he knows that another boy Wolfgang was approached. Wolfgang has refused to go there any more and Mr Schwartz has promised that he will not ask Freddy or Tommy to continue to go. Freddy has promised not to have any further contact and to let us know if Mr Schwartz asks him to go there again.

In cases where a young child was formally adopted by a family, visits were usually discontinued. At the top of Elfriede's file appear the words, 'No action! No visits!' Elfriede came to England at the age of three and stayed with the Lewis family in Newport, Monmouthshire. In 1942 she was described as 'a normally developed, healthy little girl who has no memory for any other home or country. She is as much a part of the family as Mrs Lewis's own baby sons . . . we think she is very fortunate to have found such a wonderfully happy home.'

Few cases were so simple. For Liesl whose mother had been able to escape to this country, a battle royal developed between her parent and her foster parent.

> Liesl's mother called with Liesl. The mother is in a terrible state as Mrs Wynne, the child's foster mother, came up with the child last Sunday and confronted the real mother, who is just out of hospital after an operation, with the request to sign a form handing over the legal guardianship to Mrs Wynne. Mrs Wynne said that unless this was done she did not want Liesl back and would in fact adopt another child . . . Liesl's affection is divided between mother and foster parents . . . She promised to explain to the Wynnes that she loves them and that she sees no need for a guardianship form to be signed and does not want to hurt her mother.

After more skirmishes, a compromise was reached which allowed for Liesl to stay with the Wynnes until her real mother was able to care for her.

Though those parents who were able to escape to England might have been expected to accept immediate responsibility for their offspring, this was often not practicable. Hampered by their lack of English, traumatised by events in Germany and Austria and, in most cases, with very limited resources, they were invariably in need of care themselves. Knowing the risks, Bloomsbury House kept an eye on those children who were reunited with their parents. They were anxious about seventeen-year-old Joseph:

> . . . a very squalid home . . . the boy occupies the same bedroom as his mother, though in a separate bed. Miss Smith does not think the mother is a fit person to have charge of the boy and thinks he should be removed as soon as possible . . .

In fact, Joseph and his mother stayed together, moving eventually to a larger flat.

Families were often separated, mothers and daughters being sent into domestic service many miles apart. Magda Chadwick remembers:

> My mother left a week earlier than I did with my sister. Mother went as a housekeeper and my sister at seventeen was a children's

maid. We thought if we all got out there was a chance for my father, but things happened too quickly. I remember he sent us some pictures. He was learning butlering and he sent pictures of himself with a tray of silver and glasses . . .

If a reunion with parents took place quickly enough, the result was ecstatic. Sonia Altman's parents followed close behind her *Kindertransport*.

My parents were sent for by the people they were going to work for. A car came to London to pick them up. They knew by then that I was in Middlesbrough but they didn't know where. They couldn't speak English. They got to Middlesbrough – it was a hot day in August just before the war broke out – and the car windows were open. They stopped at traffic lights and my mother heard a child screaming. She said to my father: 'That's Sonia!' They asked the driver to stop and she made her way to where the child was screaming. It was a dentist's on the corner and I was sitting in that dentist's chair. Can you imagine the reunion?

Alice Staller (now in California) was glad of her mother's support, even from a distance. She had been guaranteed by several people and entered Michael Hall School. When the school evacuated to Minehead, Alice was taken out of the classroom to become a full-time household help:

I later learned that the school's headmaster had given his wife an allowance of 2/6d for me, which she kept for herself. I was without means and recall phoning my mother in London, courtesy of a kind garage owner in the village. She then forwarded some money to me for a rail ticket to come to London and join her. The family where she was working as housekeeper let me stay with her to get my act together.

Gerda's mother was living with a man to whom she was not married. She was very anxious to have her daughter with her.

Mrs Howe of the Bromley Committee phoned stating that her committee would be averse to the child leaving her present foster mother and going to a household where there is this irregular union . . . We endeavoured to keep the child away from her mother as long as possible, but under the circumstances it might perhaps be best that Gerda now returns to her mother.

Gerda kept contact with her foster mother, visiting her in the holidays, which satisfied Bloomsbury House that the decencies were being preserved.

The strains of life in a strange country without parents could cause conflict between brothers and sisters.

> Selma called, having found out Solomon's address from their land-lady. He is now staying with a friend. Selma said that towards the end of his stay with her and Anni he had refused to speak to either of them, had not taken his meals with them, had kept his room locked and had generally ignored them completely. Their landlady, who is fond of the two girls, strongly disapproved of the atmosphere prevailing and told Selma that, unless their quarrel could be patched up, she thought they would be much better off without him. He had also taken with him all the linen, sheets, etc., which he had brought as his share towards the household.
>
> The two girls could not afford the rent which they had paid as a threesome, so they have moved to a smaller room through the kindness of the landlady. Solomon should be seen and have it made clear to him that, in these present days of separation and bereavement, it is not only undutiful but vey wrong not to maintain friendly relations with one's own flesh and blood.

Solomon might have replied (the records do not give his side of the story) that it takes two to quarrel. Having relatives in England was not always the bonus it was made out to be. Uncles and aunts were likely to be out of touch with what was happening to their family on the continent, and sometimes there were tensions and disagreements which had caused them to move away in the first place.

Elli Adler remembers the reception her aunt gave her:

> My aunt unpacked my suitcase and said what a lot of rubbish I had brought because I had brought books. My mother had packed classical books and also some of my own books, one in particular I was very fond of – a book about Greek mythology – and she deprived me of these books. She just took them away except for the *Jungle* books. I didn't get on with her very well. She said my mother should have packed more clothes, but I think my mother had packed all the clothes I had. I don't think my aunt realised just how hard up we were.

Not exactly overjoyed at the prospect of looking after her niece, Liesl Silverstone's aunt secretly attempted to shift the responsibility without her niece knowing:

> I remember being shocked when I found my aunt's letter trying to farm me out at four pounds a week to an elderly couple. But I knew that she didn't want me. I also knew that my aunt was the one sister who couldn't cope in her family and who was constantly overprotected and smothered. She found it very difficult here as a refugee. I suppose I was all she needed.
>
> In fact, I was the mother in that household, which was quite a burden. I was trying to hold it all together. I wasn't just seeing to my schoolwork, I was looking after her.

Some of the happiest memories are of small hostels that provided more of a family atmosphere than did foster homes. This was particularly noticeable when hostels were set up by individuals or by groups of sympathisers, rather than by religious or other charitable organisations. There was the contact with friendly adults, but not so close as to suggest to the children that their real parents were being supplanted – a common resentment in foster homes. At the same time, the children could draw emotional strength from a shared experience.

Among those who set themselves the task of creating a hostel for orthodox children was Sybil Wulwick. Married in the summer of 1938 to the Reverend Geza Wulwick, who had been brought up in Czechoslovakia, and who spoke fluent German, she and her husband settled in Middlesbrough and almost immediately started collecting money for refugee children. Their breakthrough was the free loan of a large Victorian house. Reverend Wulwick dedicated himself to the children's needs:

> Because the hostel wasn't ready by the time the first batch of children arrived, we had to take them into our homes. My husband brought me two girls. He said he had noticed that the male members of the committee were choosing the prettiest, so he decided to go for two not-so-pretty girls. I suddenly had twins – two Hannahs. Our hearts went out to these children. One of them, Hannah Freulich (she was a plump little thing), had a letter inside her attache case with a big box of talcum powder from her mother. The letter said: 'Please look after my little girl. I thank you from the bottom

of my heart. Bath her every night and use this powder; she is used to it.' So I did.

Meanwhile, we were getting the hostel ready. We didn't want it to be a grim place, we wanted it to be as near to home for those children as we could get. One lady said she was due to have a new dining room carpet and as soon as it came we could have the old one which was still quite good. The committee called on her and asked her when she expected her new carpet and she said in two weeks. And in front of her astonished eyes they rolled up her carpet.

The Schlesingers already had five children including one, John, who was destined to become a leading film director. Bernard Schlesinger was senior physician at the great Ormond Street Hospital for Sick Children, his wife, Winifred, a gifted musician and linguist. With their sympathetic, open-minded attitudes to young people, they came closest to the RCM ideal for a foster family. The hostel was a large house in Highgate which the Schlesingers bought with money left by a relative. A matron was installed, and three helpers, one of whom did the cooking. There was room for twelve children. One of them remembers:

Mrs Schlesinger was at Liverpool Street to meet us all and we were very impressed that she spoke very fluent German. We were taken straight to Highgate. We were well received, well looked after, wanted for nothing; we were extremely lucky. There were five boys and seven girls in the group; we got on very well. We were enrolled in the local school, where we shared a classroom with the top form who were probably thirteen or so. We must have seemed a lot of oddballs – probably dressed a bit funny, and so on. We had more or less individual teaching, but I don't quite know how they managed to teach the English children at the same time in the same room. It couldn't have been easy. I think they involved those children in helping to teach us. We were only there for one term but we did a lot of reading, we learnt our tables – pounds, shillings and pence – by reciting in chorus: quite old-fashioned but most effective. In no time at all we knew that thirty-six pence were three shillings and the rest of it. It was also assumed that we hadn't had prior schooling, which of course wasn't true. This went so far that we were taught to write in copperplate copybooks. It completely changed our writing style – we learnt again as if we were five-year-olds.

There was one more refugee helped by the Schlesingers. As a relative, Dick Levy went to stay in the family home.

On 16 March 1939 I arrived in London, excited and bewildered. I met Uncle Bernard and Auntie Win and was taken to 15 Templewood Avenue. This was to be my new home and at nine-years-old I perceived that a great change in my life had occurred.

Soon I shed my German language and customs and adopted those of my new home. Auntie Win and Uncle Bernard became Mummy and Daddy. They gave me the same love and affection and discipline that they gave their own children. I was part of the family.

As the war approached, the spacious Templewood Avenue house was exchanged for the more intimate Mount Pleasant near Kintbury. When war broke out Bernard had to go with the army, first to Norway and later to India. For the next six years it was Win who held the family together, making those years – so tragic for so many millions – happy and busy ones for us children at Mount Pleasant. During the holidays we rode horses and bicycles, made music and put on shows, played in the house and, when it became too crowded, in pigsties converted into 'offices'. Win never let us perceive how incredibly difficult it must have been for her to cope with six growing children, with a house often bursting with visitors and with all the uncertainties brought on by the war, while Bernard was at the other end of the world.

When the war ended and Bernard returned there was a big party in the country. It says much for the tolerance and humanity of the family that among the guests was a group of German POWs.

The extended family of the Schlesingers kept in touch over the years. Other foster children with happy memories did the same, though distance and new relationships combined to make contact sporadic.

Ya'acov Friedler returned from Israel to visit the Maggs family after a gap of fifty years. Siegmar Silber corresponded in the 1970s with the family he had stayed with before leaving at the age of eleven to join relatives in the States. There was so much news to exchange – careers followed, children born, marriages made. Edith Taylor's story is one of the most extraordinary. Four years after her husband died she returned from the United

States to marry her foster father, Mr Taylor, who was then a widower:

> . . . because I had promised Mrs Taylor I would look after him. She had said jokingly: 'You are the only one who knows how to make chopped liver as he likes it.' She had taught me, you see, and she wanted him taken care of. We had not quite twenty years together.

8

Evacuation and Internment

'One of our girls was reported for sketching a village green (an unlikely military target) and a boy who was overheard describing his home in Vienna was branded as a spy, though presumably not a very intelligent one.'

In the back rooms of Whitehall, where they worked on the knotty problem of what to do in a national emergency, there was a file on the likely effects of German air attacks on London. It started with the assumption that 100,000 bombs would fall on the capital within fourteen days of the declaration of war. Enormous casualties were anticipated. The partial remedy, for no one could think of exhaustive response, was to clear London and other big cities of children aged under fifteen, the sick and the handicapped: all those who were of more hindrance than help to the defence effort.

At the time of the Czechoslovakian crisis on Monday 28 September 1938, there was a temporary evacuation of schoolchildren and hospital patients from London. Just short of a year later, on 1 September 1939, came the real thing. Among the million and a half dispatched from urban Britain into the countryside were between two to three thousand refugee children who were experiencing their second dramatic upheaval within months. Fourteen hostels were evacuated *en masse*.

At the start of the operation, children went every day to school equipped with gas masks in cardboard boxes and carrying a small case ready packed – no one knew which day they would actually be leaving and the destination was secret. When the day finally came, each child was tagged with a number for identification. Iron rations were issued for the train or bus journey. Some children had last-minute treats of ice cream and sweets which made them very sick. Weeping parents bade goodbye to their offspring. It was almost a rerun of experience in Germany and Austria.

At the reception centres children were billeted by haphazard allotment or by 'cattle market' selection. They were paraded around while householders took their pick, a routine familiar to refugee children who had passed through Dovercourt. Many families had children forced on them by billeting officers. Local authorities appointed volunteers to go from door to door to see who had room and who didn't; those on the receiving end had no choice in the matter.

No child could be expected to enjoy the experience, but for refugee children there were several factors which made evacuation more than typically painful. Even those who had arrived in early 1939 or before did not as yet have complete command of English and this made communication with their new and sometimes reluctant hosts difficult. In rural areas the heavy regional accents added to the problem.

Some refugee children underwent, for the second time, a fall in living standards from those they had been used to in Europe, which added to the depression they were already feeling as the threat of invasion increased.

As Dorothy Hardisty wrote in her journal:

> . . . children were quickly moved by the authorities, sometimes with their foster parents or hosts, sometimes with children of the homes they had just entered, sometimes as individuals. It was right that they should receive just the same treatment as British children, but suddenly they were bereft of all sense of security. These blows had been preceded by long periods of unhappiness and fear – they had seen persecution of their relatives; they knew of men and boys being taken away from their homes; they had heard of the dread concentration camps; they had suffered humiliation and deprivation educationally. It was not surprising therefore that some children found it hard to settle initially. Even for some of those that did settle well, evacuation was a catastrophe.

The worst sufferers were those children who were placed in remote places where strangers were automatically suspect. Magda Chadwick, born in 1928, experienced this thinly veiled hostility:

Being evacuated away from my guardians, the Morts, was the most terrible incident in my life. Having only a smattering of English, I went to the Lake District near Grange-over-Sands (Cartmel). We went to the village hall and you stood there and people came and chose you. If your face fitted. They let brothers and sisters stay together and I stood with two sisters who were very kind to me. They asked if we were a family and I said, 'No, but I would like to be with them.' So the two girls went to a couple of spinsters, who said that the farm next door needed a girl. But they got me there to be a housemaid. They asked me to wash the kitchen floor. I said I had never done it and I wasn't going to start.

I lived in the farmhouse. The country wasn't my style. I am a town person. There were no mod cons. The two sisters had a croquet lawn at their place – it was luck of the draw. *I* had to deliver the milk. In the dark, carrying two milk cans, I walked right into the wall because there was no light and I didn't know where I was going.

For Margaret Olmer, born in Vienna in 1931, despite forebodings at Liverpool Street, rural life in Norfolk proved congenial and, perhaps because she had already had to learn to adapt, she settled in more quickly than the daughter of her host family who was evacuated with her. She loved the countryside, the dogs and the local school.

In the Blitz she returned to London and then was sent to the Midlands, until the Jewish Committee returned her to a Jewish environment in 1945:

This life of moving on and readjusting made me detached. I could easily keep starting again – I have had four children with five-year gaps in between.

In many cases 'the religious question' was exacerbated by evacuation. Refugee children naturally gravitated towards people showing them kindness, and were thus susceptible to proselytisation by their Gentile hosts. Desperate to 'belong', many Jewish children were happy to attend church or chapel with their hosts, even if there was a synagogue in the vicinity. This was especially so in the Midlands, where there was a high concentration of Quaker and Christadelphian families.

Very little explanatory information was given to householders who received refugees. The local RCM committees followed up in the wake of evacuation, but this was too late for orthodox children arriving at their billets on the evening of Friday, 1 September. Householders unaware of Sabbath conventions caused much discomfort to their young guests until they became better informed about Jewish religious observances. Orthodox pupils of the Jewish secondary school were greeted on arrival at Shefford with a welcoming ham omelette. With their lack of English they were unable to explain why they chose to go hungry rather than eat such a choice dish.

Throughout the autumn, a period of successive Jewish holidays, the Anglo-Jewish press reported a general absence of kosher food in reception areas. Some communities provided a communal hot kosher meal at noon for Jewish children, who had to make do with cold vegetables and bread for breakfast and dinner. The Home Secretary, Sir John Anderson, suggested that this should be a general measure, but few local authorities saw the need to exert themselves.

The happiest results came when householders gave their evacuees time to settle in and made some attempt to understand their cultural differences. One such family took in two sisters:

> We said please take us because nobody wants us. So they went to the kitchen and discussed us and their hearts melted and that's how they took us both. It was a wonderful thing to do because they had no idea about the Jewish problem and all their family were wondering about them taking Germans. But that didn't last very long. While we were there we spent a very happy Christmas with her parents on a farm in Hertford and after the war, when my relatives came over from Holland on a visit, they met my uncle.

Kurt Weinburg's evacuation began disastrously but, thanks to his headmaster (who had already proved his sensitivity by introducing Kurt on his first day to the only other Jewish boy in the school), it turned out better than he expected:

> . . . I just assembled with all the other children at the school and we walked to the station and then went to Burgess Hill. We were billeted with various families and I remember the first family I was sent to didn't want to take me because I came from Germany. So whoever was in charge of billeting took me next door to the home of Mr Crombie. He was my headmaster who was about to open

the school in Cornwall. As I had no family and certainly no money, he took me with the school servant, two dogs and one other boy in his old Morris from Burgess Hill to London, and then we drove early in the morning from London all the way to Cornwall. I became a boarder and Mr Crombie gave me free schooling until I did matriculation in 1942.

It was wonderful in Cornwall. For me it was freedom – I was back in the countryside I loved. The school was small – only about thirty-five children. In London there was discipline with uniforms; down there there was no discipline and we didn't have to wear uniforms. I adopted one of Mr Crombie's dogs, a black cairn terrier – he more or less became my dog. There was no electricity in the building and no running water. We spent a lot of time cutting up wood for the fires. We developed an ingenious system for making light. We trickled water over trays of carbide which then gave off gas. This was collected in a container like a miniature gasometer and fed through narrow pipes into the downstairs room to produce a naked flame. Upstairs we had paraffin lamps. It was fantastic.

I joined the Boy Scout troop and soon became patrol leader, and that gave me a lot of responsibility for the first time. I took my patrol camping and I organised the salvage collections of waste paper, tins and boxes. At the end I had the whole of West Cornwall under my control . . .

In spite of evacuation to an apparently safe area, Peter Morgan has vivid memories of a more frightening side of wartime activity:

In 1939, we were evacuated to the Isle of Wight. I can't think of a worse place to have sent children. Whatever the Germans had left after bombing London, we got the lot. We were actually machine-gunned one Saturday afternoon walking along the front at Ventnor. The plane just came in and shot at us as if the pilot had nothing better to do.

Peter went next to the Latymer School which had been evacuated from Hammersmith to High Wycombe.

. . . standing at the top of the church at West Wycombe, on a clear night you could see St Paul's and you could see London burning.

He was still in the way of stray bombs. One landed in the middle of the school playing fields.

The disruption caused by the evacuation extended through to

Bloomsbury House. It was clear that the records department could not remain in London. The files not only contained the family details of each child but also their Home Office permits, passports and other certificates. A country house, The Grange, was rented at Hindhead and the aftercare department was transferred there, together with the records and a staff of fifteen. Three girls and two boys from Germany helped in the house and the office and another boy worked in the garden.

Refugee children under the age of sixteen were liable to be evacuated; refugee children over sixteen risked being interned.

★   ★   ★

From the first day of the war the security forces went in fear of the unseen enemy: agents and provocateurs smuggled into the country under the guise of fugitives from Nazi persecution. Voices were raised in support of rounding up all foreigners, but the government was unwilling to go the way of its predecessor in the first world war and order a general internment. Public opinion, it was argued, would react unfavourably to such an extreme measure. Instead, a nationwide network of 120 investigative tribunals was set up, headed by lawyers who were empowered to call before them all adult foreigners living within their jurisdiction. The plan was to categorise aliens under one of three headings. A small number were assessed as category A – German and Austrians with specialised military knowledge which could be used to hinder the British war effort. They were immediately interned. Category B covered those who had lived in Britain for some time and showed no obvious signs of hostility. They kept their basic freedom but were not allowed to own a car, a camera or any large-scale maps, and were forbidden to travel more than five miles from home. Those who could produce evidence of 'character, associations and loyalty' were placed in category C and were left to their own devices, at least for the time being. Home Office guidelines suggested that refugees from religious, racial or political per-secution had the strongest case for a C registration.

The tribunals began their work in October 1939. Since they met behind closed doors and no provision was made for legal representation, decisions were heavily dependent on the sensitivity of individual chairmen. Not surprisingly, their deliberations

revealed wild inconsistencies. In Leeds, aliens of whatever background were given a B label, whereas in Manchester they were
designated grade C. Several tribunals put the unemployed into B
category, telling them to apply for a transfer to C when they found
jobs. One tribunal decided that all women qualified for a B rating
on the entirely erroneous assumption that domestic servants were
a prime source of disaffection. It was not until the Home Office
called the tribunal chairmen together to clarify the guidelines that
the ratio of Bs to Cs began to fall. Even so, the RCM had to
accept that some 300 of its boys were stuck with a B rating.
Protests were made on their behalf but, as Henry Toch discovered,
self-help was the only effective recourse.

> When the war broke out my brother and I went to a tribunal at
> King's Cross Police Station. My brother went one morning and I
> went the next. My brother was classed as 'B' (dangerous enemy
> alien). I thought this was unfair. I went on my own to the police
> with our registration books and told them they had got it wrong.
> They asked me what I wanted and I said: 'I'm the dangerous one
> and he's the friendly.' The police sergeant, seeing an unusually small
> boy of sixteen, laughed and said: 'I'll see what I can do.' He went
> to the judge, took both books in and he came back and said, 'You're
> both friendly now.'

After a few weeks of relative calm – the 'phoney war' – chauvi-
nism was revived by the German invasion of Norway. The bad
news persisted. With the fall of the Netherlands, Belgium and
Luxembourg, anti-alien feelings mounted to near paranoia. Addled
by the speed of events which sent him scurrying from The Hague,
the erstwhile British ambassador, Sir Neville Bland warned
that:

> Every German or Austrian servant, however superficially charming
> and devoted, is a real and grave menace . . . when the signal is
> given, as it will scarcely fail to be when Hitler so decides, there will
> be satellites of the monster *all over the country* who will at once
> embark on widespread sabotage and attacks on civilians and the
> military indiscriminately.

In fact, the Germans experienced limited success with their Fifth
Column in Holland. They did install agents in The Hague with
instructions to guide paratroopers to the Dutch seat of government.

But they were not successful (Queen Wilhelmina and the government escaped) and they were certainly not disguised as servant girls. However, Bland's nightmare vision had a powerful effect on the government's thinking and on public opinion. Anyone with a foreign accent, including refugee children, were labelled as potential saboteurs.

> One of our girls was reported for sketching a village green (an unlikely military target) and a boy who was overheard describing his home in Vienna was branded as a spy, though presumably not a very intelligent one.

The light-hearted tone of Elaine Blond characterised Bloomsbury House policy of not taking minor problems too seriously. There was a war on; inconvenience could be expected and not only for youngsters. Travelling the country, Lola Hahn-Warburg found that her pronounced German accent caused a lot of trouble.

> On a tour of inspection in North Wales, an innocent request for directions attracted a police escort which followed her, at a safe distance, for several miles.

But as the war intensified, the jokes wore thin. It is still with a sense of amazement at the flights of human inanity that Ruth Michaelis relates the experience of her brother Martin, who found himself in serious trouble with his foster family:

> They discovered he had built himself a crystal set and he was listening in German in the night when he thought nobody was about – he wanted to hear his mother tongue. They accused him of being a spy (he was eleven) and they called the police in. From that time both Martin and I were regularly interrogated by the police.

One of the first decisions of the Churchill government was to tighten security along the vulnerable south and east coasts. Starting on 10 May, all male category B and category C Germans and Austrians living in these areas were detained, among them boys just past the age of sixteen who were taken from foster parents or schools without explanation.

We found ourselves arriving at Seaton in South Devon and were taken to a holiday camp with chalets, dance-halls, swimming pools, etc. But the atmosphere was not pleasant. The whole camp was surrounded with barbed wire, electric fences, armed guards, screened with canvas and dotted with look-out towers. We were herded in; the officers had their revolvers drawn. Whenever the sirens went – which seemed to happen frequently – they drove us, blowing their whistles, into the chalets.

It was a brief stay at Seaton. The next stop was Bury in Lancashire, where home was a disused cotton mill.

It was empty; long halls supported on cast-iron pillars; there was oil and dirt everywhere and there were our 'beds' – straw palliasses, meagre ones and blankets, laid out in rows along the pillars. When we arrived our suitcases were searched thoroughly – this had already happened in Seaton but here they were more thorough. Everything was emptied on to the floor; a few essentials were returned to us; the rest was heaped in two piles, one for the officers and one for the men; they seemed especially keen on toilet articles and stationery. This was a symptom of that time but was not legal: a year later the commandant of that camp was sentenced to a term of imprisonment for these thefts.

A warning against a panic reaction to the Bland report came from the Home Secretary, Sir John Anderson. He pointed out the enormous differences between the Netherlands and Britain, starting with the absence of a common frontier with Germany. Britain had exercised tight control over the entry of aliens for as long as anyone could remember and, anyway, there had been little contact between Germany and Britain for at least nine months. Moreover, the vast majority of the 73,000 Germans and Austrians in Britain were refugees from Nazi oppression. It was ludicrous to see them as a threat to security.

But prejudice triumphed. The order to intern all male category B aliens was posted on 16 May. A week later the order was extended to women and their children. Then a start was made on rounding up the C grade, those who were known incongruously as 'friendly enemy aliens'. By July, more than 30,000 men and women were interned, among them some 1000 refugee children registered with the RCM.

Elaine Blond joined the chorus of protest from Bloomsbury House:

They were sent to hastily constructed camps, the biggest of which were at Huyton, near Liverpool, and on the Isle of Man. Life there was miserable. Young and old were thrown together, sharing rooms and beds. A Jewish adolescent who had every reason to hate Nazism could find in his closest companion a devotee of fascism who counted Hitler among the saints. And nobody knew what was going on.

Our complaints, though vigorous, were not at first taken seriously. I was not the only one at the RCM to be told by a Home Office official that refugees wanted to be interned; how else could they be protected from the angry natives who blamed them for causing the war? Making the best of a bad job, we sent in books, recruited volunteer teachers (there were internees preparing for their school certificates) and explained to the supervisors the intricacies of the kosher diet. One group of *Youth Aliyah* boys were allowed to grow and prepare their own food, a form of self-help which did something to alleviate the tedium.

The refugee organisations now found themselves in a difficult position. Once again they were besieged by applicants – desperate relatives of the interned – seeking information and reassurance. But little information was available from official sources such as the Home Office bureau at St Stephen's House in Westminster. Eventually, a central department set up jointly by the refugee committees helped to alleviate major problems like the treatment of refugees as Nazis, refugees and Nazis being kept in close proximity, inadequate accommodation, lack of adequate medical care and the separation of families.

Most of the RCM internees were packed off to the Isle of Man, a late addition to the list of camps drawn up by the War Office in 1939. In fact, it came as a complete surprise to the hoteliers of Ramsey when they were given notice to quit their premises within six days, leaving behind 'all furniture, bedding, linen, cutlery, crockery and utensils'. In Port Erin, where a women's camp was set up, landladies were asked if they would accept internees at 3/- a day. As the summer tourist trade was looking gloomy, the offer was taken up enthusiastically.

For one early arrival in Ramsey, where the internees were cordoned off from the rest of the town by barbed wire:

Those first few days were the most depressing of my life. It was my first – and so far only – experience of being imprisoned. For the first time I became conscious of how utterly alone I was in the world. The few friends I had made were either in the same position or could not help me anyway. This was the only time when I strongly felt that emotion which is usually called 'homesickness', but the emotion turned sour since there was no home for which to be sickening.

The mood soon passed. Refugee children had proved their ability to adapt. Once they found their bearings some of them even discovered a few side-benefits to internment:

Apart from the daily roll-call, we were left entirely to our own devices. These were in some ways quite remarkable. The number of professional men, artists and intellectuals among the inmates was disproportionate and soon made itself felt. For me this became a time of intellectual awakening, or rather re-awakening.

Walter Friedman, who was running a hostel in London and who himself just managed to avoid internment, points out:

Surprisingly enough the life behind barbed wire, with all the in-herent disadvantages, was not too bad for the young people . . . They had to learn to live together with people whom fate had thrown together and who came from a great variety of backgrounds. However, there were adults, Jewish refugees belonging to all classes of society. Many of the young people found contact again with congenial older people, such as they had no chance to meet since they arrived in this country . . .

In almost all of the internment camps lectures and school classes were held. Youngsters who had hitherto been isolated on farms and factories could now take part in informed discussion on a wide variety of subjects. Politics was a favourite topic.

Fred Dunston remembers a particularly heated discussion:

A very interesting man called some of the younger ones together and asked each in turn how they visualised their own personal future after the war. There were some convinced Communists and Socialists, who thought that they would like to return to Austria or Germany. There were quite a number of Zionists, who were hoping to go to a kibbutz in Palestine. Some of the people said they would like to stay on in England. I said I did not know, as the future was too uncertain. Then the man said: 'Supposing there is a huge earthquake and the whole of Palestine becomes submerged in the Mediterranean Sea, so that it no longer exists. What would you do then?' Pandemonium ensued. 'It is not possible! It can't happen! You cannot make such ridiculous assumptions!' The point the man intended to make was obviously missed and the meeting broke up without any conclusion being reached.

Visiting the Isle of Man for the RCM in November 1940, William Simpson was impressed with the efforts being made to give youngsters an education, though he was anxious that an 'English' influence should be maintained. Often, all education was conducted by the internees themselves – English lessons being given by people who had been in this country for a number of years. At Onchan:

> The camp university has an average of thirty courses running each day, with some 600 internees out of a total of 1200 in the camp attending. Up to 19 October, the total number of classes, lectures, tutorials, etc., was 3900 and the total attendance over the same period numbered 78,000.
>
> There was also a youth college offering farming, commercial, technical and general courses. In the technical section both elementary and advanced training is given, while in the general section students are prepared for the matriculation exam.
>
> The number of boys in the camp between sixteen and twenty-one years of age was 231 at the time of my visit and the average attendance at the school was about 100. About fifty of the boys were unable to attend, so I was told, because it was necessary for them to work in order to earn pocket money.
>
> The college is housed in a quite small house without proper blackout arrangements and without furniture. Students are urged to bring their own chairs and the roughest of desks have been knocked together from rough boards. These desks are quite useless for lessons in machine drawing, etc. There was also difficulty about heating the school, since the Island authorities would only allow coal for dwelling houses, and therefore would not make any allowance for a house used entirely for cultural purposes.

Reporting on a common complaint, Mr Simpson noted a serious shortage of football boots.

Billeting arrangements were subject to strain. The promised allowance to cover extra heating and lighting was not forthcoming, and as the days lengthened and winter approached there was understandable bad feeling between landladies and their reluctant lodgers. Mr Simpson spoke of the unaccustomed burden the landladies were having to carry and stressed the need for 'good public relations work'.

But ex-internees remember well the monotony of the boarding house diet:

> Herrings three times a week. We did our best to ring the changes; baked, boiled, fried, even as roll–mops, but in the end imagination failed us and we tipped a whole day's supply down the drains. We got away with it. Other houses tried it too and got found out because the drains blocked up.
>
> (Lewis Erlanger – copyright reserved.)

Ya'acov Friedler was interned in the women's camp at Port Erin with his sister, who had asked for him and his brother to join her there. He remembers a culinary repertoire consisting of kippers alternating with macaroni in tomato sauce. Internees did the work of chambermaids and waited at table:

> It was not of course our business to worry about the hotel owners' finances, but the fact that we were not wholly a burden on them did give us a better feeling. I cannot recall an instance of any of the owners recriminating with their long-staying, if involuntary, guests.

However, emotional tension did occur in the camp on another front:

> . . . the hotel next to us housed true enemy aliens, several dozen German women who in 1940 were still openly flouting their support for the victorious Nazis.
>
> In their wisdom the authorities boarded next to each other a group of women who were self-confessed Nazis and another who were refugees from Nazism and opposed to it with all their hearts . . .
>
> Our next door neighbours thus wore a permanent smirk as long as Hitler was gaining his easy victories in Europe. Sometimes they would make a show of greeting each other with the raised arm Nazi

Jewish refugee children on a train, shortly after crossing the German border

Photo: Wiener Library

German refugee children embark in Holland for the journey to England

12 December, 1938. Children from Vienna arrive at Harwich, most of them Jewish, the remainder 'non-Aryan' Catholics and Protestants, or the children of anti-Nazis. They were than taken by a special train to Pakefield Holiday Camp, Lowestoft

The children arrive at customs in England
Photo: Wiener Library

A distressed teenage refugee on arrival in England
Photo: Wiener Library

Two of the youngest refugees: the boy is five years old and the girl six
Photo: Wiener Library

*A little girl from a party of children drawn mainly from Berlin
and Hamburg clutches her doll. Arriving in Harwich on
2 December, 1938, she was then taken to a holiday camp at
Dovercourt, near Harwich*

Photo: Wiener Library

A party of refugee girls at an English reception camp
Photo: Wiener Library

Refugee children wave from their chalets at a holiday camp in Dovercourt
Photo: Wiener Library

Dorli (now Dorothy) and Lisi Oppenheimer in Vienna, December 1938, before they left for England, where they stayed with Theo and Tilly Hall in Leeds

Photo: courtesy of Dorothy Fleming

Dorothy and Lisi sent these pictures to their parents in Vienna to reassure them that they were healthy and happy in England

Photos: courtesy of Dorothy Fleming

Otto M. Schiff, CBE, Founder and Chairman, Jewish Refugees Committee 1933-49; Honorary President, CBF 1949-52

Registration card of refugee Liesel Fischmann

SURNAME F I S C H M A N N
No. OF CHILDREN
CHRISTIAN NAME Liesel
DATE OF REG.
37, Brondesbury Rd., London NW.7
No.
NATIONALITY Czech
ENGLISH ADDRESS CSR.
HOME ADDRESS CSR.
EXP. OF PASSPORT
BIRTHPLACE
DATE OF BIRTH 16.6.1927 OF PROFESSION
GUARANTOR - NAME and ADDRESS FISCHMANN - CF. 131.046
see:Friedel Bedriska CROSS REFERENCE
H.O. No.
ARRIVAL DATE MARRIED
LEFT U.K. FOR
DATE

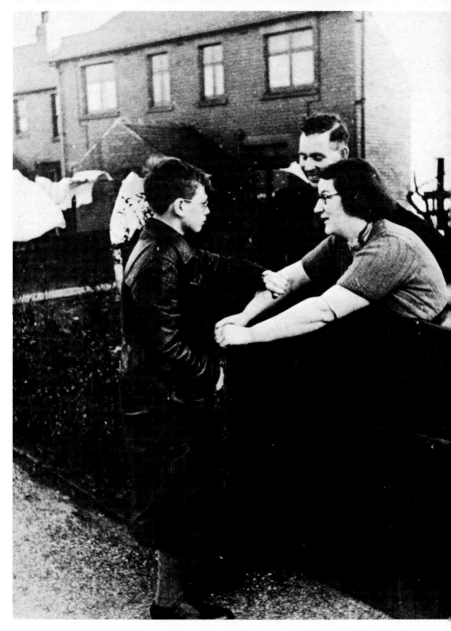

December 1938. Hubert Pardo, aged 13, from Hamburg, and Mr and Mrs H. Ogilesby, the couple with whom he stayed

Photo: Hulton-Deutsch

salute when they saw one of us in the offing. While we ground our teeth and prayed for the Allies, they strutted along the seafront, their heads held high. Needless to say, none of them were Jewish.

The women in the camp made Ya'acov and his brother Solly the focus of their affections:

> Though Solly and I had been separated from our mother for a long time, we got all the mother love boys could take from the enemy aliens of Port Erin. They diverted to us all their pent-up affections, expanded by their idleness and sharpened by their sexual frustrations. After having been motherless for so long we now found ourselves mothered with a vengeance. We were hugged and fondled, kissed and stroked. Many was the embrace we didn't manage to wriggle out of that would have been better appreciated by older males. We brushed them off as a nuisance.

For some Movement children, the hardship of internment was compounded by plans to ship 'enemy aliens' to Canada and Australia. At a cabinet meeting on 24 May 1940, Churchill stated in an aside that he was 'strongly in favour of removing all internees out of the United Kingdom'. In June, Canada volunteered to take 6000 to 7000 and Australia 10,000 prisoners of war and dangerous internees. Lumped together, these two groups were no more than 4000 strong. By no stretch of the imagination could the majority of internees be described as 'dangerous'. Nonetheless, it was decided to make up the numbers with category B and C refugees.

In early June, the RCM was summarily informed that the *Duchess of York* with 2600 passengers, including a handful of teenagers from Huyton, was on its way to Canada. At the end of the month, the *Arandora Star*, once advertised as 'the world's most delightful cruising liner', set sail with nearly 1200 internees and 200 British troops to guard them.

The ship, carrying two and a half times its normal load of passengers, was sunk by a German U-boat off the coast of Ireland at 6 a.m. on 2 July 1940. Amongst those who lost their lives were 143 Germans and Austrians and 470 Italians, but the total number of casualties, which included members of the crew and some British troops, was not revealed.

The only message survivors were permitted to send, a postcard with the words 'I am safe', puzzled the recipients, who knew nothing about the deportations. Distracted relatives, not knowing whether their menfolk were interned in this country, interned in Canada or drowned, were directed by the Home Office to the War Office and from there to the Admiralty, who sent them back to the War Office. Such was the official secrecy, or confusion, that it took several weeks to confirm that no RCM boys were among the casualties.

Despite the tragedy, the deportation continued. The *Dunera*, an 11,000 ton former troopship, bound for Australia, set sail on 10 July. It carried 2543 men, of whom 2100 were category C aliens, refugees from the RCM and *Youth Aliyah* were on board. Alfred Cooper was among them:

> I was on the *Arandora Star* first but that got torpedoed. I don't really remember much – it was early in the morning. I don't know how I got out because I can't swim. A naval destroyer picked us up. There weren't many Jewish people on the *Arandora Star*; it was mostly Italians and political refugees.
>
> Then we went on the *Dunera*, about a week after being torpedoed. They didn't tell me that I was going to Australia, they just put me on the boat in Liverpool and off we went. We had trouble on the *Dunera* . . . the guards used to urinate in the porridge; we all had dysentery. I think five people died. It was so crowded that some people used to sleep in hammocks and some on the mess tables. There were no proper toilets on the ship – there was one long board with different holes and water flushed through all the time and of course that made the dysentery worse . . .
>
> We were kept down below all the time but once a day they used to take us for a walk. We were behind barbed wire . . . I saw Table Mountain at Cape Town – everyone was allowed a minute at the porthole. We were not allowed off the boat until Australia.
>
> The man in charge of the men who guarded us was Captain O'Neill. He had the VC from the First World War. He used to rob the rich Jews. I saw him do it myself. When I first got on the boat the first thing I saw was a lot of suitcases opened. They used to beat us and tell us to hurry up and they would rip open the suitcases with their bayonets. Everybody made a claim when they got off the boat. My brother made a claim and the War Office repaid him for everything he had lost.
>
> The *Dunera* was very bad. There were suicides. One of them walked in front of me and just jumped overboard. And one got killed in a fight over a hammock.

Conditions were no better, and possibly worse, on the *Ettrick* which made for Canada with 220 RCM boys on board.

We were herded together in the bows of the ship in a three-tiered space with a shaft in the centre. The three tiers were connected by companion ways – the top tier was at about sea level. Most of the space was taken up by dining tables, benches, the shaft and the companion ways. At the top level, over 500 people lived and slept for twelve days and nights.

In the event of an emergency the only way out for the internees on the lower tiers would have been the companion way and from there to the lower deck, but at the top of the companion way there was a barbed wire barrier which left a space of some four feet for passage during the day but was entirely closed and under military guard during the night. To reach the upper deck and the lifeboats we would have had to get through another barbed wire barrier and two further companion ways, which were always heavily guarded, while the doors at the top of the companion way were kept locked.

The only supply of air came through the ventilating pipes which ran through the body of the ship.

Not enough hammocks and blankets were issued to the internees; people slept on the dining tables, on the benches, on the floor, on the companion way, literally on top of each other.

For two days we were not allowed to emerge, for we were not to see any part of the Scottish or Irish coast. After that, congestion was relieved during the daytime by two-hourly shifts of half the complement on deck. There were two inadequate meals a day, one at 8 a.m. and one at 6 p.m.

Many people were seasick almost the whole time and a few buckets were allotted to them and put down among the people who had to lie on the floor at night. During the second night a sudden epidemic of diarrhoea broke out. The gangway leading to the lavatories was closed by barbed wire and, as the guards refused to open them even in an emergency, people had to relieve themselves wherever they stood or happened to be. This situation was repeated during the following night and the prisoners were finally granted another few buckets, for which there was hardly any room left on the floors where people were lying.

After their arrival in the Canadian camp all the refugees' belongings were taken away by NCOs and privates. They were told that everything would be returned the next morning. However, when two days later the luggage and confiscated goods were returned, it was discovered that money and such things as watches, pens, lighters had disappeared. While the luggage was laid out for examination and collection, the thieving continued.

The *Dunera* almost shared the fate of the *Arandora Star*. Early in its voyage it was grazed by a torpedo, but thereafter she avoided the attention of the German U-boats, docking at Melbourne Bay on 3 September, where some of the *Arandora Star* survivors disembarked. The others continued to Sydney, where they were taken to an internment camp at Hay, three miles up the railway on the Murrumbidgee river. For Alfred Cooper, as for his fellow passengers, journey's end came as a welcome relief:

> The only trouble was the flies. It was very hot. I used to hang the washing out and by the time you had put the last bit out the first bit was dry. We had everything there. Football teams, lectures, good entertainment. The guards were very good to us. The commandant used to give us virtually everything we wanted. There were two camps opposite to each other. At the beginning we were all together, but then some wanted kosher food so they went off to the other camp.

Back in England, as the scandal of the *Arandora Star*, the *Ettrick* and the *Dunera* filtered through to the public, opinion shifted from 'intern the lot' to 'free them now'. On 31 July, the Home Office published a White Paper listing headings under which internees could be released. The first two groups covered those under sixteen and over sixty-five years of age and young persons under eighteen who had been resident with British families, or in an educational establishment prior to internment. Young people under RCM care were therefore among the first to qualify for release. This was the case for Peter Prager:

> I stayed at Lingfield for three weeks, sleeping in the racecourse stables on straw, then I was transferred to Huyton for another three weeks. Then I was told that anyone under eighteen could be released, but it had to be an outside agency which applied. I was then under the care of the Refugee Children's Movement and I was told that I was the first one for whom they had applied. They thought I was the safest because I had lived with an English family beforehand. So I was released.

Casting around for a suitable envoy to go out to Australia on behalf of a contrite British government, the choice fell on Major Julian Layton, an active promoter of the refugee cause whose experience encompassed several weeks on the Isle of Man liaising with the civil administration. He departed with authorisation to release all young internees who were willing to join the Pioneer Corps. The remainder either remained in Australia for vital war work or joined the labour units of the Australian army. Six *Youth Aliyah* boys managed to secure emigration permits for Palestine.

Although compensation was given to the deportees for possessions stolen from them during the journey, no compensation was offered to the schoolchildren who were forced by internment to leave school or job training to which, in most cases, they were unable to return.

The official view remained faithful to the spirit of a memorandum issued to the internment tribunals in 1939:

> While it is desired to avoid any unnecessary hardship to individuals, nevertheless the interests of the individual cannot in present circumstances be a primary consideration; they must be subordinated to considerations of national security.

Even when the collective paranoia of the early months of 1940 subsided, this attitude prevailed.

9

Board and Lodging

'*A* remark made at the opening of the Hostel has given
rise to the suggestion that the Hostel is a somewhat luxurious
place. It was referred to as a palace and the garden was
likened to Eden. These are figures of speech and should not
be taken literally.'

At a time when property prices were distinctly flat, the influx of
refugees created a boom in one sector of the market. From 1938,
enticing offers appeared in the small ads section of the Jewish press:

> Upper Clapton, large freehold property containing 24 rooms, suit-
> able for housing 50 children. Price £3250.

RCM hostels sprang up across urban Britain with the highest
proportion in London, Manchester and Leeds. They housed children who could not find foster parents or who were too old to fit
easily into a new family environment. Run by members of the
RCM local committees or Jewish Refugees Committee, they
relied on state allowances and charitable appeals to cover the costs
of upkeep. It was calculated that each child needed one pound a
week for food and clothing. Donations in kind were as welcome
as money. A boy's hostel in London received mattresses from a
shipping company, blankets from another firm and food from the
Deserving Charities Organisation. London's East End traders were
particularly generous.

A large part of hostel administration was in the hands of volunteers who were themselves refugees. Although they spoke German
and came from the same backgrounds as their charges, they were

often young and inexperienced and unprepared for the demands of the work.

Harry Katz spent several years in a hostel in Leeds:

> It could have been better but I reckon the reason was that the people in charge weren't competent. They were not trained to do the job. The children did just what they wanted.

Lottie and Freddie Freedman, a young married couple, came to England with a *Kindertransport* from Berlin via Hamburg in 1939. Freddie, who worked for the youth department of the Jewish community in Rosenstrasse, had organised and travelled with many transports, until finally he was warned: 'You either stay in England or you've had it.'

Intending eventually to travel on to America, the Freedmans had nowhere to go and were unable to take work. Bloomsbury House sent them to help out at a hostel. Lottie was thrown in at the deep end:

> After a week the cook ran away and I, who could barely boil an egg, had to take over cooking for forty children. It was a disaster but I learned. The committee decided to give me pocket money and then they paid for a little home we had, so we were quite well off . . .

Freddie then applied to be a hostel leader with Lottie as matron. They were interviewed by Mrs Norman Bentwich and other leading lights of the Jewish community. At 22, Lottie felt she had few qualifications for such a sensitive job, but after his time with the *Kindertransporte* Freddie was more confident. The appointment committee was impressed.

> We became leaders of a hostel in the deepest slums of North Kensington. We had forty boys aged fourteen to eighteen at the Western Council Training Hostel on St Mark's Road.

At the start, Lottie was confounded by the garden:

> I thought, Goodness, they have funny flowers here – because the soil was stuck with knives. The cook before had muddled up the kosher kitchen – the milk and the meat and so on.

Lottie did her best with the disorientated and often distressed inmates.

> The children in the hostel came from all kinds of backgrounds and all corners of Germany, Austria and Czechoslovakia. As soon as they opened their bags, I could see a picture of the parents and I knew just what the background was. I was detached then – today I know so much more about development and psychology. I just had common sense then.
>
> One boy would cry for his mother when he had tummy ache – and I would just say 'She isn't here.' Today I would handle it differently. I think I was a mixture of a surrogate mother and a good friend and fun. I wanted to have fun too.

In the early days of the war the Freedmans lost all their boys aged over sixteen to internment. Throughout the Blitz, Lottie regularly trooped down to the Anderson shelter at the bottom of the garden with the boys and her baby daughter in a Moses basket. When her husband was spotted, torch in hand, prowling the garden at night, the neighbours accused him of spying. But the Freedmans had less trouble with overconscientious citizens than with their local synagogue:

> They were very concerned that we should be kosher. A terrible row blew up one day because my husband refused to buy black-market meat – he would rather have fed them not kosher. That was the end of our hostel days.

Generally, children from orthodox homes were placed in hostels controlled or strongly influenced by the Chief Rabbi's Religious Emergency Council led by Solomon Schonfeld. Among those he approached to help with finding accommodation for the orthodox children he was bringing from Germany and Austria was Mrs Annie Wolfson. She and her husband bought a house in Victoria Park Road in Hackney to convert into a hostel for twenty girls. Intended as a clearing house for girls who could not immediately find other homes, the hostel was managed by the Hackney Aid Committee for Refugee Children, who recruited a matron and staff from the ranks of the unemployed refugees. Judging by the loud protests when the girls had to be evacuated to Norfolk, the enterprise lived up to the best expectations. It reopened in 1941 and was active until the end of the war.

Circumstances were less favourable for the Home for Jewish Refugee Children at 5 The Avenue, London NW6. This orthodox hostel was opened in December 1938 to receive children from Dovercourt. One of the early arrivals was Zita Hirschhorn (Sonia Schmitzer):

> We had open house every Sunday, when families came to pick children to stay with them, in order to make room for additional children to be brought over from Europe. I myself went to two different families but always asked to be returned. Although I was treated very well I was very lonely for my friends in the hostel. After the evacuation, in 1940, we were allowed to return to the hostel for *Pesach*, at our own risk.
>
> We were all billeted with non-Jewish families in Stotfold, Bedfordshire, and wanted to celebrate *Pesach* in our own home, in a kosher way. We were all orthodox kids. Then the bombing of London started and soon we were hit by a landmine and had to leave the house. We ended up in another hostel in Hackney.
>
> There, too, we were heavily bombed out. It was a miracle we were not killed. Half the house went with a direct hit. We were in the basement sleeping on mattresses on the other side of the building.

Zita Hirschhorn stayed with the hostel until it closed in 1948.

Low down in the popularity stakes was Cazenove Road in London's East End. Even after experiencing the spartan life of a training farm, Käthe Fischel found conditions at this orthodox hostel hard to take.

> It was an old, dark Edwardian house. I was horrified. Most of the girls were from poor Jewish families, including English Jewish girls from the East End, and all they did was sew buttons on garments in factories. There was a lot of praying but the girls had no education. I presume the idea was to find them husbands. My friend and I both remember, each girl had a little personal pot of jam but no one ever offered us any.

Claire Barrington also remembers Cazenove Road:

> The other, English Jewish, girls had jobs and prided themselves on their hair and clothes, while we refugees had straight hair. Because we didn't look well groomed, there was a feeling against us, they

resented us. They were very religious and they thought themselves a little bit superior. I was unhappy there. I had been given sixpence a week pocket money at the Hachsharah Training Centre and of course I didn't spend it. I had just managed to save one pound when I left my purse in one of the dormitories at the hostel. Of course, when I came back, it was gone. I needed that pound, it was a lot of money. I always felt that because I was alone, everything was twice as bad. I was so vulnerable.

Hard conditions were not necessarily a bar to enjoying hostel life as Martha Levy discovered:

I was just eighteen when I went to the hostel – there were about 30 or 35 other girls there, all the same age. I was very happy and made a lot of friends.

I got a job sewing on buttons. My English was still not very good and one day I went to the foreman, who was on the phone, and asked him if I could 'destroy' him rather than 'disturb' him. For weeks after he would say, 'Well, Martha – do you still want to destroy me?' Then I bettered myself and went to be a machinist in a factory in the East End. The manager was Viennese and terribly, terribly strict. All the people who worked there were English. They were all very interested in my background and sympathetic, but I didn't socialise with them because living in a girls' hostel with a boys' hostel opposite there was no need.

We had regular duties such as washing-up. We had to get up at 5.30 so that we could get a workman's train ticket. If I didn't do this, by Friday I didn't have the money for a bar of soap. I had to be at work at 8 o'clock. The food at the hostel was not too exciting, because one day my manager came home with me and complained bitterly: 'These girls should have something more substantial than sandwiches of beetroot or watercress. How can they work on this?'

An English couple ran the hostel. The wife liked me very much and was in tears when I left. I went with two other girls and we took two private rooms. I had met my husband-to-be by then and we left the hostel because we had to be in by ten and we wanted more freedom.

Hostel food was a regular subject of complaint for RCM visitors:

. . . Heinz was rather nervy and fidgety and says he has been suffering from headaches recently and also from occasional nose-bleeding. It transpires that he has no regular dinners at school and just manages on a few sandwiches provided by the hostel which, of course, are not substantial. He says he cannot afford 5d every day for the school dinner. He only has 2/- a week pocket money.

A contributor to Karen Gershon's book *We Came As Children* remembers two very different hostels:

I was fortunate to be sent to Ramsgate Hostel, a place with a family atmosphere, one that was designed to minimise any problems of homelessness and homesickness. It housed about fifteen boys from Germany and Austria. There were the usual petty rivalries and fights amongst the boys, as well as minor division along nationality lines. Apart from eating well and enjoying our environment by taking long walks, we did little but study English, read, write letters, listen to the radio and, last but definitely not least, clean the house . . .

After the beginning of the war, we were transferred to the Chiltern Emigrants Training Colony at Benson, near Reading, which was operated by the Christian Service Union for mentally retarded British boys. We took our meals (and very bad ones they were too) in a common dining hall and occasionally played soccer and cricket with the British boys, but otherwise had little contact with them. They seemed harmless and pleasant enough. About sixty of us refugee boys were housed in three rather primitive, heatless barracks. Some worked in pigsties and cowsheds; others trimmed hedges and built fences or roads. I was put in a sort of unskilled labour battalion which worked in a gravel pit. The contrast between Ramsgate and Benson could hardly have been greater. The warmth and security of family life were replaced by the impersonal coldness of army-style living, and at sixteen I was not ready for this.

Walter Friedmann describes the difficulties experienced by young people struggling to educate or better themselves, while coping with hostel life and trying to make a living:

At first, having settled into the hostel, they would plan their spare time very carefully, studying serious books to improve their unfinished education, or taking up hobbies like stamp collecting. But circumstances were against them.

When they came home from work they had their dinner, then they sat around for a while, a little tired perhaps, talking of this and that. Eventually one of them would make the effort and say, 'Well, I have to go to my room now to get on with my reading.' But then his room mate would start talking about his day at work, his boss, the increase in wages he should have got but didn't. His friend goes downstairs again and finally sits in a quiet corner to start reading. It is now late and he is really tired and cannot take it in any more, so he puts the book down and says to himself: 'Tomorrow is another day. Tomorrow I shall finish this chapter.' But the next evening is not very different – perhaps the discussion is on another subject but something is always going on. There is always the feeling of tiredness, and tired people need quiet so they can concentrate. But where can you find peace in a house full of young people? There is always noise! So after a while, even the efforts of this keen youngster to do some studying by himself come to an end and he becomes just like one of the others, one of the crowd, who just waste their valuable spare time . . .

In March 1939, a group of thirty boys from Frankfurt took over The Cedars, an eight-bedroomed former nursing home on the 6000-acre Waddesdon Estate of James de Rothschild. Nearly all the boys had started life in rural Germany but, to escape anti-Semitism, had been sent to Philanthropia, a Jewish school in Frankfurt. Here they stayed in a hostel run by Hugo and Lilli Steinhardt, which was attacked on *Kristallnacht*. A desperate letter of appeal from the Steinhardts to Lord Rothschild in London resulted in the handing over of The Cedars.

Among the other famous names who set up hostels for the *Kindertransporte* was Harry Jacobs, the head of Times Furnishing. He took in ten children up to five years old and guaranteed their upbringing and education to the age of eighteen. During the war he moved children to his home in Surrey, where a wing was converted into a nursery, and he engaged a cook and nurse and a maid to look after them. When he was called up, the children moved to Hemel Hempstead. Eva Minckes, now aged eighty-five and living in Israel, worked at the home. She was actually the real mother of one of the children, but was never allowed to say so – 'to avoid sadness for the other children'.

Lord Sainsbury took twenty-five children, paid for their education and kept in touch with them afterwards. The Salmon family (Harry Salmon was chairman and Julius Salmon a director of J. Lyons), together with the Glucksteins, accommodated twenty-three children in The Haven above Burton's Tailors on the Kentish Town Road in London. Peter Morgan remembers being taken out to lunch at the Trocadero and visiting Cadby Hall, the headquarters of J. Lyons.

Of the hostel he said:

> It was new. It was magnificent. Everything was run almost on hotel lines. After all, they were hoteliers – they had the Strand Palace, the Regent Palace and the Cumberland. We lived a life of luxury, as I recall it today!

English names were adopted to speed up the process of assimilation. That was when Peter Morgenstern became Peter Morgan. To the same end, the clothes brought over from Germany were quietly removed.

'On the train from Harwich to London our cases were taken away as our guarantors did not want us wearing funny clothes,' one girl remembers. 'Even at the age of eight years old, I knew how much love had gone into that case . . .' Gifts of cuddly toys were no compensation. Peter Morgan had no complaints, however, and went on to work in the hotels and restaurants of the Lyons empire.

Among the non-Jewish organisations responsible for hostels, the Christadelphians were to the fore. With their faith rooted in Jewish law, the Christadelphians had a long-standing interest in cooperative ventures, contributing generously to attempts to re-establish the Jewish people in Palestine. When the exodus of children from Germany and Austria began, they were among the first to respond.

A refugee mother and her two teenage sons were the founder residents of one of the earliest Christadelphian hostels – Little Thorn, on the Bilton Road in Rugby. Here a small group of Jewish boys were given a home and were trained for careers in leather manufacture, cabinet-making, and engineering. The hostel also became a focal point for refugees to gather and socialise at weekends.

Also in the Midlands, Elpis Lodge ('Abode of Hope') opened in April 1940 at 117 Gough Road, Edgbaston. Managed by Birmingham Jewry, the running of the hostel was funded by the Birmingham and Coventry Christadelphian Ecclesias. Dr Hirsch, previously headmaster of a school in Frankfurt, and his wife were wardens of the hostel, which accommodated twenty teenaged boys.

The atmosphere of the hostel was orthodox. Aside from the practical aspects of caring for the young people, there was much talk of spiritual care and regeneration, so that the young men at Elpis Lodge would go out into the world 'imbued and enlightened with the hope of a better future', and not embittered by the ill-treatment and injustice they had experienced. In the years up to 1945, forty-eight boys learnt woodwork, tailoring, engineering and many other trades, often carrying on the work traditional to their families.

Evidently there was some feeling that life at Elpis Lodge was too comfortable. A contributor to *The Christadelphian* of January 1941, set out to correct the impression:

> A remark made at the opening of the Hostel has given rise to the suggestion that the Hostel is a somewhat luxurious place. It was referred to as a palace and the garden was likened to Eden. These are figures of speech and should not be taken literally. The house is old. So is the garden. The presence of an old cedar tree lends dignity to the garden and there is a rockery which has been beautiful and could be made so again. The house itself is very simple in design inside and out. There is nothing palatial about it and in its furnishing and equipment it resembles a hospital. Any suggestion of luxury is completely absent.

If comfort was at a premium in the average hostel, in the agricultural training centres it was entirely absent, often as a matter of deliberate policy.

Käthe Fischel, who was at the David Eder Farm in Kent throughout the harsh winter of 1939, remembers:

> We were in barracks with no floors, just earth stamped down. We washed in jugs and ewers and the water was always frozen. We crawled into each other's beds for warmth. The food was terrible – no-one knew how to cook. A friend of mine, who afterwards married a well-known German journalist, was working in the kitchen. Potatoes were boiled and stood in huge buckets. Someone came in in wellingtons and stood in a bucket and those potatoes were still served. They had huge packets of dates but they must have bought them cheaply because they were as dry as dust. They

looked like camel fodder, which perhaps is what they were supposed to be.

The centres were mostly run by *Youth Aliyah*, in cooperation with the RCM, but there was one notable exception where the RCM took all of the responsibility – and all of the blame.

Barham House, just outside Ipswich, on the Essex–Suffolk border, started life as an overspill camp for Dovercourt. It had accommodation for 200 boys.

There was no mistaking Barham House. Built as a Victorian workhouse, it had a grey, forbidding look which must have deterred all but the neediest applicants. Its defects were emphasised by its proximity to Shrubland Park, a splendid Palladian mansion with a long drive and imposing gatehouses, which first-time visitors sometimes mistook for the RCM building. They were soon put right.

According to the book of 'daily happenings', life at Barham House was a model of domestic harmony.

> We have a nursery of 18 boys aged nine and under. Most of these have short lessons in the morning. They are taken for walks, play games and are generally supervised by competent workers from the time they get up to the time they go to bed.
>
> Boys ten to sixteen years of age have school all the morning . . . the basis of teaching is English and they are grouped in accordance with their knowledge of English.
>
> Boys sixteen and upwards do field work all day. This is done under the supervision of a trained agriculturalist. At the moment they are preparing the ground for the reception of seeds in the early spring, and in the summer of next year we shall be more than self-supporting in potatoes, greens, beet, celery, etc.
>
> With the exception of cooking, all the domestic work of the building is undertaken by children supervised by staff. The laundry, except for sheets and towels, is done by boys under the supervision of a washerwoman.
>
> There is a tailor's shop, carpenter's shop and a bootmaker's shop, all run by boys under supervision. Special classes for carpentry and bookbinding are being commenced in the New Year under a trained teacher.

The camp was run by a staff dedicated to the belief that young people thrived on fresh air, early morning runs and cold showers.

Even assuming the truth of this, the experience of some of the inmates suggests that it was possible to have too much of a good thing.

> Our headmaster, Mr Percival, fixed our windows so that they could not be shut at night. In that cold winter I got sciatica and one morning I couldn't move my legs.

That is what happened to Ernst Sicher. Others recall the plague of rats ('They tore away the bottoms from the boys' trousers and at night you could hear their squeaking very clearly') and the epidemic of scabies.

> Two doctors, one from Vienna, the other from Berlin, were in daily attendance. But there were also cases of diphtheria and scarlet fever. This meant that all of us had to be kept in quarantine and with all the new cases, the quarantine was extended for weeks.

With the spring, there was a dramatic improvement in the quality of life. The damp retreated down the walls, the gardens came back to life and there was fresh food in the kitchen. But relations between the youngsters and their adult minders did not change for the better. A stream of complaints to Bloomsbury House led to the sacking of the more objectionable roughnecks. One of them made a farewell address:

> Whoever's behind this can count himself lucky. If there was a war on, I'd shoot him.

The new regime consisted of a triumvirate of English Protestant, Irish Catholic and Jewish interests, with each representative chasing hard for jobs and foster homes for their charges. It was not an ideal arrangement, but it worked well enough for youngsters to feel that Barham House was on their side. In fact, the only serious problems at this stage involved children who did not want to leave the security of the one home they knew.

> Two boys had such a strong resistance to leaving, they made themselves ill, one by eating a large portion of butter, the other, more drastically, by eating soap.

With the first days of the war came another change, a retrograde one this time, in the way Barham House was managed. By a mysterious logic which was lost on the majority, a retired military officer took command, demanding total obedience from all foreigners in the camp.

'There's a war on now and all of you are in enemy territory,' he announced to a general assembly. 'Whoever criticises my authority is criticising the government and will be interned.'

Once again, Bloomsbury House was inundated with complaints. The reaction was to try to speed up the reallocation of those remaining at Barham House (a process which was unintentionally assisted by the activation of the internment laws), to provide the best possible reason for closing the place down. The last residents moved out towards the end of 1940, leaving Barham House to be taken over by the army.

Youth Aliyah would not have given up quite so easily. The concept of *aliyah* – immigration to Palestine to live on agricultural settlements – was a passionate ideal which took priority over all other considerations. The children were split into two age groups, *Youth Aliyah* for the fourteen to seventeen-year-olds and *Hechalutz*, the adult movement, for the rest. The younger children, who had completed nine years of school but who were not quite old enough to join the *Hechalutz* training programme, combined a half-day study syllabus with agricultural work.

Youth Aliyah was opposed to the very principle of fostering refugee children. It was an article of faith which led to disputes with the RCM and lively discussions between Rebecca Sieff and her younger sister, Elaine Blond.

> There were those like Becky who believed that hostels, with their minimal standard of comfort, were the best training for a hard pioneering life in Palestine. I think she had visions of a strict regime of early morning runs and cold showers. It was not my idea of a proper upbringing . . .

The appeal went out for the loan or gift of farms or country estates where *Youth Aliyah* children could live, learn and work collectively. If this was not possible, then they had to be placed as 'hands' on conventional farms where they were close enough together to meet in the evenings with their *Madrichim* (group counsellors) for cultural communion. A former worker at *Youth Aliyah*'s London office argued:

> While the RCM cared mostly for the children's physical wellbeing, we cared also for their values and gave them a purpose in life, a goal to work towards.

Contact between the various *Youth Aliyah* training centres was chiefly by newsletters published by the London office, but some groups brought out their own monthly bulletin with such exalted titles as *The Plough, Seeds* and *Our Life*. At first written in German and Hebrew, these publications soon turned to English.

Within *Youth Aliyah* there were several competing Zionist factions ranging from the strictly orthodox *Bachad* to the moderate *Maccabi Hazair*, the Zionist scout movement. All these groups were keen to add to their numbers, which could lead to problems when more than one faction was active in a locality. Still, for all its divisions, *Youth Aliyah* provided a sense of cultural identity and companionship which the RCM was not capable of offering.

Yoash Kahn, who has taught in England for many years but who also has strong links with education in Israel, recalls his hostel days with affection, even if he did have problems adjusting to the regime.

> At first I had difficulty settling down – I was a pain in the neck. I went to one of the three hostels in Devon – Exmouth (which closed), Teignmouth and Dawlish, which were run by a Jewish youth movement called *Habonim*, a socialist Zionist movement leading to Kibbutz life. They were keen to further the aims of the movement. They were very democratic, in that there was a general meeting and committees to make all the decisions.
>
> The warden, the matron and the staff were not all that much older than we were. They were mostly *chalutzim* (potential kibbutzniks) who had been on their way to Israel but were stopped by the war. They came with no training; all they had was ordinary common sense. But somehow it worked. We had rotas for all the usual domestic chores – sweeping, peeling potatoes, darning socks . . .

In the early days Yoash was a natural rebel, refusing to make his bed with a proper hospital corner, throwing the blue collection box for the Jewish National Fund at a fellow student, and taking up almost permanent occupancy of the bed-wetters room.

I remember particularly, because it was an extreme measure, that they persuaded the general meeting to send me to Coventry. They were doing their best, but they couldn't see that ignoring me would just aggravate the problem . . .

Yoash ran away and was returned to the hostel. With time he began to settle and his school work improved:

They managed to get me into Teignmouth Grammar. The *Batim* (the Hebrew generic name for hostels) had a large number of pupils in this school and in my form there were about thirteen or fourteen of us out of thirty pupils. The competition was ferocious. Our form marks were calculated to a second decimal place in order to sort us out. Finally, in my last exams, I came top in the class. It all turned out for the good. There was a change of leadership at the hostel; I don't know whether they left all together or one by one, but with the second generation of leaders I established a good relationship and things went well.

Yoash became an ardent flag carrier for *Habonim*.

By the beginning of the war, there were around twenty *Hach-shara* centres in Britain. The best known was Whittingham House, twenty miles from Edinburgh, described by an admiring non-resident as 'a little Jerusalem in Britain's green and pleasant land'. Once the home of Lord Balfour, it was offered by his son, Viscount Taprain, for the training of 200 children in agriculture, horticulture and forestry. Children from *Youth Aliyah* and the RCM were housed there.

Almost immediately, there was a conflict of values between *Youth Aliyah* and the presbyterian governors. The school matron, herself a refugee, acted as an intermediary:

There was, for instance, the question of pooling all the pocket money, decided on at one of the school meetings. That smacked too much of communism to please the Edinburgh businessmen. Or – of less importance – I ordered cake for Sabbath breakfast. 'Cake for breakfast?' It seemed awful to the Edinburgh people (including the baker). But it came punctually every Friday.

Well-meaning sponsors in London could be no less insensitive:

I hardly believed my eyes when I unpacked some sample clothes for the children – they were all khaki-coloured. So I sat down and wrote in my best (not very good) English that design and quality of the garments were excellent, but that I could not ask continental children to wear brown uniforms after their experiences with the Brownshirts . . .

Teachers were in short supply and those who did volunteer were naturally steeped in the Scottish tradition of education.

. . . For some, these foreign children were as strange as beings from another world. They had never seen such a lack of conformity, which resulted from the fact that they not only came from very varied social backgrounds and every part of middle Europe, but also had not undergone the levelling training of a British school.

The attempt by the first headmaster to run Whittingham as a Jewish Eton was not appreciated by the children. Erich Duchinsky, a *Youth Aliyah* worker, led the campaign to have him removed.

He had no understanding – a very old man with no idea of what it was all about. I persuaded the Whittingham committee he should go.

One of the younger teachers took over. Nonetheless, an inquiry by *Youth Aliyah* in the autumn of 1940 revealed a persistently unsatisfactory state of affairs. It was understandable that most of the staff had no previous experience with Jewish children, but there seemed to be little effort to make contact. Lessons took up only two hours a day and the farm work was badly organised. But the faults were not all on one side:

There was laziness and indifference amongst the children, especially in the first year of their stay, most probably aggravated by long times spent waiting in reception camps with hardly any work or tuition or leadership. So it was not a rare sight to see a group of boys playing football when they should have been in class learning English or arithmetic – there was much less absenteeism from practical work.

Two new teachers were engaged and six *Madrichim* drafted in to inspire greater devotion to Zionism. Nonetheless, the lack of cohesive leadership took its toll, and by late 1939 thirty of the original 166 students had reneged on their undertaking to emigrate to Palestine. By 1941, places at Whittingham were left vacant by departing eighteen-year-olds. A year later, the school closed. Those children remaining went to Dalton House near Edinburgh.

Despite the high praise lavished on Whittingham by Norman Bentwich, among others (he called it 'the most romantic of the agricultural centres'), it was hardly a success story either for *Youth Aliyah* or the RCM.

Conditions were just as tough at Great Engeham Farm in Kent. Handed over in 1939 by its owners in response to an advertisement in *The Times*, *Youth Aliyah* decided to use it as a transit camp for refugee children who were waiting for permanent *hachshara*. The farm itself housed twenty-five Czechoslovaks who were part of the overspill from Whittingham. The R C M placed fifty children, the agricultural committee of the Council for German Jewry another thirty, and the Women's Appeal Committee sent a small group of Polish children. They were all sent to work on neighbouring farms where pickers were in great demand. Out of season they helped build up local defences by filling sandbags.

Fred Dunston (Fritz Deutsch), a *Youth Aliyah* worker and former Scout leader from Vienna, was drafted in as an organiser of the transit camp, which was to be built on a large meadow across the road from the training centre at Great Engeham Farm:

> Transports to this camp started to arrive at the end of June 1939. The last one arrived one day before the outbreak of war, bringing the number of children at the camp up to about 300. Although they were not to stay at the camp very long about 60 were still there at the beginning of December. As these transports had been put together in a great hurry, quite a number of children were included, who did not belong to the *Youth Aliyah* at all.

Accommodation was provided by big marquees, high enough to take double-decker bedsteads. Later on some old railway carriages situated on the farm were also used. A kitchen, washing facilities and lavatories were to be built, camp style, in the open. It was hoped to accomplish all this within a week. This did not prove possible, but all the same the camp was soon in full swing. A few army bell tents were put up quickly, but the marquees remained packed in huge bales while lorries kept arriving with yet more gear. Arrangements were further complicated by the arrival of an orthodox *Bachad* group who demanded a separate kosher kitchen all of their own, which they maintained right up to the time of their departure to Gwrych Castle at the outbreak of war. Arguments between different factions of *Madrichim* and competition for the children's allegiance caused more headaches:

> There were children belonging to at least six or eight Zionist Youth Movements, all with very different ideologies. *Madrichim,* or youth leaders, all had their own ideas of how the camp should be run. Instead of running it jointly they went all out for indoctrination and made lots of promises to attract recruits. Unfortunately, the *Madrichim* had more political knowledge than practical experience in dealing with children and of camp craft.

During the first two weeks about 180 children arrived at Great Engeham. They went short on just about all the basic resources including water, which had to be transported over the fields in a two-wheeled handcart. As there was no proper path, half the water was lost on the journey. To keep up with demand, teams of carriers worked in shifts throughout the day.

There was consolation in knowing that others were worse off. A party of girls who went on an outing to a local Guides' camp were surprised to find that the accommodation there was even more primitive than that at Great Engeham. The only difference was that the Guides could look forward to returning to comfortable homes.

The abundance of physical work prevented *Madrichim* from spending enough time with the children, let alone helping them with their education. This meant that the troublemakers, including many who did not want to come to Great Engeham in the first place, were given a pretty free run.

Fred Dunston and his fellow workers can recall children who 'turned our hair grey', they were so difficult to handle.

> Many children did not understand why they were there. They were certainly not expecting to spend up to two years training for a life on a kibbutz. Not surprisingly, they were very unhappy and unsettled when they found out. It was a difficult task for us to calm them down. They said they had been sent by the *Kultusgemeinde*, Vienna and not by the Palestine office. They had been promised

they would go to foster parents . . . Some of the girls were crying their eyes out, refusing to go on *hachshara* with the type of louts who were on their transport. We had full sympathy for these girls . . . There were at least four or five boys who were not suitable either for our camp or for *Youth Aliyah*. We simply did not know what to do with them . . .

Even those who were prepared to join in found it difficult to understand what the camp was trying to achieve.

The motto of the Kibbutz is 'everybody gives as much as he can and receives in return what he needs'. However, some of these children came from well-to-do, middle-class families who had no sympathy with this philosophy. They were here because their parents were desperate for them to escape from the Nazi tyranny. They were not necessarily the most clever or the most suitable for *Youth Aliyah*. To try to forge a community, the *Madrichim* simply pointed ahead – 'When we are in Palestine it will all be marvellous' – but you can't keep children going on promises like that. It would have been better to have concentrated on proper English, Ivrit, history and geography lessons and maybe some other type of training – but that was impossible under the given circumstances.

With the approach of war, the children responded to the danger by working more closely as a group, by exceeding their targets for filling sandbags, and by camouflaging their tents with foliage. At this point the first contingent of *Bachad* children was sent off to their own training centre, Gwrych Castle, in Wales.

Soon the weather turned to almost constant rain. Living conditions deteriorated steadily and the tents had to be pulled down as life under canvas became almost impossible. The remaining children had to move into the old railway carriages as well, making them rather crowded. They had to stay on till their respective training centres were ready to receive them.

At the beginning of December 1939, Fred Dunstan was one of the adults who went with the last group of children from the transit camp to 'Bydown', not far from Barnstaple in North Devon. This was an old country house with large grounds providing room for about sixty to seventy people. Accommodation there was good in every respect and there was a good staff ratio so that agricultural work and educational lessons could be organised properly in half daily sessions. The local Refugee Committee took great interest in the centre, and visits to the pleasant town of Barnstaple were much enjoyed.

> It was a sort of country home for about sixty children. Accommodation was good, cooking facilities adequate, and Barnstaple a very pleasant town. Here we established a proper *Youth Aliyah* centre, with half-day lessons and half-day farm work. In March 1940, some of the children went to Braunton on the other side of Barnstaple and worked on a smaller farm there.

In March 1940, Fred, together with some adults, members of the *Hechaluz* and about twenty children from Bydown and other centres, moved into a house at Braunton, which was also not far from Barnstaple. The work for this group had been arranged on a large but highly specialised farm, which concentrated on growing bulbs, flowers and potatoes. However, from the *Youth Aliyah* point of view, the general conditions on this farm as well as the work demanded from the children was totally unsuitable:

> The work consisted in walking up and down flowerbeds of an enormous length, carrying a basket on your arm. You had to make up bunches of daffodils or simply cut off the blossoms of tulips and put them into the basket, which, when full, had to be emptied into a lorry. This went on without change day in day out. It was hard labour, not an agricultural training of any kind. The children had to leave the house at 5.45 in the morning (with special permission from the police, because all 'enemy aliens' were under curfew restrictions). The walk to the farm took about an hour, so they just arrived in good time to clock in before seven o'clock in the morning, when the foreman blew his whistle and work had to commence. There were only two half hour breaks during an eight to ten hour day. This would not have mattered so much if the children had been older, but the farm did not want to employ seventeen-year-olds and older ones as they would have had to pay them much higher wages.

Under such unfavourable circumstances it was clearly not possible to pursue the *Youth Aliyah* dream of creating a genuine community and to run it on democratic lines like a Kibbutz. Everybody was far too exhausted. It was hard enough for Fred Dunston in his capacity as treasurer to decide on priorities for what little money was to spare.

> For instance, the children who let their clothes and shoes fall apart due to neglect had to be kitted out afresh. Complaints came of course from those who conscientiously looked after their own things with great care. They found that they were always last in line for anything new to be bought for them. It was not fair, but there was not much that we could do about it.

After careful consideration, Fred Dunston explained the intolerable conditions to those concerned and it was decided to arrange for the return of the children to Bydown.

By and large, it was the same story at many of the smaller training centres. At Hales Nurseries near Bournemouth, which took in over fifty children, conditions were very similar to those at Bydown. The nurseries closed down in February 1940, with many of the children and adults moving on to Bydown and Braunton.

At Llandaff Castle near Cardiff, children from *Gordonia*, *Young Macabee*, Zionist Youth and *B'rith Kodesh* (all Jewish youth movements connected with Zionism) divided their days between agricultural work, housework and study. At the outbreak of war, forty-five of these children were evacuated to the best known of all the agricultural training camps, Gwrych Castle in North Wales.

Gwrych Castle was offered rent-free by Lord Dundonald – who also made a grant towards rates and taxes and paid half the cost of repairs – a necessarily generous offer since the castle had been uninhabited for over fifteen years. (Ignoring the dereliction of the building, Norman Bentwich described it as 'one of the stately homes of Britain'.) For *Youth Aliyah* the greatest virtue of the castle was the land that came with it – 500 rough but serviceable acres. The first residents arrived from Kent on 31 August 1939, a preemptive move against the imminent mass evacuation. Erich Duchinsky was looking after them.

> One of my functions was to fetch children from Harwich and take them where they had to go . . . We were loaded onto a coach and, by-passing London, drove direct to Gwrych Castle. We arrived at midnight. Everyone was asleep. The driver banged on the gate, but we couldn't make ourselves heard. So then someone climbed over

the gate and found the caretaker, who said we were at the wrong place and that we had to go to the main gate to be let in. The caretaker was very grumpy at being woken up and we were not made to feel at all welcome. On a dark night Gwrych was a forbidding place with its high walls and towers and narrow slit windows. Very cold and very gloomy.

Striking images for the exhausted new arrivals! But there was more to come. They found that their only means of illumination was the collection of antique paraffin lamps and that there was only one boiler – which worked intermittently. One of the latest inmates noted ruefully, 'Too much water runs down the ceiling and walls, instead of the usual way, through the water pipes.'

Forty-six years on, John Edelnand, now living in Luton, re-visited Gwrych Castle and the neighbouring village of Abergele and found his memories of the local people still clear:

My first call was at the sheep and cattle auction market just off Market Street . . . I stayed for about half an hour then walked along Market Street and stopped outside *Siop Bach*. Mr and Mrs Jones used to be in that shop. I believe Mr Jones had a glass eye and he frequently presented me with a bar of chocolate without [asking me for] payment as he was aware that we did not receive any money for our work, nor from the Gwrych Castle management . . . This reminds me of a Mr Parry, who was in charge of the local cinema. He allowed me entry on my own, twice a week, free of charge. In return I had to rewind the films in the projection room ready for the next performance. I must say I enjoyed this very much as it was certainly very different from my daily chores such as tree felling, gardening and working on the farm.

I took the familiar Tan-y-Gopa Road and stopped at the Nant-y-Bela Lodge. Mr and Mrs Appleby and their four daughters and one son resided here. I had tea with this family many times, without the knowledge of the Castle management because this was strictly forbidden – only kosher food was allowed.

Tan-y-Gopa Road has a particular significance for me as it was here that I met my first local gentleman. I later learned that his name was Wil Davies, always dressed in wellington boots and chewing tobacco. I was walking down Tan-y-Gopa Road towards Abergele on the very first morning after my arrival in 1939 when Wil Davies came striding towards me. 'I must practise my English,' I muttered to myself, having learnt the language for a short while

in the private Jewish school in Germany. 'Goot mornink,' I said in
a very crude German accent. He looked at me and after a pause
said: '*Bore da, boi back. Sut 'dachi heddiw?*' I was utterly amazed, not
realising that Wales existed with its own language and culture . . .
Wil Davies taught me quite a bit of Welsh, including most swear
words, and he took great delight in listening to me when I tried to
repeat them.

Whatever their achievements in stimulating Zionist beliefs, and
their powerful impact upon individual pupils, the farming centres
failed in their immediate objective of providing a loyal and dedicated labour force for the emerging Palestine. How could it have
been otherwise?

In July 1939, a group of fifteen children from Great Engeham
and Whittingham Farm School left for Palestine, but they were
the last until after the war. Meanwhile, those waiting for the chance
to go soon passed the age of seventeen, the upper limit for *Youth
Aliyah* emigration visas. No wonder that after the intense psychological preparation for the big move which never came, many
became disillusioned with *hachshara* and left.

Gwrych Castle was abandoned by *Youth Aliyah* in 1941. The
casualty list soon spread to other centres such as Clonin Castle and
Millisle Farm in Northern Ireland, where travel restrictions made
communication with central office in London all but impossible.

Finance too became a problem. Before the war public appeals
had raised sufficient money to keep *Youth Aliyah* afloat, but, when
it became clear that large numbers of children would not soon be
leaving for Palestine, the question arose as to who would care for
them during their prolonged stay in Britain. In theory, those who
worked on the farms were capable of supporting themselves. In
practice, the employment was seasonal and ill-paid, covering little
more than the necessities of life. In 1940, Lola Hahn-Warburg and
Elaine Blond for the RCM joined with the Council for German
Jewry to appeal for a state support for *Youth Aliyah*. They were
unsuccessful. For the rest of the war *Youth Aliyah* depended on its
own brave attempts at self-sufficiency and, when these failed, on
charitable appeals and grants from the RCM.

10

Willingly to School

'When asked what I wanted to be I said a doctor. The woman who was filling in the form said: "I can't put that down – you must remember you are a refugee."'

Middle-class children from a German Jewish background were weaned on a faith in learning as the way to a prosperous and fulfilling career. In Britain, their sights were lowered. They were expected to leave school at fourteen and go out to work to earn a living or take up technical training. After all, that was the prospect for the vast majority of British children. Why, it was argued, should refugees be treated differently?

As a senior Home Office official put it to an RCM conference in October 1942: 'A refugee should have treatment comparable to that of an average English child in receipt of free education', adding, 'It is not possible to provide continued education except in highly exceptional cases of brilliancy.'

All children were entitled to free elementary education up to the age of fourteen. Thereafter, a limited number of free places at secondary and university level were open to stiff competition. As newcomers to the British education system, not to mention the English language, refugee children started with two obvious disadvantages. But even when these were overcome, and 'brilliancy' was proved beyond question, there was a psychological impediment which held back all but the most single-minded. Dorothy Hardisty, General Secretary of the RCM, knew the problem and advised making the best of it:

The general rule of the Movement is that at sixteen the young people shall enter some vocational training to fit them for a future which must, in the best circumstances, be arduous. It is recognised that few of them will have the opportunity, either in this country or elsewhere, to enter the liberal professions . . . and though this bears hardly on some, especially in view of the aptitude of Jewish children for intellectual pursuits, it is wise to take a realistic attitude to their future careers.

Quite simply, refugee children, however gifted, were not encouraged to rise up the economic and social hierarchy. The general view, extending to some members of the RCM, held that refugees belonged to the lower orders, and that no amount of hard work or intellectual promise on their part could alter their self-evident assumption.

One young refugee remembers: 'When asked what I wanted to be I said a doctor. The woman who was filling in the form said: "I can't put that down – you must remember you are a refugee."'

The prejudice was compounded by some foster parents who had a bias against education:

The main reason for moving Jean from school, as Mrs Gross puts it, is that 'she does not believe in education'. Her own daughter is a shorthand typist and has not got matric., so 'there is no reason why Jean should have a better education; on the contrary, it would be much better for her to get a shorthand-typing training and start work as soon as possible.'

Jean's headmistress did not agree; nor did Bloomsbury House. After a long argument, an offer from the Movement to take over financial responsibility for the girl's education persuaded Mrs Gross to change her mind, Jean stayed on at her grammar school.

When she came to England, aged five, Hannah was described as a bright if naughty child. The pattern continued throughout her time at school, leading her foster father to conclude that her education was a waste of time:

Accompanied by Hannah to see Mr Max Wolf to discuss her future with him. He is determined that Hannah leaves Stoatley Rough at the end of the summer term. Feels that it is no disgrace to Hannah that she has not made more progress at school, there is not much point in her carrying on and that she should receive some proper training.

What he did not know, until an RCM visitor winkled it out, was that Hannah wanted to study art.

> After some discussion he agreed that, provided Farnham Art School find Hannah's work sufficiently good to admit her, he has no objection.

Hannah was duly offered and accepted a place at Farnham.

With evacuation and the Movement's preference for rural settings for foster homes and hostels, younger children were often isolated in small village primary schools, where they were a curiosity to the other children and to the staff. Struggling with an unfamiliar language, the simplest conversations were misinterpreted, as when Herbert Hobden (Holzinger) failed to understand why 'yes' was pronounced 'yessah' at school until someone explained that it was the respectful way to address the teacher: 'Yes, sir'.

Many experienced the feeling of guilt by association.

> I didn't want to be known as a foreigner, having by that time learned something of the common English attitude to foreigners, and I especially resented being called a German. 'Austrian' was not too bad, for after all Austria herself had been a victim of Nazism. I was furious when I was nicknamed 'Girder' at school, and wished I hadn't such a silly name as Gerda and a surname which I had always to spell out to people.

And again:

> I used to feel terribly embarrassed when people asked me to say something in German and always refused.

Sensitivities were sharply attuned. Vera Coppard, attending St Christopher's School at Letchworth, found it hard to take the persistent jokes about her being a Germany spy. The not unfamiliar childish jape of depositing a stink bomb in her locker caused her great anguish. Did they really hate her so much?

Another layer of guilt was added for brighter children who acclimatised sufficiently to start pulling ahead of their classmates. Said one: 'I lied about my birth but I realised I was different and always coming top of the class did not help.'

Teachers were by no means free from prejudice. Even those who prided themselves on liberal views found it hard not to score points off the Germans, including refugee Germans. 'British soldiers are the best in the world,' a schoolmaster told his class, adding, for the benefit of the *Kindertransporte* pupils, 'You people did not think we had it in us.'

The natural tendency was to lie low:

> I just went on at school – trying not to be noticed. Occasionally, by some obscure and innocently intended action, one would be picked out. I remember an incident when we all went into a room which was rather cold and I shivered. The teacher with us said in her wonderfully piercing upper-class voice: 'People in England don't shiver when they come into a cold room. There isn't enough coal because *we're* fighting the *Germans.*'

Probably the greatest difficulty for the RCM was in satisfying the needs of the older children, who had already achieved a sound basic education at home in Germany or Austria. By rights, as Dorothy Hardisty pointed out, these young people should have been destined for college or university. A British youngster from a poor background who gained higher school certificate had at least a chance of going on to university or technical college, with fees and maintenance paid.

Young refugees, however, were not eligible for state scholarships or state bursaries. This effectively cut them out from higher education. Their only hope was a university scholarship or exhibition and, though a small number of refugees did find their way into university by this route, it was more common for those who wanted to continue their studies to attend evening classes or sign on for correspondence courses. Even so, cleverness and dogged determination were not always appreciated.

Klaus was a boy with a good school certificate who wanted to join ICI to work in chemical engineering. His RCM contact could not resist a snide comment: 'It is extraordinary that a boy of fifteen should have such a very high opinion of his capabilities.'

A happier story is that of Edward. Born in 1936, he came to England three years later, followed shortly afterwards by his mother. In 1944 he was awarded a free place as a weekly boarder at Rowan House School. By the time he returned to Germany in 1948, his progress was such that his teachers were inspired to proclaim: 'He is a brilliant pupil . . . An example to us all.'

Among those who campaigned tirelessly for gifted youngsters, knowing full well that there was more at stake than mere survival, was Greta Burkill. As chairman of the Cambridgeshire Committee – in effect, covering the whole of East Anglia – some 800 youngsters came within her province, although at the height of the evacuation this figure increased to 2000.

German born, her father a left-wing journalist, Greta went to school and university in Britain and married a Cambridge don, Charles Burkill, in 1928. Always the true internationalist, Hitler's advent was her signal to pitch into refugee work.

The Cambridge Refugee Committee started life in the Quaker home of Hilda Sturge. In 1935 the Committee moved to 35 Hills Road and then was given the large house next door – number 55 – by Jesus College. Hilda Sturge took on responsibility for the adult refugees, while the Committee, with Greta acting as honorary secretary, looked after the children. The Cambridge Committee brought over at least seventy guaranteed children from Germany, mostly teenagers, who were all given a decent education. Private schools in the area were persuaded to offer places at reduced fees.

With two daughters of her own, Greta expanded her family by taking in the son of a German socialist who had been sent to a concentration camp, and a Viennese boy who adopted her name by deed poll. She helped a succession of youngsters to take part-time degrees by getting them jobs as kitchen porters or trainee cooks. In one year alone she was overseeing twelve undergraduates, of whom eleven emerged with first-class degrees. One of her helpers was Nina Liebermann:

> I learned many things from Greta Burkill, not the least of them never to give up on your original goal . . . Many a physicist, mathematician or legal scholar owe their career opportunities to the tenacity of Greta Burkill. Indeed, when thwarted by bureaucrats, she could be like a tigress fighting for her cubs.

The early months of the war and the threat of an air attack on London brought a number of educational establishments to Cambridge – the London School of Economics, Guy's Hospital, St Bartholomew's and Bedford College among them. It was difficult to imagine a more stimulating environment for bright children who might otherwise have lost out on their education. But life was never easy for the young refugee, as Greta Burkill later recorded:

> The refugee child on the whole was ambitious and eager for knowledge. Having missed schooling in the home country, so many of them, after a day's work, went to night school and worked for Matriculation and for Higher School Certificate and so gained qualifications to enter university and polytechnics. Today these children would be called especially gifted and everything would be done to help them overcome their frustration, but then life was too hard and the country was under great pressure.
>
> To combine a daytime job (however carefully it was chosen) and to work for examinations as well was very strenuous, though one must not forget that some British children also had to fight to reach university status, though not in such lonely circumstances, for grammar school education had to be paid for and there were plenty of parents who were not prepared to do this. It was only after the 1944 Education Act, with its 11-plus examination, that grammar schools became more open, but even then it was only ten per cent of elementary schoolchildren who were successful.

Friedrich Bettelheim was one of the young people who benefited from Greta Burkill's efforts. He came to England aged ten years old and at seventeen was taking his higher school certificate in physics and hoping to study medicine as a Major scholar at King's College. He was young to be going up to Cambridge, but was taken on there and gained a first in Preliminary Natural Sciences. Greta Burkill did not confine herself to looking after his education, but fought for him to spend a summer with his parents in Venezuela – a country not keen to grant visitors' visas to Jews at that time.

Despite such success stories, Greta Burkill's persistent correspondence with universities, the Education Ministry, the Home Office and the International Student Service (ISS) suggests a frightening lack of imagination in high places.

As the secretary of the ISS wrote to her in November 1943:

> I may be too cautious in my attitude for, although I entirely agree with you that exceptionally brilliant refugee children should be given the same chances of higher education as an English boy or girl, I am rather doubtful whether the population of England at

large has advanced sufficiently far in this direction to agree to open the chances of state scholarships to refugees. My feeling and that of my own Relief Committee is that we should, where possible, urge the county education authorities to exercise their discretion sympathetically where consideration was being given to refugee applications. Some counties have been giving Major scholarships of £60 or so to refugees, and these grants, in conjunction with University scholarships and School Leaving scholarships, are about as much as a British child would be able to get. If there are any children which you would like to refer to me, I should be glad to do what I can in the way of getting them funds from other sources, although, as you know, our own grants are intended primarily for older students.

George Alexander Gruen was accepted by Winchester School and was about to sit for his Cambridge entrance when he was interned and shipped off to Canada in 1940. Greta fought for his rehabilitation. Returning in 1941, he was given lodgings by the Vicar of Trumpington, a grant by his school and £52 by the Movement. He achieved a First in his preliminary examination at Trinity College, Cambridge and went on to also get a First in the History Tripos Part 1. His studies were again interrupted, this time by a spell in the Intelligence Corps, from which he returned to Cambridge to complete Part 2 of the History Tripos.

D. K. Haymann gained a scholarship to St John's College from Gordonstoun, the school founded by Kurt Hahn, the brother-in-law of Lola Hahn-Warburg. But the scholarship was worth only £100 and, though his school plundered its scarce resources to add £20, it was not enough for the boy to support himself at Cambridge. Hearing of his difficulties from Greta Burkill, the College contributed a further £50 and the Self-Aid Society for Refugees another £50. His tutor raised what more was needed for financial security.

The constant battle for funds is echoed in the case of Fritz Buchwitz, a talented young mathematician. He gained a £120 scholarship to Sidney Sussex College in Cambridge in 1943, but had no other financial help. He was told to go up to Cambridge, despite a shortfall of £60 in his funds, and that his college would do its utmost to ensure that he could carry on with his studies.

Georg Kreisel gained a Major scholarship to Trinity College from Dudley Grammar School in 1941. No other money was available. His housemaster wrote to Lord Baldwin asking for help, which led to an extra £150 per annum towards Georg's keep. Lord Baldwin's generosity was well rewarded as Georg gained a double First in Mathematics in 1942 and went into research for the Admiralty.

Wolfgang Graetzer was another gifted pupil. He went to Bedford Modern School in 1939 and, after only four terms, gained four distinctions and five credits in his School Certificate. He was then sent out to work, first at a toy factory in the East End of London and then at an estate agents. The International Student Service came to the rescue with a place at the Northern Polytechnic, with lodgings in a hostel guaranteed by the RCM. There he gained an Intermediate BS, and then worked washing up plates and studying in the evening so that he gained a scholarship to Imperial College, where the ISS agreed to support him. But the strain proved too much and Wolfgang became ill. This was put down to his experiences in Vienna and the intense strain of his life after leaving school.

Eighty-one refugee children went to Bunce Court, the school Anna Essinger had brought over from the Schwäbische Alb mountains of the Danube to Otterden, a large manor house standing in twenty-five acres of Kent countryside. Bunce Court was a progressive school. The emphasis was on self-reliance, with the children free to work out their own solutions without a close-knit family environment. Staff and pupils were on first name terms, so that Miss Clifton was Cliffy to her face, and Anna Essinger, who had been dubbed *Tante Anna* in German, was known simply as TA. The children contributed to the maintenance of their school, to the extent of making furniture and cleaning and repairing the building. But, unlike other progressive schools, classroom teaching was firmly rooted in the German tradition with the highest priority given to academic excellence.

Clever, imaginative children like Leslie Brent did well at Bunce Court.

> At first I shared a bedroom with five or six boys in the main part of the school building on the top floor. The school had very beautiful grounds, a lovely garden and a small wood; a large playing field, an open-air amphitheatre, which had been built by the children themselves in earlier years, in which plays were performed . . . The

children did a lot of the work that needed to be done and it was an important part of the philosophy of Anna Essinger that children should be involved on a practical basis . . . My duties tended to gravitate from doing kitchen work (through that I got to know the non-Jewish German cook, Gretel Heidl, extremely well and we became lifelong friends – she was a sort of mother to me), to working in the workshop and in the garden. In the afternoon there were sporting activities – we unfortunately did not play cricket; that came very much later. We played hockey and football in the main and, of course, had athletics. We didn't play other schools as we didn't have much contact with them – we were geographically quite isolated. In the mornings we started off with gymnastics before breakfast, which some children found hateful, and once a week we organised a relay race. I enjoyed the physical side very much indeed.

I was one of many children who were very happy at Bunce Court. To me it was a safe haven where I was treated with affection and respect; where I was taught well and made friends . . . It provided me with a very secure environment and a very good springboard for life, despite a total lack of teaching in the physical sciences. Although I was only there from early 1939 to the end of 1942, the influence it has had on me was out of all proportion to the time I spent there.

The eldest of a family of nine, Anna Essinger was a dominant personality with the physique to match. A former teacher at Bunce Court, remembers her as:

Very tall – massive almost. Not a beauty at all. She had very poor eyesight – all the Essingers did – so she had to wear thick glasses. She always wore dark clothes. She had straight brown hair – with not a single grey hair to be seen . . . there was a certain lack of warmth, although there was always a strong feeling for the good of the children. She did not teach because she was always too busy with the administration. She would walk around the school twice a day inspecting everything, including the kitchen and the garden which she was very keen on (the biology teacher, who was a graduate from Reading, not only had to teach biology but was also in charge of the garden), and that garden kept the whole school in vegetables.

Bunce Court took a broadminded approach to religion. According to Leslie Brent, Anna Essinger was:

. . . quite anti-religious; at the very least agnostic. We were taught scripture and our teacher made the Bible come alive in an extraordinary way. There were some children from an orthodox background and they formed a little group that celebrated the Sabbath on Friday evenings and had services on Saturdays, but this was highly improvised.

Nor was Anna Essinger much interested in Jewish nationalism. But she did have an acute social conscience which Lucie Kaye, a former colleague, describes as 'a Quaker mentality'. And she was, without question, a very courageous woman.

While still in Germany, the Nazis told her to put up a swastika flag and she said she would not do that. They said she had to and they would be back to see if she had obeyed them. On the day, they returned and there was no flag. She told them: 'The children have gone on a hike for the whole day; there's not much point in showing a flag when there is nobody in the house.' After that, they left her alone.

Those who found difficulty in settling at Bunce Court had to sort out their own problems. There was no time for laggards. Pupils and staff were under enormous pressure.

Everybody had to work like hell. The teachers had no free time at all, our days were about twelve hours long, and she didn't care, because the less overheads to pay, the more children we could bring over from Germany.

From the earliest days in England, Bunce Court was open to children whose families were victims of Nazi persecution. At least a dozen pupils were educated free of charge on a promise that fees would be paid when the parents' situation improved. (Some, who got to America, conveniently forgot their pledge.) When the *Kindertransporte* began to arrive, Anna Essinger led a party of teachers and older pupils in trying to inject a semblance of education into the chaos that was Dovercourt. But she soon fell out with those who dictated RCM policy. She disapproved of the haphazard selection of foster parents (she would have much preferred the children to go to hostels run on the lines of Bunce Court) and, when the Movement pressed ahead anyway, she concentrated on plucking out from the crowd the children she identified as especially gifted and on salvaging those who had been packed off to unsuitable foster homes. A former pupil at the school remembers:

> Anna chose these children on the basis of her private feelings; she thought they would fit in and she would like them and she could give them something . . . Anna wanted young ones she would have for some time. Some three- and four-year-olds she took in because they had an older brother or sister at the school.

Private benefactors enabled the school to build two new dormitories, while thirty of the youngest children were accommodated in an old farmhouse. There was never enough money for essentials. Hardly a week passed without Anna Essinger setting off for London on a fund raising mission, invariably returning with promises to sponsor more refugee children. The sharpest financial blow came in mid-1939, when the owner of Bunce Court decided she wanted to sell the freehold. It was a choice of buy up or get out. Somehow a mortgage was raised, but the diversion of resources frustrated Anna Essinger's attempts to add further to the number of admissions. In May 1940, her problems were compounded by an evacuation order which transposed Bunce Court from Kent to Shropshire and by the internment of some of its best teachers. The school occupied Trench Hall, a stately home which, having stood vacant for seven years, showed all the obvious signs of neglect. This was when Anna Essinger's philosophy of self-help came into its own, not least in transforming the jungle of a garden to provide food for the entire school.

How Bunce Court got through the war it is hard to imagine, but get through it did and with flying colours, if the testimony of former pupils is anything to go by. The school was that rare achievement – a family within an institution. There was greater contentment there than within the average hostel or foster home and most certainly a greater sense of personal fulfilment.

The irony of Bunce Court was its failure to survive for very long after the war. Anna Essinger's commitment to refugee children was extended into the peace by the arrival of youngsters who had survived the concentration camps. But when they moved on the school lost its reason for being. There were not many families with young children who welcomed a school with Teutonic associations, however liberal, and the refugee label was a further disincentive to parents canvassing the choice of private education.

Having retired to a cottage on the estate, Anna Essinger appointed a successor, who fought a losing battle against falling rolls and proprietorial interference. Bunce Court, the school, closed in 1949. It reopened soon afterwards as a home for unmarried mothers.

There was a clear understanding between the RCM and the Home Office that youngsters who were already into their teens when they arrived in Britain in 1938 and 1939 should undertake some form of vocational training. But there were four conditions to be met before permits were issued. Two of them favoured refugees; their conditions of work had to be at least as good as those offered to British workers, and their employers had to provide real training as opposed to handing out menial jobs to what was essentially cheap labour. But the other two conditions were tightly restrictive. Young refugees were not allowed to compete with their British contemporaries, and the jobs open to refugees had to be specifically created for them. This meant that farming was the likeliest occupation for RCM boys, even though they mostly came from urban professional and commercial backgrounds and had a positive aversion to rural life. But the country needed food and there was a shortage of workers in this traditionally ill-paid industry.

In February 1941, the RCM circulated some 1500 fourteen-year-olds on the attractions of a career on the land:

> Farming is a fine life and a very important occupation, but it is an occupation in which training is necessary. During training you would discover all the benefits of open-air life, and you would learn about growing plants and vegetables and breeding pigs and poultry and ploughing the land in which corn, wheat, turnips, potatoes and many other things will be grown. In a year, you would be able to see the whole of the processes needed to grow and produce these things and, at the end of the time, you would have the satisfaction of seeing the results of that work.
>
> At the same time as you would be learning this outdoor work, lessons would be given to you in English, and religious instruction would be provided. You would work and live among other refugee boys and girls with the same ambition as your own . . .
>
> Think seriously about farming as an occupation and talk it over

with those who have looked after you. If, when you have done this, you feel you would like to undergo the training, let us know. We feel that if you have put your heart and soul into the work you will have derived a great deal of benefit from your training.

The letter did not mention that, having made the choice, there would not be much chance of going back. The policy of the labour exchanges towards boys who wanted to come out of farming was to refuse them alternative employment.

Clive Milton was one of the few who found that the open life did have its virtues:

We learned to milk cows. We kept pigs. They were not huge farms and we trained for about eight weeks. The farm was very good for me. It gave me time to organise myself – more so than if I had stayed with my cousin. On the farm there wasn't much to do in the evenings – it gave one time to reflect. At seventeen I felt that life was great. But I was always aware of living on charity, which I disliked.

After the training period we went out to a farmer who needed help. The first farmer I went to was a smallholder. He needed a boy to give him a hand. He couldn't afford me for very long. Then I went to a larger farm in Wiltshire. At first the family were very friendly but I think I was beginning to display my entrepreneurial instincts, which they did not like, and there was a bit of friction. I could see opportunities for making money on the farm, but the farmer was looking for a boy to clean out the stable, not a boy dreaming of renting a piece of field and rearing his own animals . . .

I was always working – I worked in the evenings at bars and doing woodwork. I got up at 5.00 a.m. and went to bed at 11.0 p.m. seven days a week. I had saved £1000 by the time I was nineteen. Then I bought a tractor and was going to be a subcontractor but I got called up.

Another occupation, essential to the war effort and which urgently needed more staff was nursing. An RCM report on girls in nursing appeared in 1944, when the number of *Kindertransporte* volunteers in the profession passed the two hundred mark.

Of course, there are some who prove unsuitable for nursing. It is found very often in the cases of those who fell by the wayside that they have entered hospital work too young. War-time needs have led the Ministry of Labour to consider the age of seventeen and a half as suitable for entry, but we continue to believe that under eighteen a girl is not psychologically or physically developed enough to undertake the strenuous and demanding life of a student nurse. The gap between school-leaving age and eighteen is best filled by a course such as nursery nursing.

Training for nursing was on strictly formal lines, with great emphasis on turning out in a neat, starched uniform and on working to the rule book. Comments in personal record cards dwell on disciplinary matters.

A talk with Matron reveals that Ruth is a very good worker, especially with small babies. She is accurate and reliable and clean in her work (unfortunately not in her personal hygiene, which is so important for a children's nurse). Matron and the other nurses have tried hard to improve this fact, but unfortunately without much result.

Many girls worked in minor clerical jobs and were encouraged to learn shorthand and typing skills at evening classes. Brigitte, aged sixteen in 1943, hoped to give up her job as a messenger to do secretarial studies full time:

We informed her that this was quite out of the question as it would prove far too costly on public funds, there being full maintenance, fees, clothing, pocket money, books, to be provided for at a possible minimum of £3 a week . . . when asked why she could not consider evening classes she said that she had to be at home and in bed between 9 and 9.30 and she would have no time to study.

Brigitte did make enquiries at Pitmans, where classes started at five in the evening, and at the Kilburn Polytechnic, where there were weekend classes, but continued to doubt her ability to study enough at evening classes.

She was interested in a correspondence course but that could not be advised for so young a girl. She says she has friends and mentioned Mr Israel, who had promised her some financial help. She asked whether, if these friends could give substantial financial help, we would have any objection to her leaving work for study. We told her if other people could give her the opportunity we could not, we certainly would have no objection.

Menial work was easy to come by, either through the local Labour Exchange or through the Movement. But the jobs were invariably dead-end and, despite the Home Office call for 'real' training, wages were at subsistence level or below, which led to a succession of requests for small loans from the Movement. Many girls and boys wandered from job to job, like Rosina Domingo:

> A friend from Vienna and I went into domestic service in a very big house near Brighton. The servants there resented us. 'The foreigners come here and they do this and they do that . . . There are plenty of English people to do the work . . .' All I got there was five shillings.
>
> Once again I was a nursery maid. My friend was a kitchen maid. We shared a room and we had stone hot-water bottles. We used to joke in the night and have a laugh. The hot-water bottle and my friend fell out of bed and the cook was in the room underneath and she hit her the next day.
>
> In 1940 I came to London with that friend and we went for a job near Tottenham Court Road in a clothes factory – a Jewish firm. They gave us jobs as machinists. At the end of the week we had to leave because the other girls would not work with Germans. The employers cried because they knew what had happened to us.

When Bloomsbury House or a regional committee acted as a Labour Exchange, it was a case of take it or leave it – there was no time for career advice. Claire Barrington worked in the tailoring trade:

> Tailoring was seasonal, which of course I didn't know. This means you are in one day and you can be out the next. There were more men than women in tailoring and I got on better with them than with the women. They were nicer. I worked for private tailors, people who were doing quite expensive clothes. They didn't pay us much, but they charged a lot. They were always screaming and shouting, but it wasn't all that bad – only the insecurity. I was forever worrying about getting a job or being out of work. It was a constant worry.
>
> I may have had a visitor from the Movement once in a blue moon, but as long as you had a job and you ate reasonably well then that was all they worried about. Anyway, they had too many to deal with so they couldn't single me out. I was completely forgotten; nobody cared whether I lived or died. I have heard some

dreadful stories of people who were domestic servants who were
treated like scum . . . I could never go through that again . . .

After going to evening classes to study dress design, Claire
hoped for better things, but was soon disillusioned when she found
that her employer expected to use her designs without paying her.
She then tried a government training course in shorthand and
typing but, lacking confidence, ended up as a filing clerk.

I was so insecure, I overworked in order to please everybody. In
the end I resented it – it was no different from tailoring. But it was
me who created the pattern. A born victim. Since you are not sure
of your ability and you lack confidence, you are willing to do
everything, and eventually it all piles up on top of you and you
resent it and eventually you leave. That was the pattern of my life.

Herbert Gale came to England in December 1938, at the age of
fifteen. While in the transit camp at Lowestoft he was offered a
choice of hostels in Belfast, Leeds or London. He chose Leeds. His
regional committee found him work:

I was sent to an upholstery firm, where I had to sew one side of a
cushion in readiness for it to be stuffed for a three-piece suite. I was
given fare money and a packed lunch – meat loaf sandwiches. I
have never stopped hating minced meat since then . . . I found
the work really boring and the people I worked with were very
suspicious of me being a foreigner. They were poor and uneducated.
My wages were 5/- a week, which I had to hand over unopened to
the hostel. I was given 1/- back.
     After a while I wanted to change my job. They found me a job
in a hairdresser's, where I was a lather boy, in between sweeping
up. I lathered the customers for a shave and, after I had proved
myself, I was allowed to put hairgrease on the customers. I was
promised that when I was more qualified I would be allowed to
shave the customers. I did get a few tips! There was a Jewish baker's
next door owned by a very kind lady who was on the Committee.
She told me to come in every day and have as many cakes as I
wanted – free!

Philip Urbach fell on his feet when by chance he met a teacher
from a school which was being evacuated to Wales. The school
was Summerhill, run by A. S. Neill, whose revolutionary views

on education have since had considerable influence on modern teaching methods. Philip was taken on as a sort of pupil-teacher, helping with the children and also furthering his own education.

> He was a wonderful man, A. S. Neill. Not only did he pay me a pound a week in the end, but I could attend classes whenever I wanted. He gave me considerable freedom to do whatever I liked with the children – I was expected to do something – but sometimes I would simply help fire the boiler, which was always a great preoccupation at Llanfestiniog. At other times I would take the children for walks or adventure expeditions, or I took them camping. It always amazes me now, looking back, because I was so young and inexperienced, the kind of trust he had in me. I took them on mountaineering expeditions, although I had no experience myself of mountains. I also took them for various sports – unlikely as it may seem when you look at me now – including some German ball games which were not very well known over here. And I began to teach a little. So I spent two years there and what English education I had, I had there.

The tensions of wartime could easily turn anger against refugees who were thought to be getting privileged treatment. Salomea was at the Cadby Nursery when, at short notice, several refugee nurses took up the chance of emigrating to America.

> At the end of last week Salomea was called in by Sister in Charge. Sister told her that she had been asked about four weeks ago to 'give the sack' to Salomea because the superintendent of the nursery felt that, in view of the departure of the other refugees, it would be best to give them all notice gradually. She added that she had put off telling Salomea for a while because she felt it was very hard on her, especially as Salomea's work was so much appreciated. She assured Salomea that she would have a very good reference.

When Salomea tried to find another job, she was turned down because she had been given notice from her previous employment. She went on to take a social science course and to train for general nursing.

Promotion for Hilde was not the cause for celebration she had expected:

. . . she is worried about the anti-alien feeling in the factory. She says the managers and directors are really good to her, but that the work people react adversely. Hilde always feels an undercurrent of ill feeling against her – the factory hands resent the fact that as an alien she is in a position of authority over them. She understands their resentment, but nevertheless it makes her unhappy and she tries all she can to combat this feeling.

The borderline between teasing and victimisation was easily crossed as Herbert Gale (Hans Groschler) discovered:

While I was working at the hairdressers, I asked one of our Jewish customers, who I knew had a large factory, to give me a job rebuilding old sewing machines, which he did. I was taught the work. A few of my workmates were very kind but some were anti-Semitic. A favourite pastime of theirs was to fill my pocket with grease and to thread a six-inch bolt through the buttonholes of my coat, put a nut on the end and damage the thread of the bolt, making it impossible for me to remove without putting it in a vice and hacksawing it.

A familiar character in the annals of wartime prejudice was the busybody who made a vocation out of telling others how to behave.

Fritz telephoned and mentioned he had had some trouble with an 'informer', who had complained either to the Home Office or the Ministry of Labour that this young man was not in uniform. The matter was taken up by the Ministry of Labour and he now has a letter from them stating that they are satisfied with the work that he is doing and will not be making any change.

There were those who took direct action against their tormentors. Paula, aged twenty-three in 1945 and working for the Worcester Brass Company in Birmingham, had no hesitation in sticking up for herself:

Paula has changed her job. In her own words: a fellow worker called her a dirty refugee and hit her, so Paula socked her in the jaw. Unfortunately, the lady fell backwards through a glass window and it was decided by all parties that it was best if Paula left . . . she has had no trouble at work since this incident. A manager of the firm pointed out that he understood Paula's point of view perfectly and agreed with her. But in view of the attitude of the employee he felt that a change would be best.

The report adds: 'Paula is living a very bright life with plenty of entertainment and dancing, but she knows how many beans make five!'

Of the reports on problem children that came through to Bloomsbury House, in at least fifty per cent of the cases education, or the lack of it, was a contributory factor.

Youngsters who were found jobs and then left to their own devices invariably ended up lonely and frustrated. They were different from other young workers and they were not allowed to forget it. Feelings against refugees and things foreign, like a German accent, caused mysterious illness and bloody-mindedness.

Karl was judged to be a normal, pleasant boy when he started as a clerical assistant in February 1943, but he was soon complaining that the work he was given was boring and that his pay – 1/6d an hour – was not enough. He was frequently sick, though the doctor could find nothing physically wrong with him, took to borrowing money which he did not pay back, and was averse to working or changing his clothes. In July he was thrown out of his hostel and ended up at the Jews' Temporary Shelter in the East End. From there he was handed on to Bloomsbury House, where Elaine Blond agreed a one-off payment to fit him out for another job. This 'last chance' produced 'a wonderful change, both in the brightness and cleanliness of Karl', and his supervisor had 'the feeling that the chance given to him will be more than repaid'.

But within a fortnight Karl was back to zero – 'as bad as ever'. Having lost one job he was interviewed at the Feltham Ordnance Factory, but was rejected as useless, 'having fallen asleep while waiting to be given instructions'.

There followed a period of over a year when Karl moved aimlessly through a succession of jobs. Then there was a police report. Karl had been caught travelling the Underground without a ticket. Bloomsbury House helped to get him off with a warning, but there was no further contact. The last heard of Karl was at the end of the war when he had a job as a waiter.

There were occasions when Bloomsbury House pulled out all the stops on behalf of children who were clearly gifted – usually in the arts. At sixteen, Edgar gained a scholarship to the Royal College of Music in 1941. Up to then he had been supported by the British Council, who now passed the buck to Bloomsbury House. Edgar was offered a grant for six months; after that he was on his own. It was long enough for him to persuade the Royal College of Music that his talent was worth taking seriously. His scholarship was extended, but he was without maintenance until Bloomsbury House put him in touch with a sponsor. In 1943 he was still doggedly pursuing his studies.

Help of a more immediately practical nature was given to Marian, a young pianist who was without a piano. Bloomsbury House had the answer. 'When the weather gets warmer she will be able to go and practise on the piano in the home of the Misses Montague – we will let her know when this is possible.' Though not in the best of health, Marian was determined to make her own way, accepting little else from Bloomsbury House except tickets for the occasional outing to the Wigmore Hall. Her last entry reads: 'Letter from girl thanking us for concert tickets. Informs us that she has managed to buy a piano with her savings.'

When no other funding was available, one or other of the wealthier members of the RCM could be relied upon to chip in a contribution. Awarded a free place at Birmingham University to study music for three years, Peter was short of basics like clothes and books until Elaine Blond gave him £30 and arranged for Peter to work at Bloomsbury House in his holidays to help make up any shortfall.

Hans was sitting his finals, at the London School of Economics in 1947, when his father called Bloomsbury House and asked if his son could have a fortnight's convalescence at their expense as he was over-tired and very nervous. The father had only been in the country six months and had no means of supporting his son. Hans was sent to Bournemouth for a fortnight.

Also at the LSE, Hella was guaranteed £60 a year for the first two years of her course by Professor Harold Laski, the brother of Elaine Blond's first husband. When he was no longer able to provide this, Dorothy Hardisty persuaded the International Student Service, who were already paying Hella £20 a year, to increase their grant.

Shortage of money was not the only impediment to higher education. When Hannah declared her ambition to be a teacher,

Bloomsbury House replied that it was doubtful 'if she could be released from essential work to take up full-time study'.

Undeterred, two months later Hannah enrolled at University College, London to read French, having obtained her release from war work on medical grounds. She had also found herself a sponsor to support her to the tune of £100 a year. Bloomsbury House, asked to contribute £35 towards books, told her she was too late that term (it was November) and that she might possibly get a small emergency grant for the summer term (six months ahead) if she still needed it. The case was passed on to German Self Aid, who gave £50.

Would-be actors and actresses were rarely taken seriously by the Movement. Having fallen in love with the theatre in the Free German Youth, a left-wing group dedicated to rebuilding Germany for socialism, Ruth called Bloomsbury House to say 'she was very interested in dramatic work and hopes one day to take it up as a career'. The weighty hint was ignored.

In May 1944, Ruth called again:

> She is going through an 'I want to be an actress' phase. She attends the theatre school at Morley College on five evenings a week . . . She knows she is apt to be nervy and feels that this is due to striving after the unattainable. She is always restless and on the move. Her work affords her no satisfaction and it becomes merely mechanical – all her thought and interests are centred round the stage.

Two years on, Ruth made yet another bid to launch herself into her chosen career:

> Miss Abrahams of the Jewish Board of Guardians rang to let us known that Ruth has called at her office asking for financial help in order to take a full-time training at the School of Dramatic Art. The girl apparently went there without an introduction from us and explained to Miss Abrahams that a friend had advised her to call. Miss Abrahams wanted to know whether we had any objections whatsoever against Ruth's being helped by the Board, but pointed out the grave difficulties in obtaining permission for work on the stage.

The records peter out before telling us if Ruth achieved her ambitions. But if single-minded determination is a qualification for a stage career, Ruth had a better chance than most.

Another aspiring actress bitterly resented what she considered to be interference from Bloomsbury House. Of Sonja, her RCM adviser wrote:

> The girl has no previous stage training or experience beyond some lessons in step dancing, but she says it has always been her ambition to go on the stage and that we have always promised to help her, though no mention of stage or histrionic ability appears in her dossier. We are strongly of the opinion that the Movement could not subscribe itself to encourage employment of this description . . . The girl is inclined to be hysterical and says that now she has the opportunity of realising her ambition we are frustrating her.
>
> I have promised to ascertain if Mrs Laski (Elaine Blond) or Mrs Hahn-Warburg have any theatrical connections to whom the girl could be introduced. It is a most impractical and ridiculous suggestion but, before damping the girl's ardour completely, we feel that it would be wiser for her to be damped by a celebrity.

One month later, however, Sonja was working at Amersham Repertory Theatre as a student trainee – receiving no wages, but getting her maintenance paid by her ex-employer.

> She was most indignant at the thought of any improper relations between her and this man. She has no conscience about accepting his money, as she feels it is her only opportunity of gaining a foothold in the theatrical profession, and she is not going to let this chance slip through her fingers . . . She says the man is fabulously wealthy and will in no way miss this small sum and that he seems fully prepared, from philanthropic motives, to help her along the way.

Of all the obstacles put in the way of young refugees entering the learned professions, none were higher and bulkier than those erected by the medical fraternity. Very few beat the system and those who did were not much encouraged by Bloomsbury House.

Vera was a brilliant member of a very clever family of sisters. At sixteen, having taken her Higher School Certificate, she was already preparing for her first MD examination. Encouraged by Mr Lacey, her guarantor, who firmly believed that, young as she was, Vera would find a medical school to accept her, she applied to Kings College Hospital, the Royal Free Hospital and Glasgow Medical School. Bloomsbury House reacted sceptically with a half-hearted inquiry as to the Home Office attitude to refugee medical students. But Vera did not wait on a Home Office ruling. Having passed the equivalent of the first MD examination, the universities could hardly turn her away, though places were made conditional on her waiting for her eighteenth birthday before going up. To occupy the intervening months she took a job in a hospital.

There was a lot to be said for knowing your place if you wanted help from Bloomsbury House. Hermann clearly went about his interview in the wrong way:

> A most unpleasant young man. He had a long story to tell of his misfortunes, beginning with a statement to the effect that he was dismissed from Garners under suspicion of sabotage (this boiled down to statements that he had made a drawing of some machinery and the other workers did not like him, or what he had done, and made trouble). He then accused us of refusing him financial help, causing him to take up part-time work without a permit for Miss Wagenaar of Frognal Lane. This led to unsavoury accusations against Miss Wagenaar, in addition to which he said she owed him £5. He has now obtained a work permit from the Willesden Labour Exchange . . . to work for the London Provincial Film Company as a mechanic-driver. The young man spun a wonderful story of his need for money next week, until his first pay day in the new job, his driving licence need renewing, he owes to his landlady and he has not a penny . . . He became so insulting that he had to be asked to leave the office . . .

The brush-off seems to have had the desired effect. Subsequent entries on his report card show Hermann enjoying his new job delivering films to cinemas, paying off his debts and making toys in his spare time.

Appeals to Bloomsbury House to support job training and applications throw up some curious details: 'Ruth needs 2 prs. knickers and 1 apron' – she got the first items but not the apron. One frequent request was for containers in which to put belongings which were to be stored at Bloomsbury House: 'Alice needs 2 wooden boxes and 1 cardboard container in which to put all her belongings . . .' Very often special clothes were needed for work – gumboots and waterproofs for those working on the land, aprons and overalls for those in catering.

On the lower end of the job market, the most popular employer, certainly for girls, was Lyons. The smart Corner Houses had an undeniable glamour in those dull days. As Peter Morgan remembers: 'Waitresses at the Corner Houses were called Nippies – all in black with a frilled apron and a frilly hat. You couldn't get a job as a Nippy if you had anything more than an eighteen-inch waist.'

Bloomsbury House tried to dampen down the enthusiasm for Lyons – the uniforms were very expensive to provide – but many ended up working there. Peter Morgan himself went on to be a waiter in London's foremost hotels.

As ever, the saddest cases were those where no amount of educational funding could improve their life's chances. Margot was slow at her schoolwork, and, with little chance of improving, it was hoped that she would eventually emigrate to Palestine with her sister. But in 1944, at the age of fifteen, she was judged to have the mental age of a child four years younger. There was still some hope.

> Her doctor states that there will be a change in her glands between the ages of sixteen and seventeen and her health will improve.

It was not to be. In 1947:

> The headmistress reports that Margot is progressing but has a mental age of a girl of twelve. Is in an old-fashioned private school but no doubt this suits the special case. She has a speech impediment but understands English well.

Later in the year, a report from St George's Hospital was quoted:

> Margot's mental age is 10 years 6 months, so she is at the bottom of the borderline class. Her performance tests indicate that her practical abilities are a little higher. As she seems happy and well looked after at her present school, the doctor advises that she should remain where she is. Margot herself has no realization of her limitations and will always need a secure and sheltered background.

When the 1945 Education Act broadened the entry to secondary and higher education, it became much easier for Bloomsbury House to deal with the more able children. Susanne was one of these. She gained the best School Certificate results at her school in

Norfolk and went on to take science subjects for Higher Certificate. Now eligible for a county scholarship, it was no problem to encourage Susanne to think about a university course.

> At present she wants to be a schoolmistress after a four-year training course, but she will very likely have other views when she realises the potentialities which university training will give her.

But for most, persistence and endurance were still the prerequisites of educational advance. And even then, there was no guarantee. Eva Maria, born in Berlin 1927, had a long and difficult struggle to get her higher education. Described as 'weak and difficult to deal with', she was nonetheless accepted for Oldham Grammar School while living in one room with her mother – a 'mentally weak person' who worked night shifts. Eva Maria wanted to be a teacher and was offered a place, after a couple of years, at St Katherine's Training College. She struggled to get finance together and qualified in 1947. In 1951, she received an LCC grant and was able to study full-time at London University. For Eva Maria, persistence and endurance paid off. She was one of the few.

11

War Effort

More than a thousand Kindertransporte *refugees served in the armed forces, among them some three hundred girls. Thirty lost their lives.*

When Peter Prager left his family on 23 December 1938, he had only one thing on his mind:

> I was convinced there was going to be a war and I was convinced Britain, America and France would fight Germany and would win and I wanted to be in the occupation army . . .

He was aged fifteen at the time; seven years later his dream came true. In 1945 he joined the army as a civilian in the censorship division and worked in Berlin.

His teenage resolution was shared by many young refugees, though when it came to offering their services they found that joining up was not as simple as the recruiting posters had led them to believe.

> Gert called with his form for the RAF. I took him to Captain Davidson to act as witness. The Captain reinforced my statement to the boy that, though he has got as far as his medical, he won't get into the Force. Gert still wants to try . . . Captain Davidson told him to come along and offer for the Pioneers as soon as he gets a refusal.

Captain Bernard Davidson had been one of Otto Schiff's adjutants on the Refugee Committee before his appointment by the War Office as recruiting officer for the aliens and refugees. At first, there was not much to do. It took some time for the War Office to be persuaded that fugitives from the enemy could usefully serve their adopted country. In 1940, any refugee of military age was less likely to be called up than to be sent down, to an internment camp. But as the fear of invasion receded and the public outrage at the scandals of the *Arandora Star* and the *Dunera* made itself known, refugees moved up in the War Office estimation. It was not far, it has to be said, but far enough for enrolment with the Auxiliary Military Pioneer Corps, later known as the Royal Pioneer Corps, to secure release from internment.

The Pioneer Corps was non-combatant, though volunteers had to accept the risks 'of being employed in any theatre of war'. It was the least glamorous sector of the army, undertaking labour of all kinds: construction work, handling of stores behind the lines, digging latrines. British subjects who were too old or otherwise unsuitable for active service found their way to the Pioneer Corps. From 1940 they were joined by thousands of refugees who were keen to serve in some capacity, however lowly, and equally keen to escape internment.

The first training centre for refugee recruits to the Pioneer Corps was the Kitchener Camp at Richborough in Kent. From there, five companies, each of 300 men, went to France in the early months of 1940. When the British Expeditionary Force was ordered to retreat, the Pioneers were issued with rifles, machine-guns and anti-tank weapons to help fight the rearguard action on the withdrawal to Dunkirk. All five companies returned safely and, with the prospect of invasion looming nearer, the training centre was moved from Richborough to the West Country. Alien soldiers, who might be treated as traitors by invading Germans, were too much at risk so near the south coast.

The fear of invasion was a powerful factor in many refugees' lives. Kurt Weinburg, evacuated to Cornwall with his school, was active in the Boy Scouts, spending much of his spare time on salvage collections. Naturally, he was on the lookout for more exciting activity.

> When the Home Guard was formed, I joined, but Mr Crombie (my headmaster) was told by the police that under no circumstances was I to have anything to do with the Home Guard as I was an enemy alien. So I had to leave.

Mr Crombie made me one of the Boy Scout spotters and we took it in turns to sleep at the local vicarage because there was a telephone there. Once there was an invasion alarm over the whole western part of England. I shall never forget it. It was during the holidays and the headmaster was away in London and I was one of the few older boys left at the school.

I wasn't on duty that night at the vicarage, but at about two o'clock in the morning the boy in charge of the telephone burst into my room, crying: 'Kurt, invasion, invasion!' He then dashed off to warn the others and I got up. I had a 2.2 gun (I wasn't allowed the 303 which the Home Guard had) and we barricaded the front door. We expected the parachutists to land at any moment and we waited and waited. Eventually we went out, but it was two days before we heard that it had been a false alarm. I took a boy over to a nearby farm in the morning – he was carrying a jug to collect milk – and I walked with him with my loaded 2.2. At night we patrolled the cliffs watching for any boats that were trying to land.

Kurt was able to sign up without first enduring the humiliation of internment. Older boys, who had a spell on the Isle of Man or in one of the other internment camps, had first to be interviewed by Captain Davidson. With only one medical officer on hand, their release took some time. Passed fit, they were encouraged to anglicise their names before filling out identity cards and soldiers' books. The warning was clear. If they kept to German names and were captured they would be treated as traitors.

One of the funniest incidents was the pay parade following our change of names, because no one could remember his new name. Myer became Montgomery, Stuertzel became Stephens, and so on and to top it all, the last man on the Pay Parade every week, Zell, changed his name to Avent so that he could be first to collect his pay.

Many members of the alien companies of the Pioneers chafed against the restrictions of their service. They wanted to join one of the fighting services and be eligible for promotion like British soldiers. But, in the early days of the war, even the most gifted were spurned.

Here is Fritz Braunthal who, judging by his letters, was a highly intelligent eighteen-year-old. He was, he told Greta Burkill, intent on persuading the Cambridge University recruiting board to offer him a place on an officer training course.

> That would be, as you know, the fulfilment of my most daring dreams. I do hope it comes off.

Two months later he got his answer from Colonel Murray of the Cambridge University Senior Training Corps.

> I regret to say that we have been unsuccessful in arranging for your posting to an OCTU [Officer Cadet Training Unit]. The War Office say that the only opening for you at present is enlistment into the Pioneer Corps.

Fritz turned again to Greta Burkill:

> This was rather a blow to me, particularly as everything had gone so very well up to the last moment . . . Do you think that there would be any point in either myself or you (if you would be so kind) urging the matter with Colonel Murray again, or do you think I should just join the Pioneer Corps straight away?

As always, Greta was prepared to take up the challenge ('We might put pressure on the War Office at this end'), but was forestalled by an offer from another direction.

'I have not yet joined the Pioneers,' wrote Fritz on 15 November, 'but I have got myself a job as a radio reporter with the United Press of America. It is tremendously interesting and suited to my qualifications as a knowledge of languages is essential to the job.' He added, 'But I would chuck it immediately if I could get into the army.'

On his behalf, Great Burkill made one more assault on the establishment, only to receive from the university the final brush off.

> I can sympathise, as you do, with refugee students' wish to undertake work more directly connected with their special training and interests. However, there is, in fact, nothing more for them to do than to join the Pioneer Corps. After all, our own young men, whatever their intellectual and other qualifications, have to go into the army, and it is little hardship that the Pioneer Corps is the only opening for young men from other countries.

Those who could not take the Pioneers at any price had the option of training for essential civilian work. This is why Victor, with his higher school certificate in physics, chemistry, maths and German, ended up on a mining course at Chesterfield Technical College. He spent his war at the Bolsover Colliery in Derbyshire. Others became farm labourers.

Towards the tail end of 1942, the military embargo on refugees was beginning to weaken. The prospect of a long war with the inevitable increase in demand for service manpower was a critical factor. But the realisation that the refugee community was not riddled with spies and fifth columnists helped to soften official attitudes. Volunteers with technical qualifications were accepted for the Engineers, Ordnance and the Service Corps. The first fighting unit thrown open to refugees was the International Commando Unit. Those who joined knew full well that they were liable to be dropped behind enemy lines. As Lord Mountbatten said of them:

> They were a group of Germans who believed in democracy and liberty in their own country and were fine soldiers. None of them let us down and half of them lost their lives.

With the refugees giving such good account of themselves, the case for the surviving restrictions was fatally weakened. By 1943, they were free to offer their services to any part of the military except the Signals; 800 Pioneers went into technical units, 650 to combatant units of the infantry and armoured corps, 450 to the Intelligence Corps and specialist formations, 300 to the Commandos, the Airborne troops and the special forces, and over 100 to the Navy and the Royal Air Force.

Leslie Brent, who was young enough to have avoided internment but was nonetheless classified as an enemy alien, joined the forces in 1944:

> I joined the infantry, the Royal Warwickshire Regiment, because of my association with Birmingham. I was sent to Glasgow for my general service training for five weeks, and for the first time I was exposed to the rough and tumble of life; working-class lads whose every third word was a four-letter word. I had not experienced this before. It was traumatic, but quite educational! I was thought to be a rather strange fish – I still had my German name and a bit of a

German accent. I didn't smoke and when we fell out for a smoke I tended to pull out my book of *Anna Karenina*, so I was rather an odd man.

At the end of the training I wanted to join the Royal Ambulance Corps, which is probably indicative of my not wanting necessarily to kill Germans though wanting to do my bit towards the war effort. I was told I could not – 'You are too intelligent and too fit. We would like you to go into the infantry and would like you eventually to become an officer.' I continued with my training in Warwickshire and became a lance corporal. In the autumn of 1944, I finished up at an officers' training camp in Heysham, Lancaster for three or four months. I was then sent to Ireland to a training camp in County Down and spent some time there training soldiers. I was well liked by the men because I had some empathy for them and I did my best to safeguard their welfare.

I was sent to join the 5th Division as a full lieutenant in Trieste in northern Italy. From there I was sent to Germany, which was a very strange experience – to enter war-torn Germany as an officer.

Many refugees found themselves in the same position. As the Allies advanced across the continent, there was a huge demand for interpreters and for interrogators to interview German and Austrian prisoners of war.

The Intelligence service was even prepared to give young Hans a second look, even though he was not a prepossessing sight. He had been working at tar processing and the fumes had given him an unpleasant skin complaint. He also seemed to be rather boastful and above himself. But his appearance was misleading. In an interview with the Intelligence Department of the Foreign Office, he showed great promise as an interpreter. He joined the Civilian Branch of the Army of Occupation in Germany and in 1945, at the age of twenty-two, became an interpreter with the US Air Force. The final comment on his report card reads: 'Still the same old boaster . . .'

Howard Franks interrogated German POWs in England and Norway:

Some of the naval and airforce POWs had studied in Oxford and their English was as fluent as, if not better than, mine and they asked me how I spoke German so well. And there I used to lie. The lie was carefully made up. I said I had studied in Innsbruch because I knew these people were quite clever enough to detect a Viennese accent in my English. But I think the clever ones guessed my background.

Clive Milton, too, worked as an interpreter:

> I was sent to Oslo with a 28-strong unit to take over the raw materials the Germans had left. We employed those Germans who were left – this was my first contact with *Wehrmacht* personnel.

Later he returned to England to work in a POW camp:

> In the camp the English workers were mainly in the Pioneer Corps – not refugees, but mostly people of below average intelligence level. They were a fairly mean lot, especially at non-commissioned officer level. They would not think twice of kicking a German or forcing him to do unpleasant tasks. Fortunately, they were acting under orders of officers of exemplary character. Left on their own they could have committed atrocities.
>
> I felt . . . not hatred, as such – I have never been able to hate individuals, as such – so I could interrogate quite dispassionately. I am sure they knew I was from a Jewish background, but I would never discuss this with a prisoner. It was a business relationship. They would give me presents and stuff – there was nothing for them to do so they would make little things. Also, my office was staffed by Germans.

Some of those who served with the Forces on the continent were brought close to areas where their families had lived, or where friends and relatives had last been heard of. Sometimes the compulsion to try and trace them was irresistible, as Alfred Cooper found:

> I went with the Pioneer Corps (this was around D-Day) to France, where we were attached to a Canadian Forestry Corps. They were cutting timber down to make huts. Then we went to Belgium and I went absent there for two weeks because I tried to trace my brother who escaped to Belgium. He had hidden in the coal mines as a miner. I went to the Jewish Committee, but a fellow told me not to deal with them as he thought they cooperated with the Germans. So I went to the Palace of Justice and in the end, after I created hell, they gave me the information. So I virtually walked from Brussels – along the railway line (I did have lifts too, but you had to be careful about taking lifts because of army intelligence), and I found him. I hadn't seen him since *Kristallnacht*. He had escaped from a

camp in France – he speaks fluent French – and he had gone back to the camps (which was where you were sent before going to Auschwitz) and brought out his wife and daughter.

Towards the end of the war, Alfred joined the Jewish Brigade. Recruitment was mainly in Israel, but the Brigade was part of the British Army and was stationed in Italy, Holland and Western Germany.

Alfred went to Germany with the Brigade after the war and was stationed at Bielefeld, a German army camp taken over by the British:

> I asked the Sgt Major for two weeks leave to see my sister. But the leave wasn't granted. So the Sgt Major asked me how long I had been in the army and, when I said six years, he said: 'Don't you know what to do?' So I went over the fence. I was AWOL for two weeks and when I came back I had to paint the barrack railings. I found my sister in Hamburg. She had had a hard time. My brother-in-law was not Jewish and they had to hide in the fields. She gave birth to her second child in a forest. They had no ration cards, nothing.

The Jewish Brigade was composed of ardent Zionists who carried their missionary zeal through the displaced persons camps of Europe. It seemed like home to Henry Schwartz, though it came as a surprise to find that he was not immediately accepted.

> . . . I was an Austrian and they didn't want me, I became an Englishman and they didn't trust me, so what was left? I had to become a Jew! So when the Jewish Brigade came up I was just about the first volunteer. When we went out to Italy in the Brigade I discovered that anybody who wanted promotion had to be born in Palestine. I thought, 'I can't win.'

After VE day:

> You couldn't get any parcels sent to you from home. All the parcels went to the displaced persons camp – where there were only Jewish people. It was the only time there was no anti-Semitism. We used to pick up boys who were illegal immigrants, put them in British uniform, issue them with a paybook and send them off to Palestine. It was fantastic.

We were near Antwerp and the Flemish were a very anti-Semitic group. They showed a newsreel in a cinema of American troops going into a displaced persons' camp and attending Jewish religious service, and the audience started laughing. Well, they didn't laugh any more because we broke the cinema up – nobody laughed at the Jews when the Jewish Brigade was there.

There was another incident I remember. We used to have a group of seven (they were real thugs – one of them was a Spaniard who used to appear in the music-hall as a tough guy. I think people used to stand on his chest), and we were at a dance (this was in Holland) and one of our boys went up to a girl and asked her to dance. She was sitting with a Polish soldier and she said she couldn't dance. When asked why not, she said her boyfriend told her not to dance with Jews. There were thirteen in hospital that night.

We were absolutely feared. It was a different type of Jew from what I had ever met before.

Discipline in the Jewish Brigade was of a sort unknown in any conventional army:

A colonel found one of his junior officers, a major, cleaning shoes while his batman sat talking to him. The colonel was outraged. He threatened the junior officer with a court martial. The major said: 'Do you know what happened to your predecessor? Let me tell you. One day he went into the storeroom and there were no reserve arms, so he asked where they were. When he couldn't get any answer, he lost his temper and shouted that all Jews were liars and crooks. So a deputation went to the brigadier and said, 'Remove him in two hours or we will bring him back in a coffin – what is it to be?' So he was removed. The major cleaning the shoes said: 'This is the Jewish Brigade – forget your discipline. We are both from the kibbutz and we have decided that one day I am the batman and the next day he is. Don't interfere. When we are on duty fighting, I am the major and he is the batman, but when it comes to cleaning shoes, we are both in the kibbutz. So either you accept it or do what the other bloke did and leave, because this is the Jewish Brigade.

Soldiers serving elsewhere in the British Forces were liable to encounter problems with their Jewish identity. Clive Milton:

When the Germans capitulated I worked as an interpreter and was promoted to a staff sergeant. There was a lot of anti-Semitism amongst British soldiers. Many were regulars, having served in Palestine, and hated anyone who was not British. When two British sergeants were hanged in retaliation for the hanging of Jewish terrorists, there was a fight in our sergeants' mess. We were fighting each other with knives.

Herman Rothman found that his religion and the army were ill matched.

It was difficult for me to live in a kosher way. Although I received the chief rabbi's food parcel, it took two months to arrive. I had to work on *Shabbat*. I suppose I had a sort of compulsion neurosis in the army. People admired me. In the morning I put on my *Tefillin* and said my prayers. I did this even when I was in the front line.

Lothar, one of the RCM's more difficult cases, had troubles of a different kind during his time in the forces. While working at Lyons Corner House in April 1942, he came out in spots. This was diagnosed as impetigo, an unpleasant and contagious affliction. At the end of 1942, out of work, he was advised to apply for the Pioneer Corps and was accepted.

However, the Pioneer Corps sent him straight back, insisting he was suffering from VD. Lothar replied that he simply had a skin complaint that could be cleared up in a few days. Then Bernard (now Major) Davidson was informed that Lothar was suffering from scabies. The recruiting officer stuck by this diagnosis, although Lothar's specialist at the Charing Cross Hospital passed him A1. Eventually he enlisted.

In February 1943, the RCM received several desperate letters from Lothar, who was in hospital, but would not say what was wrong with him. Two months later:

Major Davidson's secretary showed Mr Ruppin a letter which Major Davidson had received from his friend at the camp. It is to the effect that Lothar has been in the VD ward of the military hospital since he arrived in Bradford Training Camp, and that his state of health is such that he will be discharged from the army soon. The writer warns Major Davidson not to waste his sympathy on such an undeserving case.

The truth was never revealed, though it seems likely that Lothar suffered an injustice. In any event, he left hospital to resume training on 15 April and later in the year was planning on getting married.

Young refugee women enlisted in the Women's Auxiliary Territorial Service. (The RCM annual report for 1940–1941 lists eighty of their girls with the ATS.) Lady Cohen, wife of Lord Justice Cohen, was appointed senior commander in that Force, with the responsibility of recruiting alien women and looking after their welfare. Other girls joined the Women's Auxiliary Air Force Service (WAAFS), the Land Army and the National Fire Service. Many more, of course, were helping the war effort in the nursing profession.

Ya'acov Friedler, interned with his sister on the Isle of Man, remembers the first signs of the change of heart towards enemy aliens:

> . . . we were informed that any young woman among the internees was welcome to join the Forces. Indeed, Princess Elizabeth joined the ATS as an example to the girls of Britain, and photographs of her doing her duty were widely circulated . . .
>
> Our ranks thinned out as the young women who had been accepted left the island for military camps on the mainland . . . One of the girls in our hotel who joined the ATS sent letters describing her experiences, and the women were tickled by the information that everything she wore was khaki, from panties to bra to greatcoat. She happened to have been a particularly good-looking girl and sent us a photo of herself in uniform, with a wink in her eye and the caption, 'A Girl With a Will to Win', which she had purloined from a recruiting poster. I do not know how much her contribution to the war effort added up to, but the mere sight of her must have done a lot to raise the morale of the fighting men.

Lore Selo, working her fingers to the bone as a maid-cum-housekeeper in Finchley, was thrilled to meet a cousin of hers in uniform:

> She said how about me joining the Army, and my father, although he was very attached to me, said it would be the ideal solution for me to get away from the drudgery of being in domestic employment.
>
> So I applied, feeling very patriotic and wanting to do my bit for England. In 1942, at the age of eighteen, I was accepted for the ATS . . . At the time I was not a British subject and aliens were only offered menial jobs – preferably cooks or mess orderlies. I

plumped for the latter – although they tried their hardest to persuade me to go for cooking. I had quite a giggle to myself when the interviewer said that my continental cookery skills would probably go down well with the men. I did my initial training in Lancaster and still remember the first day in the huge dormitory after we all had our vaccinations. The after-effects were most depressing . . .

Lore was shocked by the general standard of hygiene:

Many girls had to be deloused for nits and other vermin. I noticed this with the male intake too, and I also observed that many of the men were illiterate and could only put a cross by their names.

Starting as a mess orderly, Lore was eventually transferred to North Wales.

As mess orderlies, we had to deal with two sittings each mealtime – either early or late duty. Running around with piles of plates and jugs and so forth. Once, in the rush, I slipped in a sea of gravy and fell down hard on the stone floor. Two soldiers jumped up and helped me to a table, where I sat for another half-hour with my head whirring. I felt such a fool, especially when they asked me to give a repeat performance. I think it must have been my thick hair that saved me . . .

After a while the army authorities realised that many people were in the wrong jobs and they conducted intelligence tests. Although I had never been to school in England, I passed my spelling test 100%. However, I did not do that well in maths. But they apparently felt I should be more usefully employed in an office.

Lore went as a receptionist to an army hospital in Abergele and then was posted to Canterbury, where she worked for Personnel Selection.

. . . A most interesting job. While in Canterbury, which I loved, I did many other jobs. I had a few boyfriends, but I kept my wits about me. Many nice girls got themselves involved with soldiers who turned out to be married. Some were expecting babies and, of course, were left in the lurch. I was careful and in that sense came out as green as I went in.

Summing up my army experiences – it was a good life. Going on parade and route marches didn't do a healthy young female any harm. I made many good friends and enjoyed the comradeship. Also I felt useful in contributing to the war effort. Alas, the uniform did not suit me. For other ranks there were two sizes – too large or too small. My hair should have been well above the collar and somehow it never seemed to be. That was very important. It barred promotion if one's appearance was not up to scratch. So I remained a glorious private. I became an expert in shining up shoes and brass buttons. Thinking back, I realise there was much more to it and I learned a lot more about the art of living.

Six alien companies of the Pioneer Corps accompanied the allied invasion. Many refugee servicemen were decorated and many gave their lives to their adopted country.

In 1943, men who had been invalided out of the Pioneer Corps formed an ex-servicemen's club, identified by the initials N B – non-British. The club survives and organises reunions every year.

12

Short Straws

'. . . Such failures exist where so great an upheaval has taken place and it was not to be expected that the Movement's records should be free from shadows.'

Children who were required to go out to work at fourteen, that is, the great majority of British teenagers, could hardly be blamed for assuming the right to lead their lives as they saw fit. In reality, their freedom was closely confined. Those who came from more or less stable families were generally restrained from the wilder flights of liberty by parental influence, an influence reinforced by the economic advantages of continuing to live at home.

But for refugee children these social conventions seldom came into play. An overcrowded hostel was naturally keen to dispose of its more mature residents to make way for a fresh intake, while the foster parent was, by definition, a temporary parent offering short-term security against long-term uncertainty. With rare exceptions, refugee children were expected to leave home as soon as they could fend for themselves. With only the staff at Bloomsbury House and their regional offices as the long stop for advice and modest practical assistance, it is not surprising that a high proportion of *Kindertransporte* veterans, possibly as many as one in ten, found themselves up against the police or other bastions of social authority.

The personal files held by the RCM reveal a sorry procession of young people who tried to solve their problems by turning to petty crime. A typical example was Gert, a complex boy who confused Bloomsbury House visitors. To one he was 'highly intelligent and showing creative ability'; to another his 'intelligence was not above the ordinary'; he was more the show-off who had an 'exaggerated idea of his age and importance'. Both observers were disturbed by Gert's laughter, 'which appears to ring with hysteria'. A few days short of his fifteenth birthday, Gert attempted suicide, cutting his wrist and jumping from a third-floor window. He had been caught stealing from a friend and had reacted 'hysterically' to the inevitable reprimand. There followed a succession of minor criminal offences, mostly against youngsters with whom he shared lodgings. No record of medical or psychiatric treatment appears in Gert's file, though there were persistent efforts to persuade him to pay off his debts from his earnings as a packer on an assembly line.

By August 1941, when he was sixteen, he had an evening and weekend job as a trolley boy in Lyons Piccadilly Brasserie. Whatever he was doing with the extra money, he was not settling accounts with those he had defrauded. The police were called in. Gert had been reported for selling torch batteries, which he said his employer had given him. He was put on two years' probation. The last heard of Gert was in 1943 when he tried and failed to join the RAF. Bloomsbury House urged him to settle for the Pioneers.

At this distance it is impossible to tell if Gert could have made more of his early life if he had been given the chance to make use of the 'creative ability' spotted early on by one of his helpers. But it is a fair assumption that many young refugees fell foul of authority out of sheer frustration with undemanding and tedious work, usually at subsistence wages.

The intervention of Bloomsbury House forestalled a likely prison sentence for Otto, who stole money from his landlady and his employer. What made the case stand out was the motivation for Otto's pilfering. The proceeds went on tickets for West End theatre, where the boy spent all his free evenings. Predictably, he wanted above all else to be an actor but, when he had the chance of realising his ambition by working overseas, for some reason the Home Office refused an exit permit. But in 1945 he was allowed to join the US Army – as a civil censor.

Because it was hard for young refugees to find decently paid jobs (all else being equal, refugee status was a disqualification in the eyes of most employers), they were frequently in debt. The more assertive and imaginative found honest ways to supplement their regular wage packet.

Margaret and her friends collected old clothes, converted them into dusters and sold them out of a suitcase in the Camden market and to old clothes dealers. Others just continued borrowing until they ran out of luck or excuses. Then came the blustering denials of any intention to act dishonestly, which did little to help their cause though many were sincere.

Appeals for advice on how to handle this boy or that girl who owed money arrived daily at Bloomsbury House. The appeals were made as often in sorrow as in anger. What more, for example, could Mr Marshall have done for Helmut? Out of the kindness of his heart he had let him have a job in his shoe repair shop. The boy showed little talent for the business and hardly earned the £2. 10s Mr Marshall paid him at the end of the week. But his employer recognised that, after Helmut had paid for his lodgings (fifteen shillings for a room and 'a rather meagre breakfast'), there was little enough to live on. No wonder Helmut was seen 'loitering around after working hours'; no wonder he burst into tears at the slightest provocation; and no wonder he was in debt. Little was done for him in the three years up to his seventeenth birthday when, like so many others, he found companionship and, ironically, the security he craved for by joining the army.

Helmut's problems were compounded by an unsatisfactory relationship with his landlady who 'is just on eighty years of age and has a large house to keep clean with no help whatever'. Predictably, she was not sympathetic to the boisterous ways of a young teenager, though she did not go so far as a Mrs Dudley who complained to Bloomsbury House that one of her fifteen-year-old lodgers, Willy, had 'broken the beading on a wardrobe and had also broken a chair', offences which most parents of healthy teenagers would have accepted as part of growing up.

Friction led to furious rows and the rows led to Willy demanding that he should be allowed to take a room where he could look after himself. The RCM seemed to be prepared to go along with this, until they discovered that Willy was also in trouble with his employer, a jeweller who caught the boy pocketing a silver cigarette case. No excuses were offered. Willy voiced the philosophy he had learned by experience – it was everyone for himself; if you didn't take what you wanted, no one was likely to give it to you.

It was only because his employer did not want to waste his time in court proceedings that Willy escaped probation and a possible jail sentence.

There were those in the Movement who regretted that the police were not brought in. This was not so heartless as it might seem. Before the Guardianship Act of 1943, the RCM had next to no real power to restrain a youngster who showed signs of getting out of control. The police and the probation service, on the other hand, could impose sanctions, though whether they would have had any effect on Willy, who 'was extremely rude and behaved very badly towards all authority', is open to doubt. In the end it was Dorothy Hardisty, ever patient but determined, who persuaded Willy to take up agricultural training in North Wales. In this way, she reasoned, he would be removed from the temptations of the city. Willy agreed to go as long as he was given a return fare. He wanted to be sure he could return to London if he didn't like his new job. His file closes with his departure to Brecon in March 1942. Since further complaints against him would almost certainly have been recorded, it is a fair guess that he took to the open life.

As a first cause of resentment against authority, falling out with employers was as common as falling out with landladies. Too often a job, any job, for a refugee child was seen as bestowing a great favour in return for which sacrifices were expected. Heinz was a sheet metal worker. In January 1945 'he was welding a tank which contained two gallons of paraffin. The heat of the welding compressed the air inside the tank which, together with the acetylene flame, blew the tank open, causing a flame to shoot out and burn Heinz.' It turned out that the foreman had not warned Heinz that the paraffin might explode. Indeed, he had categorically denied that there was any danger. This may have been because he was ignorant or stupid but, reading between the lines of Heinz's file, it is more likely that the foreman had taken against his young charge who was 'very intelligent and conceited'. (How often are those two descriptions juxtaposed in RCM reports, the apparent 'conceit' paraded as justification for distrusting cleverness.) In any event, Heinz was off work for two months before embarking on a steady descent of menial jobs, ending up as a kitchen cleaner. In 1948 he was found guilty of breaking and entering. Despite representations from the RCM, Heinz was deported to Germany.

It was, as one refugee worker put it, 'the easy way out' and it solved nothing.

There were many cases where Bloomsbury House was involved not at all, or only at the last moment when it was generally too late to offer any constructive help. When Max 'lifted' some cash at his hostel in north London, 'the only person who appeared at court was the German who ran the hostel. I didn't like him at all and we didn't get on. He wanted to tell the judge how to deal with me, but fortunately the judge was more understanding. I had to stay in prison for a couple of weeks before going to an approved school in Hayes, Middlesex.'

The first the Movement knew of Beno's trouble was when a sharp-eyed refugee worker spotted a news item in the *Evening Standard*. Beno was brought up before the magistrate at Bow Street, accused of posing as a Russian Air Force officer, and being in possession of eleven rounds of rifle ammunition without a certificate. As the case was held over there was just time for Dorothy Hardisty to intervene. She told the court that she had known eighteen-year-old Beno for three years, that in 1941 he had lost his power of speech when his lodgings suffered a direct hit, and that thereafter he had lived with the fantasy of becoming an air force officer. Beno was fined five pounds and told to get a job more suitable to his talents.

While Bloomsbury House sensibly avoided general rules for dealing with problem cases, there was one guiding principle in the campaign against delinquency. 'At all costs', wrote Dorothy Hardisty in one of her reports to the RCM executive, 'we must try to dissuade our boys and girls from believing that London is the answer to all their prayers.' Her concern was entirely understandable. The big city was a powerful draw to youngsters who were looking for the chance to better themselves. By the spring of 1943, there were nearly 2200 RCM children in London, an increase of one-third on the previous year. With the labour force depleted by the military, there were jobs to be filled, and at better rates of pay than elsewhere in the country. But London offered too many hostages to fortune at a time when all foreigners were suspect, and the police were inclined to arrest first and ask questions afterwards. The most common offence was to break the curfew, aliens were not supposed to be out on the streets after eleven. Seldom was any harm intended but, however genuine, excuses were invariably noted by the police under the heading of suspicious behaviour. When Philip Urbach was pulled in, he was on a tour of discovery of the East End.

> There had been these terrible air raids in the Jewish district and I wanted to see what had happened. Maybe it was foolish but I went out of concern. Well, I was wandering between bombed houses almost in a dream and someone asked me what I was doing there. When they heard my foreign accent, the police were called.

A more ambitious escapade took Johnny Blunt and a friend on a hitchhike from London to Glasgow. Here they were committing two sins of omission – the failure to be indoors by 11 p.m. and the failure to notify the police of a change of address.

> At about midnight Henry and I slipped out of the hostel, walked to the main road and started thumbing. We got to Glasgow early the next morning and went to the local refugee committee. There we had the biggest telling-off of our lives. 'Don't you know you're breaking the law? You could get into serious trouble. We ought to tell the police.'

But luck was with them. The row blew over as it did for Kurt Weinburg, who was taken out by an older friend for a night on the town. They had dinner at the Trocadero in Shaftesbury Avenue before taking in the late show at the Windmill Theatre.

> When I got back to Camden Road it was near midnight. I didn't have a key and everybody had gone to bed. So I knocked, but not too hard in case I woke up the neighbourhood. But I was heard by a policeman on patrol. He walked up the garden path and shone his torch in my face. He wanted to know what I was doing and asked to see my registration book. He knew I should have been in by 11 p.m. Then he started knocking so hard I thought he would break the door down. At least he saved me from a night on a park bench. The next day I had to report to the police station and promise not to disobey the rules. But no further action was taken.

Less fortunate was Karl, whose troubles were noted at Bloomsbury House.

> Karl called, unkempt as usual, pale and highly nervous. He had
> received this morning a summons to appear before the Hampstead
> Police Court . . . on a charge of having failed to notify his intended
> move . . . In view of a previous conviction he is very worried and
> asked to be given legal help.

Subsequently the boy was held in Brixton Prison for several weeks
under a deportation order while Dorothy Hardisty lobbied the
Home Office. Eventually Karl was released and the deportation
order lifted on a promise by the RCM that accommodation and
a job were waiting for him.

The punishment for trivial offences could go well beyond
the magistrate's ticking-off or the nominal fine. When Charlotte,
'a delicate and capable young person', was caught travelling
on the Underground without a ticket, it was not the 3s 6d
fine that bothered her so much as the magistrate's warning that,
in consequence, her application for naturalisation might be
rejected.

Once more Bloomsbury House made a timely intervention, as
often happened when the Movement could be persuaded that the
offender was basically good at heart. Judging by the records a full
confession accompanied by a fair amount of grovelling was the
surest way to create a favourable impression. Thus, Kurt got away
with receiving stolen goods to the value of £3 10s by pleading an
unselfish motivation to help his girlfriend and her three-month-
old baby, while Nissi, whose bearing 'was very humble and
apologetic', was discharged after being caught red-handed taking
cigarettes from a bombed-out tobacconist's.

Less fortunate was twenty-year-old Leo who, in early 1944, set
up as a freelance photographer without first obtaining formal
documentation from the Home Office. The Movement took
against him, not so much because he had neglected the bureaucratic
niceties, but more because he was 'a weedy, conceited, unattractive
young man' who did not respond to exhortations to join the war
effort (presumably by swapping his camera for a pick and shovel).
When he applied to the court for permission to marry, as he was
required to do since he was under twenty-one and did not have a
recognised guardian, the magistrate at Bow Street refused 'as he
was not in favour of a British girl marrying an alien'. The RCM
expressed itself powerless to intercede. Thereafter, Leo's relation-

ship with his adopted country dipped to the point where he was charged with stealing a car, sentenced to six months and recommended for deportation. By now he was of an age to make his own decisions, the first of which was to marry the English girl to whom he had been engaged for two years. This did not prevent his deportation. In July 1947 he returned illegally and appealed for help to the RCM, whose representative advised him to give himself up. On his record card appears a brief, dismissive comment: 'It is pointless for the committee to intervene.' Leo was sent back to Germany.

When boys tried for easy money they generally sold what belonged to others; when girls were similarly tempted they were more inclined to sell themselves.

> A policewoman rang to say that Anita had been noticed loitering in Piccadilly at times during a whole week, both in the evenings and on three afternoons. The police had spoken to the girl and asked us to add our warnings . . . Anita came in and, as was to be expected, stated that it was all a mistake and that she had been waiting for a girl friend, etc. She begged that I would not mention the matter to Mrs Brodowitz as it would cause gossip at the hostel . . . I did warn the girl most seriously.

The warning had no effect. Within days sixteen-year-old Anita was again in a police report. The accusation of soliciting was avoided, but she did appear to be on friendly terms with rather too many American and Canadian soldiers. It was time for a straight talk from Dorothy Hardisty.

> A long discussion ensued, during which Mrs Hardisty impressed upon Anita the serious obligations and responsibilities which she had towards herself and her men companions, and the necessity for leading a decent and moral life. It was also impressed upon her that it was undignified continually to accept presents from men, and that no man would continue to give a girl presents without eventually demanding something in return.

It was wasted effort. Less than a fortnight later a panic call from Mrs Brodowitz revealed that Anita was engaged to a man she had known for only two days – 'a real Cockney, who appears to have a lot of money'. The story went that he was a dealer in jewels and furs who had been discharged from the army after Dunkirk.

There was barely time for Dorothy Hardisty to draw breath before Mrs Brodowitz, now, understandably, 'in a state of nerves', came back with more news. Anita's fiancé was not as he described. For one thing he had discharged himself from the army and was listed as a deserter; for another, he had a wife and two children 'somewhere in Norfolk'. The only consolation and the reason why Mrs Brodowitz was so well informed was that the man had been spotted by the military police and was now in prison.

Anita took all this in her stride. Back at Bloomsbury House for another chat with Dorothy Hardisty, she gave a dramatic rendering of 'a blazing row' with the other woman. 'It was very apparent that she had thoroughly enjoyed acting the lady', noted Mrs Hardisty. But while Anita 'maintained an indifferent and callous manner' towards the affair, the RCM could do no more than appeal to her better instincts. Dorothy Hardisty had no doubt that she was wasting her time.

> Anita has now decided to finish her relations with all men; in fact, she is tired of them and wishes only to be left alone . . . She is fully aware that she can do exactly as she pleases and that the Movement has no legal power over her at all.

Shortly afterwards, Anita left the hostel and took a room of her own. Thereafter for three years, her RCM file records without comment a succession of job and address changes. In 1946, Anita married an American army lieutenant and left for the States. Her file was closed.

There were girls who persistently stayed out late, girls who kept bad company and girls who drank too much. No doubt many more boys were up to the same tricks, but convention ruled that they were better able to look after themselves. Hence, their files give little indication of misdemeanours, which take up whole pages when girls were involved. This was bad luck on Helga, who got drunk with an American soldier and was not allowed to forget it, and on Hildegard, who was taken in by the police when she was seen talking to an ex-convict, but worked in favour of Martin, who made quite a business out of playing cards for money but who was judged 'on the whole to be doing no worse than any other boy of his age in his particular position'. This opinion had soon to be revised. Martin was arrested in possession of an unloaded revolver. He had planned to hold up the cash desk of an Oxford Street store.

Getting caught before the crime designated Martin as an amateur. He might have learned a thing or two from twin brothers Walter and Theo who began, successfully, to take what they wanted in 1944 when they were eighteen. Walter made quite a business from stealing rationed food from the grocer he worked for and selling it on the black market, while Theo dealt mostly in men's clothes which he shifted on to a second-hand dealer who paid ready cash. The partnership came to an end in 1947 when Walter got away to the United States. Theo took a shorter journey – to Wormwood Scrubs, where he did four months' hard labour. Curiously, he was not deported, a sentence which in the two years immediately after the war was handed down to at least fifty young people who had come over on the *Kindertransporte*. Once a recommendation for deportation had been made it was rare for the Movement to try to reverse the order, though the irony of sending youngsters back to the source of their unhappiest memories was not lost on refugee workers. They seem to have taken the view that deportation was justified as a last resort when the victim had persistently ignored warnings, and when nothing further could be done to achieve his rehabilitation. But deportation was also an option for shifting a problem to another authority. The temptation to take the easy way out was well-nigh irresistible with youngsters who had failed to make their way (probably through no fault of their own) and who showed their resentment.

> We told Joseph that we wished to settle the matter amicably but, if he was not prepared to tell the truth and confess (to stealing from gas meters), we would place the matter in the hands of the police. The boy stated that this would not worry him. His whole attitude was anti-British, in that this country had failed to bring his parents over, and anti-Movement, in that he charged us with having turned him adrift on 35 shillings a week which was insufficient for his needs.

Joseph was a prime candidate for deportation. It would have needed a later generation of social workers, free from the prejudices of war, to detect the frustration behind the mask of ingratitude and disloyalty. In 1945 the superficial judgement invariably carried the day. Joseph had to go.

By far the greater part of the RCM's counselling work was with youngsters who suffered physical and mental breakdown. This was wholly predictable. Being on a *Kindertransport* was, in itself, a traumatic experience that left its mark on otherwise balanced and healthy children. But other shocks to the system followed in quick succession: a new language and culture; the insensitivity, not always unintentional, of foster parents, teachers and hostel administrators; the cruelty of other children (and some adults) who equated all things German with Nazism; the coming-to-terms with the long-term or permanent loss of family and friends who had been left behind, and the awareness that refugees could not expect to be treated other than as second-class citizens – to mention only the common causes of illness and depression.

The refugee workers at Bloomsbury House, led in this context by Lola Hahn-Warburg, did their best. All of them volunteers with nothing but a rudimentary knowledge of psychology and, possibly, their own experience as parents to help them, they grappled with problems that challenged the skills of the best doctors and psychiatrists.

At twenty-one Renate did not have the most exciting job in the world, but with her German friends on a radio assembly line she seemed happy and settled. She was an active trade unionist and had lately been elected a shop steward. Then, in February 1944, her face became disfigured by red blotches and her skin started peeling. Her doctor told her she had dermatitis and recommended treatment which had no effect. When she called in at Bloomsbury House for a routine chat, her adviser noted that she 'looks very dirty and neglected and is taking no pride at all in her personal appearance'. Within a month Renate had lost her job ('the complaint was that the girl was too slow') and had suffered a sharp decline in health, having contracted chronic catarrh, nervous debility and eczema of the scalp 'which made her unable to summon up the courage to get a haircut after a hairdresser had been very rude to her on the subject'.

It took over a year of counselling and treatment to restore Renate to a semblance of ordinary life. By then she could just about face up to the knowledge she had been trying to resist since February 1944; that every last member of her family had died in the concentration camps.

Histories of debilitating ailments and depression such as Renate's occur over and over again in the RCM records. In nine cases out of ten, it did not take a professional analyst to detect the cause of the problem. It was the cure that was so elusive. What was to be done for Liselotte, who showed signs of severe mental stress from the age of five? By late 1943, when Liselotte was approaching her seventh birthday, she had taken to banging her head, a symptom which worried her foster mother more than her doctor, who 'could not be persuaded to view the matter very seriously'. What was then judged professionally to be a passing phase continued for over four years. It was not until 1946 that a psychiatrist was called in. His entry on Liselotte's file portrays her as 'a lively child but mentally backward'. After detailing her mental history he added, 'Lotte has vivid fantasies and has built a whole world of dreams. Her head banging suggests a kind of infantile masturbation. She is a discouraged child who needs love.'

It was a remedy frequently recommended but less often applied. Foster parents were not always equipped to cope with the vagaries of their own children, let alone the problems of outsiders. It was one thing to offer hospitality, quite another to extend the boundaries of tolerant understanding to dark moods and sudden rages, even when these could be attributed to horrific experiences in earlier childhood.

While children were very young it was possible to muddle through. The boy who deliberately confused English and German to create a language all to himself, the girl who pulled off her toenails, the boy who refused to speak for days on end, the girl who hid all her possessions and swore that others had stolen them – all these and many more were classed as difficult but just about manageable. It was when they grew up that the problems really started.

There was, for instance, Max who, as an early teenager, complained that he was without friends.

> He has had several introductions to various youth clubs, but he has always left them after a short time as he feels completely out of the picture.

Max was said to be in the grip of some form of neurosis, but it was assumed that he would grow out of it. A year after his first interview at Bloomsbury House, he was still saying that 'he really wanted some particular friend who would take a close interest in him'. Now, however, he wanted a girlfriend. He must have tried hard because soon afterwards there was a report of an engagement. But it was soon broken off which 'left him feeling rather lonely'. And that was it until December 1946, when Max was arrested in Hyde Park. He was charged with assault on a woman. Suddenly, his inability to attract friends took on a new significance. A psychiatrist was called in and Max was given the treatment he needed, but only after serving a month in Brixton.

The tendency for psychiatric disorders to show up more dramatically as the victims emerged from childhood helped to shift the focus of RCM counselling. As the war progressed, there was greater emphasis on professional advice, a trend which accelerated sharply after Germany's defeat when the nightmare of the holocaust made its full impact on those who had been saved from the gas chambers.

One of the many who took upon himself the suffering of his parents was Norbert. Often in trouble with the police, he was unable to keep any job for more than a few weeks. He spoke constantly of his feelings of guilt. Eventually he was admitted as a voluntary patient to Napsbury Hospital, where he was diagnosed as schizophrenic. He stayed at the hospital until 1949, when a Bloomsbury House visitor reported: 'He looks extremely well, but unshaven . . . he is in an open ward and has quite a lot of freedom . . . Said he only saw me because he knew I would bring a present.'

Norbert was sent back into the real world, but within weeks he had registered as a disabled person and returned to the hospital. There was talk of performing a lobotomy, a last-resort operation for schizophrenia involving the removal of tissues in the frontal lobes of the brain. But for some reason it was decided not to go ahead. Instead he was put in a hostel where a nurse could keep an eye on him. The final entry on his record card reads: 'Norbert reports regularly to the Labour Exchange, but has no intention of working. He is not easy at the hostel and it is possible that he will have to return to hospital, but at the moment he is not certifiable.'

The question of a lobotomy was debated in every case where the patient was diagnosed schizophrenic. The uncertain effects of the operation (though some remarkable results had been achieved) ruled out hasty decisions.

On at least two occasions a lobotomy was considered and rejected for Alfred, who became ill in late 1943. As a certified inmate of Friern Hospital, his behaviour stabilised periodically, keeping alive the hope that time would be the healer. But in early 1949:

> Alfred was in a very poor condition. He could only talk with the greatest effort, and then it was of an entirely irrational nature . . . If at all possible, his case should be discussed . . . to see if the decision on a lobotomy cannot be reviewed.

The operation took place but with little to show for it. Though 'physically improved, a little fatter . . . Alfred did not seem to understand what I said to him. Suddenly he tried to make some sexual advances. I had to ask the nurse to take him away . . .' Alfred remained at Friern Hospital. His file closes with routine entries on gifts of cigarettes and allocations for pocket money.

Norbert and Alfred are representative of the thirty-six young refugees held in mental hospitals in 1945. They were joined by up to a dozen others by the end of the decade but, since the records do not give a clear indication of how far treatment was effective, there can be no precise figure for the number of serious cases at any one time. All we know is that there were success stories, including at least one lobotomy.

> Max reacted exceedingly well after his operation and has been reported as good as normal two days after it all. All traces of delusion have disappeared . . . his memory is very good, he is calm and feeling secure.

More typical is the partial cure where the doctors could say that the treatment was worthwhile but the future uncertain. This is how it was for Regina who from 1942, when she was eighteen, suffered numerous breakdowns. First admitted to Maudsley Hospital with a 'sudden onset of schizophrenia' and given insulin shock treatment, she was soon sufficiently recovered to consider a return to work. But a factory job was out because she could not stand the noise, and her preference for a more intellectual activity 'is rather pitiful in view of the girl's lack of general education and the nature of her former illness'.

The Movement came to her aid by sending her on a secretarial course and finding her a part-time job with a City accountant. In 1947, when she was 23, Regina married. A month later this apparently 'happy and contented' young lady was back in hospital 'in a very confused state and confined to bed'. A visitor reported:

> At times she was very hysterical, shouting and raving; in her more sober moments she expressed gratitude for my visit and asked me to come again.

Regina was back home and expecting a baby by the end of the year. She was said to be 'strained and suspicious', but insisted she was well and did not need help. Her file closes with Regina and her family emigrating to Israel.

By the end of the war, Bloomsbury House maintained a small department of welfare workers whose job it was to care for the chronically ill. These included not only the psychiatric cases but also those suffering from tuberculosis (nineteen patients in 1945) and others confined to hospital for long periods. Led by Lola Hahn-Warburg, who herself was an indefatigable hospital visitor, the voluntary workers were supported by an impressive team of medical advisers who gave freely of their expertise. Lola Hahn-Warburg could call on the services of a neurologist 'who is at our disposal every second Thursday for a whole afternoon', a psychologist and two psychiatric workers. Seven other specialists were available for consultation. There was also a link through to Archie McIndoe, one of the finest plastic surgeons of his day, who was based at the Queen Victoria Hospital in East Grinstead, where badly burned pilots were sent for treatment. A close friend of Elaine Blond, who was later to found the Blond McIndoe Centre for Medical Research, it was not too difficult to persuade McIndoe to help where the removal of a disfigurement, usually facial, could boost a patient's confidence.

As head of the welfare department, Lola Hahn-Warburg had a wide-ranging brief. Some of the more difficult cases turned up at her office, where she had to cope without professional help.

> A boy of eighteen or nineteen came to see me. Nobody else at Bloomsbury House wanted him in the building. He was aggressive and undisciplined. I invited him in. When I was behind my desk, he jumped up suddenly, took out a knife and cut the telephone wire. Then he opened the window and started climbing out on the

ledge. I tried to remain very calm. I said to him, 'I am very unwell. I have bad kidney trouble. It is so cold in here with the window open. Will you please come back into the office?'

And he did. We talked for a long time. Eventually, I persuaded him to go with me to hospital. There was a doctor I knew who would help him get into a special home. He let me drive him in my car and gave no further trouble.

Lola kept track of patients whose personalities were as variable as the weather ('One minute Paul says he does not want his wife any more and the next he has changed his mind'), she listened to their grievances ('Josef thinks he is fit to work and look after himself; says he is being kept a prisoner . . . but he is very confused and deluded') and even mediated between doctors ('Dr Freymann said . . . it must be a genuine case of epilepsy . . . but . . . Dr Sommers feels that Regina has nothing to lose and a great deal to gain if she follows his advice re support for her floating kidney'). But the highest value was put on just being there, the willingness to sit by a bedside and to do more listening than talking, the patience with inconsistencies and sudden reversals of mood and the readiness to come back, week after week.

Nathan was seventeen and seriously ill with tuberculosis when he was taken in to Highgate Hospital in January 1942. He stayed there until his death ten years on. When his sister emigrated to Israel, the Movement introduced a visitor who called in once or twice every week. They became close friends, sharing an interest in politics and psychology.

The rewards of hospital visiting were not always as apparent:

> I saw Edda only for a very short time. Physically, she looked well and very well cared for. She started whimpering when I tried to speak to her. Suddenly she jumped up, screamed hysterically and ran off. Sister said that she is apt to slap people in the face. She thinks that she must have had very bad experience with adult people . . . She is a schizophrenic, and has deteriorated considerably in spite of the intensive treatment which she has undergone, and at present she is quite inaccessible mentally. The prognosis is unfavourable . . .

Just how much patience was needed is made clear by a story from Elaine Blond about her friend and close colleague.

Lola once told me about a girl she visited in a mental hospital. Each time Lola appeared she brought a bunch of flowers, which the girl took and held close for an hour or more. In this time she said not a single word. Even when, according to the doctors, she was showing signs of recovery, she and Lola never spoke to each other. But years later the girl, now a young woman, came to see Lola. Her greeting was a revelation. 'I shall never forget your visits', she said.

Unhappy endings were more familiar to the welfare workers. Moritz, a Polish boy born in Cologne, was a smiling, good-looking child when he arrived in June 1939. Aged thirteen, he spent two years at a Cardiff school, where he learned English, and then trained as an electrician. About the time he started work he became obsessed that he would never see his parents again; he feared that they were already dead. He was probably right. Authority, any authority, was blamed for the tragedy. Moritz antagonised his employer, who promptly sacked him, and refused help from his friends. In 1942 he was persuaded to go into hospital, where he was said to be schizophrenic. A year later he was certified insane. His letters spoke of torture, of being forced to sit alone all day, forbidden to move from his chair. It was not quite like that. Because no one had any idea of how to treat his illness, Moritz was kept in a locked ward for his own and for other patients' safety.

An entry towards the end of his record card describes Moritz as 'looking very thin and pale'. His visitor tried to talk with him, but 'discussion is difficult as he keeps repeating whatever I say'. In April 1946, Moritz was critically ill. He retreated into himself or, rather, into the past. 'He found great difficulty in saying anything, although he evidently tried very hard . . . He said a few sentences in German towards the end.'

Tuberculosis was diagnosed. Moritz died in November 1949. Elaine Blond observed that he had committed suicide by stages. Suicide in more conventional forms shows up prominently in the later records of the *Kindertransporte*, when the work of the RCM had been merged with that of the Central British Fund (CBF).

One interpretation of mental breakdown is that it is an attempt by a disturbed mind to create a breathing space for reassessment and balance; for conflicts which have been suppressed to emerge and be dealt with. Salomon, who had left Germany when he was nine, showed few signs of anything like this happening to him – although he was reported as 'somewhat unsociable' and disappeared at one stage for three days, returning well and happy.

In 1950, the final entry in his file reads:

> Mr Day of the Coroner's Court telephoned to report that Salomon . . . had been found dead by his landlady at midday. It appears that the boy had deliberately electrocuted himself and left a short note which, however, gave no indication of the whereabouts of his family in London. Advised Mr Day that there were two brothers and two sisters, in addition to the elderly parents living in London, and gave also the name and address of the boy's former foster mother, Mrs Smith.

Perhaps conflict between parents and foster parents, or religious dilemma (coming from an orthodox background, Salomon described himself as 'only liberal'), contributed – the records give little indication. Salomon was a studious boy, with no friends, who kept himself to himself.

Though leading outwardly normal lives, many from the *Kindertransporte* were still subject to emotional repercussions long into adult life. As Dorothy Hardisty wrote in her journal, '. . . such failures exist where so great an upheaval has taken place, and it was not to be expected that the Movement's records should be free from shadows.'

In 1950, the CBF visited one woman, then aged twenty-three, and her son.

> She was very keen to see me . . . [she] burst out with many different problems, jumping quickly from subject to subject. When I pointed that out to her, she said she was so excited that I came . . . she has heard that her brother in Australia . . . is suffering from schizophrenia. She identifies herself with him and . . . she fears that she might break down as well. She is still suffering from violent tempers over trifling things and wonders why she does it.
>
> She also has terrible fears and gets almost hysterical when her husband is late coming home, which happens periodically . . . the child wakes up screaming every night and shouts that there is someone there. The other night, her husband really thought so and

took with him his rifle. After a while the child calms down, but as
soon as the parents are back in bed he starts off again.

A haunted family. Like this woman's brother, there were many
who found the displacement and emotional pain overpowering.
From being able to cope (just about) with everyday life they were
tipped over the edge into breakdown, from which only a few were
able to re-emerge.

13

Divided Loyalties

*'Miss Mansfield is very upset about arrangements made
for Sigi to attend on Saturday afternoons at Synagogue, for
the boy in no way wants to give up his cubs.'*

The RCM prided itself on a broad-minded approach to religion.
This suited the collective temperament of the ruling body, which
was drawn largely from the liberal branch of Judaism, and made
sense in terms of practical politics. From the day of its foundation,
the Movement was committed to accepting help from whatever
source. If a Christian family was willing to take in a Jewish child,
then the offer was gratefully received. To have done otherwise, it
was argued, would have meant turning away young refugees
because there were no homes for them to go to.

At the beginning, a special effort was made to place orthodox
children with orthodox families, or with families prepared to
follow strict dietary rules, and to make generous allowance for
other religious observances. But resolution faded along with the
number of suitable offers. As early as April 1939 there were
reports that the orthodox community had reached the limits of its
hospitality.

'What were we then supposed to do?' Fifty years after the events,
the rhetorical question was put by Elaine Blond.

To hear some people talk, we should have told the children to stop
moaning and to make the best of it in Berlin. In fact, what we did
do was to accept as many children as we could get in – orthodox,
liberal and non-believing – on the assumption that all other prob-

lems were secondary and could be tackled, one way or another, as we went along.

This was not at all to the liking of conservative elements as represented by the Chief Rabbi's Religious Emergency Council (CRREC) and its offshoot, the Union of Orthodox Hebrew Congregations (Adath). Both organisations had as their chief promoter Rabbi Solomon Schonfeld, a brave and dedicated man who could take personal credit for bringing out some 250 children from Vienna and Berlin. But Schonfeld was also a shrewd politician whose fundamentalist views, forcefully argued, appealed to simple souls and frequently offended the orthodox establishment which he claimed to represent. Claiming to speak for the eighty per cent of *Kindertransporte* refugees who were clearly Jewish (though of these only twenty per cent were orthodox and at least fourteen per cent were non-practising), Schonfeld argued a policy of Jewish homes for Jewish children and, if this failed, for the RCM to devote its energies to raising money for hostels where religious supervision (of a strictly orthodox nature) could be guaranteed. Since this policy was never implemented, the question of what would have happened if the resources for new hostels had not been forthcoming remains hypothetical. But there were Schonfeld supporters who came perilously close to arguing that, if Jewish children could not be saved for a particular sector of the faith, they were not worth saving at all.

Failure to agree on the basic principles of caring for refugee children started a running battle between liberal and orthodox exponents of Judaism which lasted throughout the war and beyond. Early on, the RCM tried hard to play down differences with policy statements which leaned some way towards orthodoxy without limiting the freedom of the RCM to act in what it regarded as the best interests of individual children.

It is recognised that a child from an orthodox Jewish home should, if possible, live in Jewish surroundings, but each individual case must receive individual consideration from all points of view, and the policy does not involve the movement of every Jewish child from a non-Jewish home, nor the removal of a Roman Catholic child from a Protestant home, provided always that religious teaching in the child's own faith can be arranged.

When the Movement was caught out placing children in unsympathetic surroundings, remedial action was prompt. A list of Jewish children in Christian homes circulated by the Chief Rabbi brought an immediate response from the RCM's organising secretary.

> Of the list you mentioned, all but four children were not brought over by this Movement, nor had we anything to do with the placing of them. As regards the four in question, I have made arrangements for their immediate transfer to Jewish homes . . .

But there was trouble at Dovercourt camp when orthodox children refused to eat because the German rabbi who supervised the kitchen was not kosher enough for them. Anna Essinger, who was impatient with religious dogma, was decidedly unsympathetic, which led the camp's religious adviser, the Reverend Dr Grunpeter, to appeal to the Chief Rabbi for 'more tolerance and understanding of orthodox boys'. The limit to which the RCM was prepared to go in this matter was revealed in March 1939, when Grunpeter was told that his salary was to be held to £2 a week, a sum 'which will make it impossible to continue my work at the camp as resident minister'. Writing again to the Chief Rabbi, he reported rumours 'concerning the complete removal of all orthodox children' from the camp because 'they are too exacting for the authorities'.

This was true in so far as RCM workers were frequently driven to distraction by what they saw as unreasonable demands by orthodox children and their elders. Even as mild a personality as Norman Bentwich was inclined to utter strong words when an entire *Kindertransport* was held up by Schonfeld because it was scheduled to depart from Germany on the Sabbath.

Efforts were made to anticipate religious sensibilities. Parents who requested places on a *Kindertransport* were warned that orthodox foster homes were not on offer and were asked if they objected to Christian hospitality. A representative national committee for religious education and welfare was set up to establish youth clubs, organise correspondence classes, distribute literature and generally to keep contact with refugee children in Christian homes, offering Jewish hospitality at times of festival or fast and preparing boys for *Bar Mitzvah*. By December 1939 there were ninety centres for Jewish education, employing 107 teachers and serving 3000 children.

But the conservatives were not satisfied. In the months up to the outbreak of war a major cause of dispute was the status of non-practising Jews. The RCM held that, if the parents of refugee children had discouraged them from religious practices, their temporary guardians should not presume to treat them differently. Solomon Schonfeld was more inclined to regard the arrival of these children as a God-given opportunity to correct the errors of their families. He was at his strongest when he or one of his supporters discovered that the Movement's workers had misinterpreted the wishes of refugee children or their parents, or had simply allowed inadequate foster homes to escape thorough inspection.

In March 1939 the CRREC claimed that 'Not only are Jewish children with no particular religious affiliation being placed in non-Jewish homes and schools, utterly abandoned as far as their religious education is concerned, but even children who have been brought up in a religious atmosphere . . . are being callously placed in non-Jewish schools and homes, where they suffer mental torture which, in at least one case, has brought the child to the verge of a nervous breakdown.'

Their attack focused on St Margaret's School in Cricklewood, where they found ten refugee girls, three of whom had a religious background.

> These girls are obliged to do what is euphemistically called 'domestic training' and what, to put it bluntly, is domestic service, and those who are 'on duty' are forbidden to attend synagogue.

Letters were quoted from two of the girls who wanted to be moved. As for the other children, the argument raged over whether they were truly non-denominational or whether their parents had played down their Jewishness to avoid the attention of the Nazis. Who could say? Invariably, in such cases, the two sides ended up where they started with the RCM pleading moderation and a softly, softly approach.

With the start of the war, there was a period of silence on the religious front which lasted all of two weeks. Hostilities resumed when the order came to evacuate the cities. This was a blow to the defenders of orthodoxy, who had to stand by while refugee children from Jewish urban areas were shunted off to largely Christian rural areas.

'There was neither time nor machinery', wrote Dorothy Hardisty, 'to ensure that each child was placed in the right religious environment.'

Efforts were made to send Jewish teachers with Jewish evacuees (British and refugee), and a letter went out to all RCM children who had been uprooted reminding them of their faith and upbringing. One enterprising group prepared a correspondence course for *Bar Mitzvah*. But merely to recite examples of improvised education was to reveal their inadequacy. The Movement recognised this, as it also recognised that administrative pressures were working against a concerted attempt to preserve religious unity.

With the dispersal of the children over the country it was vital for the RCM to decentralise its activities. Final responsibility for such matters as deciding on the suitability of foster homes was devolved to twelve regional committees formed to coincide with the boundaries of the government-designated defence areas. Inevitably, Jewish influence on these committees was unevenly spread and at least two of them, East Anglia and the West Country, were run almost entirely by Christian volunteers.

Nor was this a short-term measure. While many British evacuees drifted back to the cities once the threat of an invasion had been lifted, refugee children were actively discouraged from returning to the urban life. This was chiefly at the behest of the Home Office who, according to Dorothy Hardisty, 'urged that in their own interest [Jewish children] should not all be placed in cities like London or Leeds where they would form a conspicuous Jewish enclave'. It was a view endorsed by the RCM, who feared the replication of the European ghettos with all that implied if the Germans did succeed in breaking through. A strong supporting argument was the supposed harmful influence of the cities on young impressionable minds. While Solomon Schonfeld and the CRREC were campaigning to remove Jewish children from Christian influences come what may, the Movement preferred that youngsters should enjoy a family upbringing in the country (associated with clean and decent living), rather than encounter the temptations of urban delinquency.

Partly in an attempt to neutralise the Schonfeld lobby, the RCM made a direct appeal to all Jewish organisations to support religious education, an appeal which led to the setting up of an Emergency Committee, on which the full range of religious interests was represented, and the appointment of Rabbi Dr van der Zyl to be responsible for the religious education of Jewish children in London. Van der Zyl, who had arrived from Germany with a *Kindertransport* in 1939, was a rare soul, a liberal who held the respect of the orthodox community. There were to be times when education was to be secondary to his role as a mediator.

Sniping between the forces of liberalism and orthodoxy showed no signs of letting up. With the RCM holding fast to its independence, offers from orthodox rabbis to take up peripatetic duties were firmly rejected. In May 1940, the RCM general secretary wrote to the Chief Rabbi, pointing out 'that our Regional Committees are autonomous and neither they nor the committees under them like interference in the arrangements they make for religious instruction'. He went on to argue against sending alien rabbis (chiefly eager volunteers from the newly-formed Council of Orthodox Rabbis from Germany, Austria and Czechoslovakia) around the country when they would need police permits every time they entered a protected area.

The refusal by the Movement to let orthodox groups share in decision-making was on the assumption that their real aim was to dominate. Hardly a week passed without Rabbi Schonfeld or his chief lieutenant and propagandist, Harry Goodman, mounting an attack against the RCM for dereliction of duty, implying that if they held the reins the race would be as good as won. As the leading opponent of orthodoxy within the RCM, Elaine Blond enjoyed nothing better than proving that her critics were less than perfect.

In February 1940 she was writing to the Chief Rabbi to report on two of Solomon Schonfeld's children who had turned up unannounced at Bloomsbury House.

> I do feel you ought to be aware that nobody seems to be supervising these boys. I am very much afraid that there are a great many cases such as these, and I intend to inform you about each one as it occurs.

A few months later, Harry Goodman responded with a full frontal attack, claiming that 9000 children in the care of the RCM had 'practically no Jewish contacts and that no effort had been made over a period of years to give these children some religious education'.

Urged by Elaine Blond to respond on behalf of the Movement, Sigmund Gestetner, whose name was well regarded in orthodox circles, wrote to the *Jewish Chronicle* to deny the charges while offering gratitude to 'those true Christians who felt it their duty to save these persecuted Jewish children'. As to claims that religious education was inadequate, he pledged the Movement 'to investigate any individual case referred to them' and promised 'to leave no stone unturned to make the most satisfactory arrangements possible'.

But how much were these promises worth? Goodman tried to find out by demanding to know how many refugee children had been baptised since they had arrived in this country. He was told that no answer was possible because no statistics were kept, though a quick glance at the minutes of the RCM executive would have shown that the conversion rate to Christianity was well into double figures.

Left to their own devices, young people were naturally inclined to veer away from any show of nonconformity. They wanted to be like others – and the others, more often than not, were middle-of-the-road Church of England. Who, for instance, could blame Edith and all the other girls in their mid-teens who fell in love with Christian boys and who lost their Jewishness along the way?

'Edith does not keep her Jewish faith, as she thinks it has brought her too much trouble', reported Rabbi van der Zyl. He wrote to her pleading that it was up to 'the young generation to rebuild what Nazism has destroyed', but Edith was not to be diverted from what she believed to be her only chance of happiness.

With boys there were pressures 'not to be difficult' at school or work in demanding special consideration. For example, there was not much sympathy for Erwin when his employer observed that he was 'clever but lazy'. According to the local RCM representative, Erwin's laziness consisted of taking advantage of his Jewish beliefs in asking for time off.

> The employer does respect the boy's beliefs . . . but they say they have had advice from a responsible Jewish person and feel that the

boy should realise he has to give in sometimes as he is working with so many non-Jewish boys.

Attitudes changed dramatically from one area to another.

Eva and Rolf lived with their foster mother, Mrs Payne, in Bromley, Kent. For three years, up to September 1942, the relationship was troublefree. Then Rolf complained to the chairman of the Bromley committee that Mrs Payne had hit him. The altercation had been caused by Rolf refusing to attend a church parade at a scout gathering. The Bromley chairman overreacted. Assuming that here was a case of attempted conversion, she kept the boy in her own house and sent a policeman and an NSPCC inspector to call on Mrs Payne, who in turn referred the dispute to her solicitors. Lola Hahn-Warburg and Rabbi van der Zyl worked on a compromise. As reported to the RCM executive in September 1942, the children would stay with Mrs Payne, continue to be members of the Guides and Scouts and to attend church parades, but to receive Jewish religious instruction and not to go to church Sunday school.

The same executive meeting discussed the problem in reverse where the RCM thought Ingeborg should be removed from her foster parents, who were failing to provide religious education, but where the local (Sheffield) committee refused to act, 'saying that they will do no more work for refugees unless it is established that their word is law'.

Pressures to conform were rarely motivated by a desire to alienate young Jews from their faith. More often than not foster parents, who were criticised for sending refugee children to Sunday school or encouraging them to eat proscribed food, were prompted by nothing more sinister than a desire to make their young guests feel at home. For those like Elaine Blond and Lola Hahn-Warburg, who spent much of their time following up complaints of proselytisation, it was a matter of acute embarrassment to have to explain to a rural vicar that joining his church choir was not necessarily the best way for a Jewish youngster to meet people, or to point out to a farmer's wife that persuading her husband to kill the fatted pig, so that her Jewish guests could enjoy a slap-up roast, was misplaced generosity.

The most difficult cases related to foster parents who were ideal in every way except the one essential. When in early 1943 there were reports that Jewish education was not being made available to four otherwise contented youngsters in the Devonshire village of Talaton, Dorothy Hardisty opened up a cautious enquiry. She wrote first to the Honiton billeting officer, suggesting that since the children had been born into orthodox families it was time for them to be moved to more appropriate surroundings. The billeting officer did not agree. As a stalwart of the established church, Lady Davidson possessed a clearly defined set of values which did not allow for the inclusion of other religions. She told Dorothy Hardisty that the children could not be disturbed. Six months later Dorothy Hardisty tried again, with a letter to Lady Davidson's successor, a Mr B. R. Dunning.

> I want to open with you once again the cases of the four young children who are evacuated to Talaton. These children come from orthodox Jewish families. The little ones had the misfortune to be driven into no-man's-land and in 1939 were brought to this country without their parents. None of us can know what has happened to the parents but we, who are interested in all the young people and children brought to this country by the Movement, hold it as our greatest hope that reunion with relatives may one day be effected. We realise that the parents are probably suffering the utmost hardships and that their religious belief will be the strongest remaining link at the moment between them and the children from whom they are parted. If they were to realise that the children were not being brought up in the orthodox manner, it would add yet more sorrow to their grievous burden.
>
> When the children first came to England, they attended the Jewish Free School in London, with which they were evacuated either late in 1939 or early 1940, so that for a time they remained in a Jewish environment. At a later date, the number of British children attending the School had fallen to such an extent that the Jewish teacher was withdrawn and these four children for some time have not received religious teaching, and have not been able to live an orthodox Jewish life.

The solution, Dorothy Hardisty suggested, was for the children to be moved to a 'properly equipped and very well run' hostel during the school terms, returning to their foster parents in the holidays. Mr Dunning was sympathetic but said, reasonably enough, that he could not force a decision on the local billeting officer (a rector's wife) or on the foster parents. A meeting was fixed for Dorothy Hardisty and E. T. Elton, a representative of orthodox Jewry, to meet the children. It began with them talking to Dorothy Hardisty alone. Immediately afterwards, she wrote up her impressions.

They are four grand youngsters. Josef is the most highly strung. He is very conscious of his Jewish birth and religion and most loyal, but he says his sister knows that their mother knows, through her, that he is living in a non-Jewish home and they do not want him moved. He wishes to have instruction and in course of time to be *Bar Mitzvah*. He corresponds with Mr Kayser of the Polish Refugee Fund, who sends him books and literature. Josef hopes to join his sister in Palestine and that his mother will go there also. He is obviously very much distressed at the thought of being moved before this can be accomplished . . .

The three girls cling most fondly to their homes. The sisters Frajdenreich say they have no one to look towards now but their foster home. Their family (six other children, apparently) just disappeared. They want Jewish instruction. Isa Scheider is in correspondence with her father in Spain — he knows she is not in a Jewish home but is satisfied . . .

They feel Jewish and are not being persuaded in any other direction. They say they know 'something', but want to know and understand more. I must repeat my impression of the scrupulous care that is being taken not in any way to introduce any non-Jewish religious instruction.

The children struck me as frank, intelligent and not just well primed. They are a credit to their foster parents — well grown, well-mannered, friendly, beautifully kept. The foster parents are quite outstanding in their care and sympathy. It was a real joy to meet such people.

The car which had brought me waited in the village. The owner driver told me a local man talked to him, telling him how all the village wanted to keep the children until they can be restored to their parents. They have been with them between four and five years and 'we want to win the fight for them', said the man.

The follow-up session with the children had both Mr Elton and Dorothy Hardisty in attendance.

We saw first the Frajdenreichs. They both said they wanted to have Jewish teaching, but to remain in their present homes. They agreed that they would go for a short visit at *Chanukah* to the Dawlish

Hostel. (Mr Elton thought of bringing them to London, but I said we must not put ourselves in the wrong by bringing evacuees to town and he agreed.) Mr Elton will try and go to see them there.

We next saw Josef Kamiel. He also would like Jewish teaching, but is very averse to leaving his foster home, even for one night. He refused Mr Elton's suggestion of a visit to Dawlish and, when Mr Elton said he must learn a great deal and be prepared for *Bar Mitzvah* and must be made ready to take his place in Palestine, he replied that his sister had said that could all come after the war. He broke down and wept. I watched him and noticed he was trembling, fidgeting with his hands and generally upset. Presently he got calmer – showed Mr Elton the literature he had received from Mr Kayser (which Mr Elton said was not much use), and was interested in a mathematical trick shown to him. On the renewal of the suggestion of a visit he again broke down. I took him out of the room and asked him what was frightening him. Josef told me, 'I've lost a home and want not to lose another. I am frightened. I had Nazi bayonets behind me. I can't bear it – I can't bear it.' The boy was in a very distressed state.

The upshot was an unequivocal recommendation from Mr Elton: 'These children have got to be moved to Jewish homes.' Dorothy Hardisty was more circumspect. Noting that 'Josef Kamiel's case will require the most careful handling and that the exercise of the smallest amount of pressure would be dangerous', she urged that arrangements should be made for the children to visit Jewish hostels or homes for festivals and fasts, and that a well-qualified teacher should visit at least once a week to give instruction.

Her view was endorsed by the RCM, leaving Mr Elton to persevere with his more radical proposals. He did not stand a chance, as Paula Frajdenreich made clear when she responded on behalf of all four children to an invitation to visit London to see for themselves what it would be like living in an orthodox hostel.

I'm sorry that we won't be coming. It would be the worst time to come to London as the Second Front will be starting soon. And we are asked not to travel at Easter. We were taken away from our parents and put with strangers in London. Then, when we had begun to settle down, we were put down here. And now you want us to go with strangers when we have been settling for four years. So we should be very pleased if you would leave us alone and not give us any more invitations. I am pleased with our lessons.

We next hear of the Talaton children in May 1946, when they were the subject of an inquiry by the Board of Deputies. The reason for such high-level interest was the much publicised report that three of the children had been baptised. The RCM held back from giving evidence, but it is clear from the main findings of the inquiry that Dorothy Hardisty's recommendations had received, at best, a half-hearted follow-up. The Board of Deputies did not criticise the foster parents, who were described as 'devoted Christians and regular church attendants', but had harsh words for the local Jewish community, small as it was, for the failure to 'follow up the cases at the relevant time'. It is difficult not to conclude that it would have been an unequal battle.

The chances of transferring young people to Jewish hostels were greatest when foster parents set about inculcating Christian values with a sledgehammer. Thus Edgar was only too happy to depart from a Methodist family who 'insisted on him attending church on Sundays three times, and various weekly meetings'. But Ursula had no wish to leave her Christadelphian foster mother, even though she did have to go to Sunday school. Everything else about her home she liked very much and, according to one RCM visitor, she was 'well instructed in the Jewish religion'.

Orthodox critics were liable to generalise. All Jewish children who shared a home with a Christian family were at risk, they argued; but they were frequently proved wrong, as in the case of Paul Kohn who was taken in by a Strict Baptist minister.

> The Rev Morton and his wife had no children of their own. They lived at 'The Manse', a few doors away from the Zion Chapel. Our new home was a modest house with narrow, rickety stairs to our bedroom, a small kitchen and scullery, a breakfast room, and the study where Mr Morton, as we were told to call him, would read, write and edit *Cheering Words*, a publication posted to all Strict Baptist congregations in the country, smoke his pipe and occasional cigar and play chess with me . . .
>
> On the very first day, we explained that we would not eat meat and that all cooking for us had to be done in separate dishes. From then on, Mr Morton went out of his way to learn the intricacies of Orthodox Jewish observance from the Jewish teachers who were now in the town. Jews had never lived in the small Fenland town of Chatteris before. Eugen and I were never asked to go to chapel, but we were expected to attend all the Jewish services that took

place in the separate chapel hall which Mr Morton willingly made available.

One day, some ultra-Orthodox Jews arrived at the Morton's front door. They had come to return me to the fold. They were very insistent that I go with them and I was extremely apprehensive. Mr Morton informed them that only my parents could decide about my future, and until then I would stay put. He wrote to them about the visit, and the answer from Haifa was clear: 'If you will have him, then our son shall stay in your care until the war is over.'

Equally contented with his Christian foster family was Ya'acov Friedler who, with two friends, faced the same agonised conflict of loyalties as Paul Kohn but chose the other way of resolving it.

One afternoon, as we were doing our homework in the parlour and Mrs Crook was darning socks, we were surprised by an unexpected visitor. A rabbi, dressed in the East European style, with a long dark coat, a large black hat, and a long grey beard. The three of us had never seen a rabbi like that before.

He turned out to be a very gentle man and in his quiet way explained that he had come from London on a mission to return us to the fold of the Jewish people. He had heard about the two Jewish refugee boys living in the country among the gentiles, cut off from all contacts with Judaism. He had a long talk with Mrs Crook and before he left promised to return, which he did several times during the next few weeks. He managed not only to arouse feelings of guilt in Solly and myself but to convince Mrs Crook and Vic that it was their duty to help us return to Judaism, heartbroken though they were at the thought of parting with us.

We had in fact been quite cut off from all things Jewish in Frome, where there was no Jewish community and, of course, no synagogue. At school there had been an instructor in Jewish religion, but he had left shortly before my own arrival. He had left a lasting impression but unfortunately not a very inspiring one, both on the very few Jewish boys in school and our gentile classmates. They still vividly remembered and frequently repeated for their own amusement how, on meting out punishment to an unruly boy, he had qualified it with 'God knows, I don't want to do this to you, but you drive me beyond the limits of human endurance.' Of all the lofty precepts of Judaic thought he was to have instilled in us, this is the phrase everybody remembered and I remember it still, though it was handed down to me at second hand.

After much persuasion we agreed that the rabbi from London

see our headmaster about us, and, in a long talk, the latter agreed that it would be the right thing for us to return to a Jewish environment, provided we were convinced we should. The two of us could hardly decide anything else.

The religious dispute was roughest when the missionary factor came into play. That deliberate alienation was attempted is undeniable, though whether conversion from orthodox to liberal Judaism and from Judaism to Christianity was as widespread as the Chief Rabbi's Religious Emergency Council claimed is open to serious question.

Nobody was ever under any misapprehension of the true purpose of organisations like the Christian Jewish Alliance and the Barbican Mission. As early as April 1939, the Chief Rabbi was sounding off against their activities, in particular those of the Barbican Mission who 'have brought to this country over a hundred Jewish children from Czechoslovakia'. He continued, 'It is their intention to baptise them. There is just a possibility of rescuing these unfortunate children if alternative homes or hostels can be found for them without delay.'

A quick response to his appeal was not matched by the willingness of the Barbican Mission to cooperate. Short-cutting the usual channels, the Chief Rabbi cabled Lord Gorell.

> Have just been informed that obstruction exists in way of transfer of children from Barbican Mission to the homes provided for by me. You are doubtless aware that following representations by me arrangements were completed with Bloomsbury House for the removal of the children four weeks ago. May I be advised of any change of policy.

To which Lord Gorell replied:

> No change of policy. Doing all we can. Awaiting Home Office action.

But the Home Office was unwilling to intervene when there was no evidence that the children were being forced to do anything they or their parents would have repudiated. The Davidson family who, after the evacuation, ran the Barbican Mission from a large country house near Exeter, made no secret of their missionary zeal. More to the point, they could produce letters from parents agreeing to the baptism of their children. No doubt some, if not all, of these documents were obtained under a form of duress – the signatories wanted their youngsters out of Prague and were ready to grasp at any opportunity. But this was not an argument the Home Office or the RCM were eager to pursue. Endorsing a campaign to save young Jews from Christianity was not liable to be well received by the church-going public, including many hard-working supporters for the refugee cause, not to mention a high proportion of Conservative voters.

There was also the question of the legal status of the RCM, which was not resolved until 1944 when the Guardianship Act weighted the scales in favour of the Movement. Until then, foster parents who were not easily overawed and were not acting criminally could defy Bloomsbury House with impunity.

Consequently, the Barbican Mission was left to its own devices for most of the war. It was not until March 1945 that Dorothy Hardisty took advantage of the Guardianship Act to insist on a tour of inspection. By then the Mission housed less than a dozen refugee children who were still under age.

First impressions were not encouraging.

> The house is in a very remote spot. Outside it is depressing-looking – no flowers – neglected grass and shrubs.
>
> The door was opened by an elderly and rather untidy woman to whom I handed the letter of introduction Lord Gorell had written for me. The door was pushed to, but not closed. Mr Bryce Gibson thought this an advance on the occasion when he had tried to gain access. Presently Mrs Davidson came and ungraciously asked if we would like to see the house. Craddock House had been bought just before the outbreak of war with the intention that it should form a country home. It was rented by the Mission. It is in poor repair – floorboards broken – in places makeshift repairs have been made with the lids of tin biscuit boxes, roughboard, etc. The dormitories are not overcrowded and the bedding was quite reasonably clean. The furnishing is very sparse – not enough wardrobes, etc., for the clothing – no floor covering. There are two bathrooms – adequately clean – a downstairs cloakroom and hand basin where the garden dirt is removed.

After this depressing start, actually meeting the children came as a pleasant surprise.

The youngsters are alert, friendly, healthy-looking. They were in holiday clothes but they were clean and there was a general air of wellbeing. Most of the children are still at Tiverton Grammar School, where they seem to be receiving a good education. Their English is excellent and they have plenty of confidence and seem well adjusted. Only one of the girls is employed in the house. There is training in view for the future for all.

As regards religion, almost all have already been baptised and others intend to be. Mrs Davidson told me that she wished it to be quite clearly understood that theirs was a Mission to the Jews and they were bent on conversion.

After listing four children needing special attention – two serious illnesses and two cases where attempted conversion had met with strong resistance – Mrs Hardisty concluded:

There are certain cases which need action and these are mentioned below. To sum up in general: I do not think we could raise any complaint as to the housing and general care so far as our children are concerned. All Hostels are in need of repair and this house is a temporary home taken when the Mission evacuated. Educationally, our children have been well looked after. Some are being sent to the University. There has been no shirking in this direction. Training for a proper career is being arranged for all. The great criticism is that our machinery has been used for the purpose of the conversion from Judaism. I hope Lord Gorell will write and ask to see copies of correspondence in which it is alleged parents gave permission. I have no doubt it exists but it would be satisfactory to know its form. The children have for six years had strictly Christian missionary teaching. Some were, I think, baptised before they came to Britain. Several intend themselves to become missionaries.

Should the Movement have done more? The question has to be referred to those who originally accepted offers of help from the Mission. One of these was Nicholas Winton, who was much praised for his part in the rescue of Jewish children from Prague. Looking back, he does not regret his alliance with the Davidsons.

I knew, the Chief Rabbi knew, and the Barbican Mission obviously knew, that these children were going to be turned into Christians. That didn't worry me in the slightest. What is better: a converted Jew or a dead Jew? But the Chief Rabbi and others didn't see it like that and they put a lot of pressure on me. They came to see me and I told them that anybody who guarantees a child I will accept.

As the war progressed, there was a discernible shift of sympathy towards Christian families whose concept of fostering Jewish children did not extend to providing a Jewish education. The tone was set in late 1939 by the Christian Council, to which was affiliated the Church of England for Non-Aryan Christians. As chairman of this committee, Bishop George Bell turned to the Archbishop of Canterbury for guidance on how best to provide for Jewish children who were cut off from their own people. He had in mind the possibility of writing to the clergy about the need for delicate handling of any cases they might encounter, but the Archbishop was not convinced. In his view, the clergy were well aware of the problem and could be relied upon to act wisely on their own initiative.

Thereafter, the Church refrained from direct comment on fostering until, as it were, the problem turned in on itself and there were worries from Christian families that Jewish children who had been with them for several years might be removed on religious grounds. The matter was raised at a Christian Council meeting in December 1943, just before the Guardianship Act entered the statute book. Did the new law mean that the appointed guardian could overrule the wishes of foster parents? If so, there was a warning of a probable backlash of anti-Semitism. Lord Gorell for the RCM poured oil. 'A solution will be found that is workable', he said. 'There is no cause for alarm.'

The Church Council was satisfied with these and similar assurances, at least for the time being. Not so their colleagues in Scotland, where the Christian Council, claiming to speak for all Scottish churches, wanted to give positive encouragement to foster parents to promote Christian values. Wrote the Rev Robert Smith:

> The policy of the Movement seems to involve not only a regrettable attitude of distrust as between Jews and Christians, but also the perpetuation of religious neglect. Guardians who cannot influence the religious views of children will find the task of normal education in the home very difficult, if not impossible.

The opposing case was contained in a report on Jewish education commissioned by the Emergency Committee. It spoke of a 'sense of frustration emerging in non-Jewish families' where refugee children had received a Christian upbringing and, consequently, 'feel bitter because they feel that their own people have forgotten them'.

The RCM held back, fearing that any move would only serve to cause more trouble. Inactivity, it was argued, was the safest policy. Feeble excuses for falling behind in religious education appeared in the children's record cards with increasing frequency.

> Miss Mansfield is very upset about arrangements made for Sigi to attend on Saturday afternoons at synagogue, for the boy in no way wants to give up his cubs.

> . . . .at the moment Eva is taking her School Certificate, so has no time for religious education.

The Movement did cooperate with a Christian Council survey of Jewish children who had been baptised since they arrived in Britain, but no figures were released. When the Chief Rabbi asked to be let in on the secret he was told simply that 'the number of genuine baptism cases appear to be small'. The larger category of less genuine cases included children who had converted 'whilst residing with parents who are in this country, after attending church in Germany' and 'after a previous education indifferent to anything Jewish'. Pressed by the Chief Rabbi for more detail, the head of the survey revealed that he was given access to RCM records only 'after an undertaking that no names would be disclosed to any authority outside the Movement'.

As one who was inside the Movement, Rabbi van der Zyl was able to follow up on cases where there was reason to think that a religious conversion was not undertaken freely. But while there are on file numerous examples of van der Zyl being sidestepped or overruled, there are no recorded instances of a youngster backtracking on a conversion. At most, van der Zyl exercised delaying tactics. When in December 1942 seventeen-year-old Barbara declared a wish to be baptised, he went to see her at her foster parents' home in Birmingham to urge a period of reflection. The story is taken up by an RCM visitor.

> 17.12.42: Barbara has been made to understand that in a few months' time she should leave her present foster parents and take a job in

Birmingham, where she will have an opportunity for other contacts and a broader outlook.

23.3.43: Visited her home. She is living with very cultured and agreeable people. They are all taking a tremendous intellectual interest in their religion and are in constant touch with the vicar. They have assured us that Barbara will take no steps towards changing her religion.

4.9.44: To Dr van der Zyl about her step to change her religion. We cannot refuse the consent.

26.11.44: Letter to Mrs Hardisty stressing that there are very few Jews in Oswestry.

16.5.44: Letter from Mrs Hardisty informing us that Lord Gorell feels it would not be in the best interest of Barbara to refuse consent to her baptism.

23.7.45: Letter to Dr van der Zyl informing him that Barbara has delayed being baptised because of the possibility of contact with her parents. She will wait until she is twenty-one.

While Barbara was in the religious divide she was joined by Frieda who, having declared her intention of becoming a Sunday school teacher in the Methodist church, was persuaded by van der Zyl to talk to her rabbi. He might as well have saved his breath. It took close on three months to set up a meeting, at which Frieda was given the clear impression that it was illegal to change her religion. When a report was fed back to Bloomsbury House, the Movement, having already decided that, 'considering the girl's age and her very determined attitude, there is not anything that can be done', immediately disassociated itself from a case 'so badly mishandled'. Frieda continued a Methodist. In 1947 she emigrated to Argentina.

For Rabbi Schonfeld and his allies in the CRREC, the frustration of failing to turn back the slow but perceptible drift away from orthodoxy, indeed, away from Judaism, was compounded by the knowledge that the tactics of the fanatics on the far right were bringing results. Regional reports to Bloomsbury House with, occasionally, copies to the Home Office, showed that at least three extremist groups were heavily engaged in enticing youngsters away from liberal institutions to join orthodox hostels. Frequent complaints were made against Rabbis Weingarten and Munk, the first based near Bletchley, the second in Tylers Green, but the prize for outrageous behaviour went to Rabbi Schneider, whose efforts to swell the attendance of his hostel in Upper Clapton Road, north London, fell only a little way short of kidnapping.

Two institutions which suffered particularly from Schneider's attentions were the Jewish Boys' Home and the Jewish Free School in Ely. Old boys of the school remember a tightly disciplined regime, not at all the begetter of slack living that Schneider seemed to imagine, although the tone of religious education was distinctly moderate. According to the headmaster, Dr E. Bernstein, the first clear case of enticement was recorded as early as September 1939.

> Markus Turkl had been evacuated only a month when he disappeared from Ely, and was soon after found to be living at the *Yeshivah* [of Rabbi Schneider]. He was not quite fourteen.
>
> In February 1940 Tibor Weiss – not quite twelve at the time – disappeared from the Home, and was soon after found to be living at 160 Upper Clapton Road; he is living at the *Yeshivah* at the present moment. In May of this year a youth of about eighteen – a pupil of *Yeshivah* – came to the Home and asked me if he could convey a message to Emanuel Surkiss, which he brought, so he alleged, from the sister of the boy. I allowed him to see Surkiss and had to leave just then myself. In my absence the youth and Surkiss asked our rabbi for permission 'to go for a walk', which permission was granted. The 'walk' was a walk to the railway station, when the youth took the train to London with Surkiss. Emanuel Surkiss was taken straight to the *Yeshivah*, where he is living at the time of writing. Surkiss was just under fourteen at the time.
>
> On 13 July of this year a letter was received by Eugen Lustig from Tibor Weiss, enclosing 30/- in notes and proposing that Lustig should leave the Home and take up residence at the *Yeshivah*. The letter was written in Hungarian in order to preserve secrecy. Both letter and translation were supplied to me by Lustig. I sent the 30/- by registered post to Rabbi Schonfeld, and begged him to visit Rabbi Schneider and point out the seriousness of these persistent efforts to entice the boys away from the Home to the *Yeshivah*. Rabbi Schonfeld wrote to tell me that he found Rabbi Schneider too fanatically disposed to be able to reason with him. Eugen Lustig eventually disappeared.

At this point, Dr Bernstein decided on direct action.

> Accordingly, on Tuesday 30 September, I went to London and called at the *Yeshivah* at 160 Upper Clapton Road. I was received by a young refugee girl, who acted as housekeeper . . . I asked if

Eugen Lustig had arrived there the previous night, and was now in residence. I was told that Lustig was not in the house at the time, and I then asked to see Surkiss. Surkiss duly appeared and, as he was in a state of panic, I reassured him by saying I had no interest in his case, but wished to know the whereabouts of Lustig. He willingly offered to show me where Lustig was, but several young men appeared and refused to allow him to accompany me. Surkiss then told me that Lustig was at the Church Street Baths. I set out for the Baths but, as I noticed several groups of young men following me, I took a circuitous route and eventually hailed a taxi. When I arrived at the Baths, the attendant informed me that the boy had just left. While waiting outside the Baths, a party of the young men, who had been following, came up and began an altercation.

I stated the legal position with regard to the boy, but in no way was able to pacify the young men. Eventually a warning was received from a policeman, who had been watching our dispute, that we should all be arrested for obstruction. I accordingly prepared to ride off in the taxi to the *Yeshivah* but the whole crowd tried to force their way into the car. I managed with difficulty to prevent this, and so travelled to the *Yeshivah* with the young men in hot pursuit.

The headmaster eventually managed to see Rabbi Schneider, who promised to send the Lustig boy back to Ely. When the boy failed to appear, Dr Bernstein returned to the hostel, this time with a Mr Springer of the Czech Refugee Trust, who demanded to see Eugen.

The Rabbi left the room with the intention of having the boy searched for. There was a great hubbub outside, and after much clamour a young man pushed his way into the room and demanded our business. After some explanation had been given by Mr Springer, we requested the young man to withdraw, which he did after much persuasion. I then realised that any arrangement with the Rabbi was likely to prove unsatisfactory, and a request was again made to the Rabbi to have the boy produced. Further clamour followed, and the same young man again forced his way in, and was with even greater difficulty prevailed upon to withdraw. I finally put it to the Rabbi that very great trouble could easily be avoided if he would allow us to see the boy. I made the offer to call next day alone and speak with the boy in his presence. He agreed to this course.

But when the meeting did take place it was with a gathering of onlookers, none of whom were very sympathetic to Dr Bernstein.

> I called at 3.30 next day, Monday 6 October. The housekeeper told me that the Rabbi was asleep. I asked her to tell the Rabbi I would call at 7.00. I did so, and was taken by the Rabbi to his *Succah*. I begged him to honour his promise to allow me to speak to the boy. He very unwillingly went to the *Beth Hamidrash* with the intention of bringing the boy to me. He did not return, but two young men came instead with a message that I should go to the *Beth Hamidrash*. I went along and there was asked to speak with the boy in the *Beth Hamidrash*. As the hall was filled with a great crowd, I declined to be put on parade and made a public show, possibly receiving some sort of censure or at least appealed to in some religious manner. After various attempts to persuade me to enter the *Beth Hamidrash* it was finally agreed to bring the boy outside.
>
> It was unfortunately dark by now, otherwise the scene would not have reflected great credit on the young men of the *Yeshiva*. Lustig appeared, strongly held by arms and shoulders by at least eight young men. A huge crowd followed – all jeering and apparently in high fettle. I addressed a few words to Lustig himself . . . and pointed out to the great crowd of young men that not a very seemly exhibition had been given by them, and that this jeering was utterly un-English. I called Lustig to testify that, if the position had been reversed and the Rabbi had been a visitor to our school in Ely, not so much as a suggestion of distaste would have been seen, let alone so humiliating a spectacle.

The story remains incomplete. There are no records to tell us what happened to Eugen Lustig and his friends, or to Dr Bernstein's appeal to the Home Office to revoke Rabbi Schneider's licence to run a hostel. But if the campaign against the Jewish Free School was allowed to continue, it must have come up against stronger defences.

Frequent references to the school make no mention of any further 'disappearances', though elsewhere in the records there are numerous accusations of child snatching from liberally inclined foster parents and hostels.

Drawing back from the extremism of Rabbi Schneider and his kind, the CRREC and Adath grumbled away, ineffectually for the most part, until 1944. It was then that they went public with a vitriolic attack on the 'extreme liberals' who were said to be dominating the RCM. The occasion for the publication of *The Child-Estranging Movement* was the entry of the Guardianship Act on to the statute book. This allowed for the appointment of a legal guardian for the 4000 or so RCM children who were under twenty-one and who were not with adopted or real parents.

Pressure for the change had started two years earlier, when the true meaning of Hitler's final solution made it evident that most of the refugee children were, or would soon be, orphans. Then, at least 8500 RCM youngsters were under twenty-one. Inevitably there were problems. Abiding by the letter of the law meant that a young refugee could not undergo surgery because no one was empowered to give consent. Similarly, the Movement was on shaky ground whenever it acted against foster parents who were regarded as unsatisfactory – one of the reasons, or, as Rabbi Schonfeld would have argued, one of the excuses, for not taking a stronger line on religious incompatibility.

At first, the orthodox lobby favoured a reform of the law, hoping thereby to strengthen its own hand against backsliders. But when it became clear that the Movement was unshakeably liberal and, worse still, that the only candidate for legal guardian was Lord Gorell, the Christian chairman of the RCM, the knives were sharpened. Schonfeld's idea of a compromise on the Guardianship Act was the setting up of a new body, weighted towards orthodoxy, to take over the running of the Movement. It was a non-starter. A more realistic approach was made by Rabbi Hertz, the Chief Rabbi who suggested a joint guardianship with Rabbi Maurice Swift, the orthodox representative on the RCM Central Committee sharing the responsibility with Lord Gorell. At the same time, he assured the Home Secretary that, should Lord Gorell be appointed as sole guardian, friendly cooperation would be maintained. 'I feel sure of Lord Gorell's impartiality', he wrote. Rabbi Schonfeld could not have been less sure, but he told the Board of Deputies:

> I am quite prepared to accept any solution of this problem which the Chief Rabbi and you consider quite satisfactory. I cannot promise acquiescence in a compromise solution forced upon you by other bodies . . .

Deputations to the Home Office concentrated on 'the necessity of ensuring that in the appointment of a guardian due attention should be paid to the wishes of the parent or nearest relative of the ward' on religious matters, and that the appointment of a guardian would be revoked on the application of a parent. Both points, argued the Home Office, were covered by common law or by specific provision in the bill. This apparently satisfied Rabbi Hertz, who made no further objection to Lord Gorell as the father-figure of the RCM, while hoping that 'a way may have been found for removing genuine orthodox children from non-Jewish homes'. He added, 'Five years after Anglo-Jewry failed to answer the challenge of refugee children reaching our shores, it seems almost impossible to achieve more.'

Schonfeld disagreed, as the circulation of the *Child-Estranging Movement* to all rabbis, ministers and wardens of Jewish congregations made abundantly clear. But Rabbi Hertz was right. It was all too late. Gradually, the Chief Rabbi distanced himself from Schonfeld and from Dayan Swift, who fought a lonely battle for conservatism on the RCM's central committee. For him, the last straw was when fifteen-year-old Susanne Karpathi declared her intention of becoming a Catholic. The exchange of letters between Dayan Swift and Lord Gorell tells all. Dayan Swift went first:

> Your decision to consent to the handing over of a young Jewish orphan of fifteen years of age to another Faith, in spite of the report of the Rev Fabricant and the sworn statement of Mr Usher Blumstein, has completely shaken my confidence in you as Guardian of our Jewish children. In the circumstances I must ask you to accept this letter as an intimation of my resignation from the Movement unless, of course, I hear from you that you are prepared to withdraw your consent to the baptism of this child. In the event of not hearing from you within the course of a week, I shall take it that you accept my resignation. It will then be necessary for me to make a statement in the press and present a report on this case to the religious and lay leaders of the Jewish community.

To which Lord Gorell replied:

> I am naturally sorry that you should be resigning from the Executive of the Movement, though I felt that your breach of confidence in respect of Bishop Craven's letter and your subsequent discourtesy, indeed hostility, to him at our last Executive made that almost inevitable. I had hoped that, in spite of occasional differences of view – astonishingly few when all these years and all the thousands

of children are considered – we should have all been enabled to continue to work together to the end. But that, clearly, is not to be. Of course, I cannot change my decision because you will resign if I do not. I gave it, quite impartially, as the decision in the best interests of my ward, after a most careful study of all the facts and after a long personal talk with that ward. I accept your resignation accordingly.

I am puzzled and pained, I must say, at the lack of appreciation you show, and have long shown, for the work of the Movement. I do not remember your ever saying a word in acknowledgement of the unstinted care and loving kindness which, for years on end, Christian foster parents have, in hundreds of cases, lavished utterly disinterestedly upon Jewish refugee children. Always you have shown suspicion and even rancour, and now in this case – the very first of its kind I have had to deal with in all the nine years of my Chairmanship – the moment I am compelled by the facts to differ from you, you tell me your confidence in me is 'completely shaken'. Very well; so be it. I accept that also, grieved though it makes me.

As for the formal declaration from Mr Blumstein, I can only say that, as far as I am aware (and I have gone very deeply into the case), he has never in all the years of Susanne's life in this country made any attempt at all to see or help her or taken any interest in her whatsoever.

I note that you intend 'to make a statement in the press and to present a report to the religious and lay leaders of the Jewish community'. I must therefore ask that it be a complete one including this letter.

There was not much more to be said. The case of Susanne Karpathi was settled in early 1948. By then there were less than fifty Jewish refugee children in Christian homes. The rest had grown up and moved away. They could make their own decisions.

14

After the War

> '*I came over at the age of three and a half. I still don't know where I belong. I was brought up in the Midlands. I went to a Christian school. I was no longer considered German, I was not considered English. I certainly wasn't Jewish – my Jewish background was not nurtured. I am neither German nor English. I am neither German nor Jew. I would like to know what is my identity?*'

There was no going back. Even the few *Kindertransporte* veterans who were reunited with their parents felt a natural revulsion against returning to the homes of their early childhood. Aside from the wish to block out unhappy memories, those who had spent their formative years in Britain were ill-equipped to make a living in Germany. Many could no longer speak German.

So what did happen to the ten thousand? The RCM personal files are frustratingly incomplete. No attempt was made to keep contact with those who, by age or marriage, put themselves beyond the reach of the Guardianship Act. The entries signing off each ward leave the reader wanting more than the news that this girl is *thinking* of emigrating to Israel or that boy is *hoping* to be an engineer.

The nearest the RCM came to trying to find out what had become of their charges after they had emerged from puberty was in March 1950, when they carried out a follow-up survey on a random sample of one hundred youngsters (the first ten files of each of the first ten letters of the alphabet). Of these, a surprisingly high proportion (sixteen per cent) turned out to be Christian, though whether by birth or conversion is not made clear. More interestingly, only thirty had re-emigrated, with fifteen going to America, seven to Israel, four to Australia and another four elsewhere. Bearing in mind that the ten thousand were only let in on the assumption that they would soon travel on to less populous lands, the emigration score is surprisingly low. But government policy had evolved during the war. Instead of too many workers chasing too few jobs, the fear now was of too many jobs for the available labour force. The demands of the economy put a new gloss on the claims of refugees to be treated like ordinary people. The breakthrough came in 1946 with an open invitation from the Home Office:

> Foreigners are not normally naturalised in this country while they are under the age of 21, but as many of the young people who were driven out of their own country and are now in the United Kingdom have no fathers or mothers, the Home Secretary has decided that such young people who have no parents living may, if they wish, apply for certificates of naturalisation, provided they are 15 years of age or over, but under 21, and have been living in the United Kingdom for at least 5 years.

But caution was urged.

> Consider carefully whether you want to be a British subject. It is a serious step to take and you should only take it if the British way of life appeals to you and you are sure that you want to live in British territory and to be a loyal subject of the King.

There was an enthusiastic response from the RCM teenagers who had put down roots, by settling into a job, for example, or marrying and starting their own families. Indeed, early marriage was already a well-established practice for RCM girls who could by this means circumvent the unamended naturalisation laws. It did not always work out, as a local press story for December 1942 reveals.

> With tears in her eyes, Inge Herz implored Hendon magistrates yesterday not to send her to a Jewish hostel. She said she was not religious and did not want anything to do with any Jewish movement.
>
> Herz, who came to this country in 1939, was charged with being

an alien, absenting herself from her address in Hendon without a permit, and with failing to notify her change of address . . .

Defendant said she was to have married an Englishman and had got a special licence, but when she found he had three convictions she decided not to marry him. She believed that if she had married him there would have been no need to notify her change of address as then she would have been English.

There was now another man whom she had known for some years and who wanted to become engaged to her . . .

Theoretically, the marriage of any RCM youngster under twenty-one was dependent on the consent of Bloomsbury House. The official line was to hold out against a liaison which did not fit the conventions. But that was not always possible.

Mary told me she is going to marry the father of the child. He has been most constant in his visits and is making arrangements for Mary . . .

Bloomsbury House was sympathetic, even though a year later Mary and her friend were still unmarried.

Mary came to discuss the immediate future. She has given notice at her present place as she cannot cope with the work. She has to cook for a family of four adults and six children. We will try to fix up a home for her child at Bedford – Mary will then try to find a job near the child. We tried to impress upon her the importance of a solicitor's agreement for the father to sign . . . Her attitude towards the child's father is very protective; she describes him as generous and solicitous but very much against interference from committees and any legal steps. Mary has an appealing nature but is very weak with rather vague ideas of how best to cope with life. Their relationship . . . has no solid foundation at all.

There were some sad outcomes in the inevitable love affairs with American and Canadian servicemen. Ruth, who had an illegitimate child in 1946, hoped to keep her baby while at the same time planning to marry a man she had never met before:

She says her fiancé is an American and is coming to England on leave at the end of October. Ruth has never seen this young man and only knows him through a four-month correspondence. We warned Ruth against taking any action . . .

Some months later, the mysterious American had faded out of the picture. Ruth arranged to have her baby adopted by a couple in Pinner. 'She misses him very much but realises it is best in his interests for him to have a settled home.'

Cilly also conducted a courtship by letter, but at least she had a passing acquaintance with her boyfriend, whom she had met in Hamburg before the war. Early in 1945 she tracked him down in Brazil.

> Cilly wondered if it would be possible for her to re-emigrate to Brazil [as she] is most anxious to join her boyfriend.

But her visa was denied. Her last throw was to explore the possibility of marriage by proxy as a way of gaining Brazilian nationality, but within a few weeks she had given up the idea and was corresponding with another boyfriend in Holland.

Paula had a history of being dull and backward at school. In 1944, after she had given birth to an illegitimate child, she was sent to Holloway for petty theft. The next year, she was in prison again, for what was described, curiously, as pro-Nazi talk, and pregnant again. Her second baby was adopted at the age of three months. Paula was then sent to the Lucy Gaster home at Watford, where she worked as a machinist. Her behaviour was said to be disruptive, not least because she made no secret of her intention to marry a man who was already married. Bloomsbury House took a sympathetic and enlightened view of her predicament:

> Paula called with the man she wants to marry . . . He will not be free to marry until September, when his divorce is being heard. Paula left £1 towards the keep of Brian [her son] . . .
>
> Paula's fiancé called. Had a long talk with him. He now knows of Paula's previous shortcomings. He was aware only of Brian but has since learnt of Paula's second baby . . . He says however that he is so fond of her that he is willing to forgive her and that he hopes they will start their life on a sound and frank basis of mutual trust . . .

There were other happy endings for the mothers of illegitimate children:

Regina called with her son Uri and informed me that she would be getting married shortly to Gerhard, whom she has known for many years. Gerhard and Regina have applied to Bunce Court school for employment. Gerhard was originally a scholar there and Regina knows Dr Friedmann [the headmaster who took over from Anna Essinger] very well.

In some cases, where couples urgently wanted (or needed) to marry, the Union of Jewish Women was able to provide a much-needed dowry:

Helga was married yesterday to the father of her baby. We gave them lunch afterwards. Miss Abrahams has managed to get a dowry of £50 from the Union of Jewish Women. This will be given to Helga at once. Helga is living under very bad conditions and is desperately anxious to find a flat or rooms.

Many young people were drawn to those of similar backgrounds. Living in Belsize Park, Rosina Domingo was not far away from a hostel for refugees from the Spanish Civil War.

One thing led to another. A lot of us married Spaniards. There were language difficulties but we had things in common . . .

My husband had had a terrible time. After fighting in the Civil War he escaped to France and was put in a camp where he had to live through the winter. Then he joined the Foreign Legion (it was that or die of cold) and when the war started he took part in the Norway campaign. When Norway fell, he got back to France and was evacuated from Dunkirk.

In London, the only job he could get was in demolition; he had no work permit. He got an extra 2d an hour by being a top man, working at the top of a building that was coming down. It was dangerous and many fell. But he was glad of the work.

Those like Thea Rudzinski went a step further and married victims of the concentration camps.

He was a survivor. There were eight in his family and only he and one sister had survived. He was in Buchenwald and Shleiben and Skarzysko and was liberated by the Russians from Theresienstadt. He has talked quite a bit to me about it. The memories can never go out of his mind. After hearing what he says I am amazed that

he can live normally. I am afraid that in his old age . . . perhaps it
will all come out. It has got to come out somewhere.

Margaret Olmer, too, married a camp survivor.

> My husband is very marked from the camps. He had to fill bombs
> with sulphur. If he had not judged it to the second he would have
> had molten sulphur all over him. There was no industrial clothing.
> He was very ill when he came out, but he is a clever person and he
> picked himself up.
>
> It was hard for me, having escaped all that, having to sleep with
> someone who has terrible nightmares. I thought fate had caught up
> with me and I was being punished for the fate I had escaped. I didn't
> have to marry someone from the camp. He wasn't the only boy
> who asked me. I think it was self-guilt.

Bloomsbury House was especially cautious on the question of
mixed marriage, more for internal political reasons than for any
strong feeling that religious compatibility was essential to a successful alliance.

> Leo says that he now has to marry urgently as the girl is pregnant
> in the third month. As he has no savings but needs at least some
> money to set up a kind of home, even in a furnished room, he asked
> for a loan of £10. We are not in a position to give him a loan and
> strongly advised him not to incur debts to begin a married life,
> especially when he mentioned that he wanted money to buy a
> wedding ring. He did not wish his married sister to know, as she
> was not in favour of his marriage. For the same reason, he could
> not ask her for financial help. The girl's parents are not aware of
> her condition yet. He was determined to marry the girl, whom he
> has known for two years and whom he says he loves dearly. He
> wandered out very disappointed.

But not all practical help was denied. Bloomsbury House offered
Leo the loan of a pram.

The change in the naturalisation laws did help to cut back on
the number of hasty and ill-considered marriages. But in other
respects, a British passport was not the panacea many expected.
There were still formidable problems of living in a country where
even former refugees were thought to be not quite the equal of the
home-born product.

Postwar austerity meant that living conditions were often cramped and poor. There were few clothes and household goods available and food was rationed. Interesting and well-paid jobs were hard to come by. Most of the young refugees found themselves in menial factory or office jobs, or in domestic work. There is a pile of file cases of young men and women longing for a more fulfilling life, perhaps on the stage or as a musician. Some, like Solomon, retreated into fantasy. Arrested for changing the date of his birth certificate from 1924 to 1920, he 'told different people that he was a Jew, Church of England, Roman Catholic and Atheist'.

Bloomsbury House advanced him a small loan to set himself up in steady occupation but without much hope of success. In 1945, Solomon was in trouble again:

> Piccadilly police rang asking if we know the boy . . . He arrived here today . . . very conceited, full of bluff. He is going to study music. He has only to play the violin before the authorities and his career is made. He wanted to know if we have a studio here where he can have his photos taken for his friends.

In 1950, Solomon returned to Bloomsbury House with a request for a suit. He had been offered a job as a clerk with the Ministry of National Insurance and was not at all suitably dressed.

> I gave him £3 . . . as I feel he is now going to settle down . . . he is married and has a child of two years.

So much for dreams.

Where there was proven talent, the prospects were more encouraging, though, as one of the few who made a highly successful career, Leslie Brent is the first to acknowledge that luck has played a big part in his life. His first break was to be plucked out of Dovercourt by Anna Essinger, who spotted him as a prospective star pupil at Bunce Court. After the army, he read zoology at Birmingham, which prepared him for his second stroke of good fortune. He was to be accepted as a postgraduate student at University College under Peter Medawar, one of the world authorities on immunology. He stayed on to be part of a research team whose work on the mysteries of the immune system led to Medawar being awarded a Nobel Prize. In 1965, Leslie Brent was appointed Professor of Zoology at Southampton.

Alf Dubs, who was one of the Czechoslovakian contingent of child refugees, became a Labour MP and is now Director of the British Refugee Council. His success came through an early dedication to radical politics:

> At grammar school in Manchester other people of my age weren't interested in politics. But I was passionately involved in the 1945 election. My mum took me to St Anne's-on-Sea for a week in a boarding house. The first election results came through at midday. There was a loudspeaker in the main square and people at the hotel sent me off to get the score. Since I was Labour I was delighted to be able to announce that we had 120 seats against only 30 for the Conservatives. I remember someone moaning, 'Oh, my God, it's the end of England.'
>
> I remember when they nationalised the mines and I thought it was a great thing. I was in hospital when the health service began. I had an ear infection and was quite ill. I said to the sister on the ENT ward (where I was the youngest), 'Are we getting special food today?' and she asked why. 'Because of the Health Service.' She told me not to be silly.

After national service, Alf Dubs went to the London School of Economics. He was elected to Parliament in 1979.

A few were able to draw on skills acquired before they were uprooted. For example, Käthe Fischel, now a successful artist known chiefly, and perhaps significantly, for her scenes of urban dereliction, was already an art student when she was forced to leave Czechoslovakia.

Others, like Clive Milton, had to start from scratch. Even as a young farm labourer he was saving money and making profit out of various farming enterprises, sometimes to the irritation of his employers. His fulfilment was to establish the Sheraton Patisserie chain.

Freddy Durst worked his way up from an apprenticeship to a jeweller. With his friend John Najmann, he went to evening classes at the Central School of Arts and Crafts.

> As the war progressed, we were taught how to make military instruments like bomb and gun sights for the RAF. We worked for three years for up to sixteen hours a day, saving what we could. Our aim was to put together a hundred pounds so that we would have enough to start on our own. After the war, we set up our own

little workshop. When John went off to Germany to find his mother who had survived Auschwitz, I was on my own for a while. That was when I bought my first bits and pieces of gold. I filed them up and made a few rings to sell to the Oxford Street shops. I sold six here, six there and, by the time I got to Selfridges, they were all gone. The problem was I didn't realise that after you sell something it takes a month to get payment. I should have opened a bank account but at twenty-one that wasn't easy. In fact, the shopkeepers I visited said they would talk to my father about it because they didn't really feel it acceptable to do business with a mere boy. But I got more and more orders and I had to arrange credit with the bullion dealers who knew me from when I ran errands. I was soon earning £8 a week, which was substantially more than when I was in charge of thirty or forty people making bomb sights.

It was the start of a career which led to the creation of the biggest jewellery manufacturing business in Britain.

With her special interest in the academically gifted, Greta Burkill kept a watchful eye on the advance of her protégés. Writing in 1978, and taking the country as a whole, she gave the RCM credit for one vice-chancellor, nine professors, four university lecturers, four medical consultants, a Shell executive, a deputy legal adviser to the International Labour Organisation, two judges, one silk and a senior administrator at the BBC; not to mention a leading film-maker, Karel Reisz, and several journalists, the best known of whom are Fritz Spiegl and Hella Pick.

In the early days after the war, feelings about Germany centred on hopes of finding relatives who had survived. The RCM coped with a flood of enquiries from children who were desperate for news:

> Ilse returned her Search Bureau cards, of which four sets are completed. She tells us she has heard through an eyewitness that seven of her near relatives have been murdered in Lublin and she has filled in forms for those about whose fate she is not yet certain.

Ilse heard a few months later that her parents had died in a camp. Only one cousin remained out of her whole family.

For the lucky ones, those whose parents did survive, the joy of an anticipated reunion was squashed flat by the problem of making contact. The RCM was forced to admit 'We have not as yet felt we can even write to the parents in liberated countries because we have no answer to their question, "When and where can I see my child?"'

There were simply no procedures for arranging travel to Germany.

> . . . nor is it yet possible for relations to go from England to Germany. The only practicable solution would be for parents to endeavour to obtain a visiting permit for Holland and Belgium and for the child to go there to meet them.

Reunions, when at last they did take place, were not always the blissful occasions both sides had anticipated.

The children had been encouraged to look to their own futures, not dwell on the past. Their experiences could not have been more of a contrast to those of their parents and, when they came together, they met as strangers. Even the language was different. And this was only the beginning of the emotional pressures. It came as a terrible shock to realise that fondly remembered parents, who had once offered confidence and stability, were now themselves in need of reassurance and desperate for affection. Few youngsters had the emotional maturity to cope, as Liesl Silverstone discovered:

> Eventually I heard that my mother had survived. They found her in the mortuary at Mauthausen Camp. She must have made a little sound when the Camp was liberated – so back she came from the dead. She was extremely ill. At first she went to Prague. She had typhus. No one else survived at all of all the people I grew up with.
>
> When she was well enough she came here. We met again. I saw her last when I was twelve and now I was eighteen. There was an enormous gap. One of the first things she said to me was that I was the one left to her to make life all right again. I couldn't do it. It was no longer a mother–and–daughter relationship. I couldn't upset her. How do you proceed with a mother who has been to Auschwitz? In retrospect, I realise that after the war I got a different mother back.
>
> It was all too confusing and awful. The things we needed to say we were not ready to say to each other. She died before it could happen. She never cried after the war. She just carried on coping, like I did. So we were both denying things. Two different people, with the war limbo in between. We survived as best we could.

Liesl and her mother returned to Czechoslovakia, where Liesl was the only person of her own age-group left alive out of a Jewish community of 60,000 in her home town. In 1948, when the Russians took over, she came back to England.

Francis Wahle did not realise that his parents were alive until 1945, when a cousin of his father's was forwarded a Red Cross message which had originally been sent out by Francis's parents in 1939. The cousin looked up the father's name on a list of judges in Vienna, discovered that he was alive, and passed on the good news to the children. Francis's mother was also alive, and was able to visit Paris on a conference, when she came to England very briefly, but it took another four years for the whole family to reunite:

> My mother had obviously changed. You don't survive a hunted life without that. She refused to send us photographs because she didn't like to look old. So it was quite a shock when we met. My father had changed less, strangely enough, because he was older than she.
>
> They had to adjust to having children again and we had to adapt to having parents. We had grown in different ways. It was almost shadow-boxing at first. There was a lot of tension. But we avoided ructions.

Ruth Michaelis was with her third foster family when her mother came to fetch her:

> I had really settled down after being kicked out of my own country and then shunted from foster parents to foster parents. I didn't want to be uprooted again and my foster family wanted to keep me, so there was a battle royal between my foster mother and my mother and it took some sort of legal process to get me repatriated.
>
> They did not repatriate my brother, which seemed very unfair to me. My parents wanted him to have the chance of going to Cambridge. But right through the war I had depended very heavily on my brother. He had been the one who always explained to me what was going on. They didn't realise what it would do to me to split us up. Had my mother come straight after the war and taken both of us back, I would never have resisted.
>
> My mother and father rowed all the time. My father had a job in Mainz and my mother stayed on Lake Constance, which is several

hundred miles away. My father only came every other weekend and then it was just rows.

I was fourteen and a very bolshie teenager. I refused to do anything. I refused to learn German. (I had forgotten it all and I flatly refused to learn.) When they wanted to send me to school I said no, and I was very surprised when they didn't take me by the scruff of the neck and deliver me there. I stayed six months before they gave in and let me come back to England.

My parents saw me off at Mainz. It was a difficult departure, not because I had any ambivalence about going, but because I was trying to avoid saying goodbye to my parents. At that time I could not deal with my mother's wish to hug and kiss me. I kept my mother at arm's length, which must have been torture for her.

During this year Ruth returned to her foster parents and to school in England. She gained a place at Reading University, but before taking it up she stayed with her parents in Germany again. It was not for long:

I thought my parents were having a row one day – though they were just heatedly discussing one of my father's cases – and I got fed up. I took my passport and left for England. It was a nasty thing for me to do but I was afraid of getting trapped in Germany.

Culture and background, as well as language, could prove a barrier. In 1945, Ella called at Bloomsbury House to ask if her parents could force her to stay with them. She was feeling stifled by family life.

Ella says that she always has to be in at nine, if she is allowed out at all, and that she cannot go to any dances except once a month. She always does the housework when she comes home from work and helps as much as she possibly can. She gives the whole of her wages to her father, only keeping back 8/- for herself.

Bloomsbury House acted as a safety valve. A week later, Ella telephoned to say that all was well again.

When the break did come, Bloomsbury House had invariably to try to repair the damage, not always successfully.

Bruno called at his mother's address and was very shocked at the place. He found his mother had left the week before, leaving no address. He was very upset, having had no reply from her to his letters. He seemed doubtful about our *bona fides*, thinking we knew all about his mother and were concealing it from him. By the time he left, the boy was fairly well reassured of our good faith, but we were unable to reassure him about his mother. It may be difficult for us to find her.

There was a tendency at the end of the war for family skeletons to be released. It was a time for confession, which was entirely understandable, except that, by opening up more divisions, it could make reconciliation all the more difficult. It was, for example, news about her grandmother that so much disturbed Elli Adler:

> My mother told me, years after she came over after the war, that my grandmother, who was very anti-Semitic and had disapproved of her marriage, had found out about my mother's application to leave and had gone to the office saying, 'I am a poor old lady, I am all on my own and have nobody', and they had struck my mother's name off the list. My mother did not find out until long afterwards and it finished her. She had never liked her mother, because she treated her very badly, but it was beyond her comprehension that anyone should do such a thing.

When her mother arrived in England, Elli went to meet her at Victoria Station.

> It was a very strange experience. I was a little girl when I left and now I was a woman with a baby. Although it was August, she was wearing a fur coat in order to bring it with her. She was a stranger to me; it was terrible. It didn't get any easier; it was always difficult.

Angela Carpos resented her mother embarking on a new relationship:

> My mother married a Greek, because the Germans wanted to send her back to Germany and she wanted to stay there. She used to meet British servicemen and tell them to look me up in London and take silk stockings or a cake . . . When I got a phone call in London that she had arrived and I was to go and see her, it was with very mixed feelings after eleven years. It was very difficult picking up the relationship. She was trying to put eleven years of lost mothering into me, and I was just trying to do what I wanted to do. I only really got close to her after I was married.

Ya'acov Friedler's mother was ill and confused after her time in the camps. Because of a technicality, she was not officially allowed to enter the country. Ya'acov went straight to the top, writing a four-page letter to the then Queen, now the Queen Mother.

> I do not recall everything I put into my letter, but I remember feeling confident that if her Majesty might be but a fraction as touched reading it as I had been writing, she would aid us in our distress . . .

In the event, a letter came from the Home Office informing Ya'acov that, on the command of Her Majesty, the application had been reconsidered and an entry visa granted for his mother. In 1947, Ya'acov went to Holland to fetch her.

> Our reunion was not tearful. I was too overcome and mother received me matter-of-factly, as though the seven years and the Holocaust that had separated us had not happened. She asked a few questions about my sister and brother, enquired whether we had regular mail from father, and then reverted to the torments of her mind. Quickly she became incoherent. This was much worse than we had feared. How was I going to be able to get mother past the immigration officer in England in such a state?

The flight back was Ya'acov's first but he was so worried about what would happen at the airport, he scarcely had time to feel excited.

> I was appalled by the fear that mother might make a scene and, notwithstanding her visa, be barred by the immigration officer. But my fears turned out to be unjustified. Perhaps my anxiety got through to my mother and danger was the only thing she could take care of. We got through the border control at Croydon airport with flying colours.

His worries over, Ya'acov was struck by the pathos of the family reunion and of his mother's luggage:

> A cardboard suitcase with a few pieces of clothing provided by the Red Cross and the Jewish Committee and a few necessities I bought for her . . . But there was also a battered old tin plate and water

bottle to which she obstinately clung. They were the only possessions she had been able to cling to since she had first been taken
away . . . they had gone with her through the camps and she would
not give them up or allow us to dispose of them. They were her
lifelines to the past and it took a lot of coaxing to persuade her to
start eating from normal tableware.

Later, in Palestine, Ya'acov met up with his father.

At last I knocked on father's door. Our reunion was embarrassing.
The image of father I had carried in my heart for the past ten years
was that of a self-confident stoutish man, with the expansive aspect
of middle-age success. Now I was embracing a grizzled old man,
small and slight, bent by physical injuries and years of mental
anguish. He had grown a goatee beard, which, like the sparse hair
he had retained, was quite white. I am short myself, but here I
found myself towering over father.

For the great majority, whose families were wiped out in the
Holocaust, feelings about Germany started inevitably with
thoughts of retribution. But opportunity came only to those, like
Johnny Blunt, who were part of the occupying forces and just
happened to pass through their home towns.

I went to the marketplace and lit a cigarette and the first person to
approach me was my old teacher, the one who used to call me
'Jewboy' and who used to tell the story of how a Jewish peddlar
knocked on his door and he kicked him up the backside, saying 'I
don't want to be done by a Jewish bastard!' He came over to me,
not recognising me, because I had my goggles on. I just looked like
any other British soldier. He said in very poor English, 'Can I help
you, sir?' I removed my goggles and put them on top of my helmet.
His mouth fell open as he looked at me. 'You are Johnny Eichwald,
aren't you?' 'Yes.' He said, 'I am very glad you survived the war.'
I just looked at him; I never said anything.

Later, Johnny was told that the local head of the Nazi party was
asking to meet him. Johnny agreed.

He attempted to come over to me, obviously to shake hands. I kept
my hands in my pockets. I didn't offer him a seat. He asked me if I
had been aware that he was always a good friend of my father. I just
looked at him. He went on and on. Eventually, he came to the point,

that he found himself in a little difficulty because he had to fill in his de-Nazification papers and he wondered if I would back him up in this. I had not said one single word. My mouth was completely sealed. I hadn't said yes or no, I just listened. After about five minutes he stopped talking. 'Is there anything else, Herr Burrose?' I asked. 'I don't think so, I can't think of anything else . . .' he said. I took a little pistol out of my pocket and weighed it in my hand. I looked him straight in the face. 'Herr Burrose,' I said, 'if by the time I count to three I still see you in front of me, you will breathe through your stomach – 'one,' before I could say two, he had gone.

Herr Burrose was tried and sentenced to one and a half years' hard labour. When he came out of prison he became a communist.

This shows his character. Once the head of the Nazis, then he turned completely the other way. I think he is a pitiful character. If it had not been for the Nazis, he would have been nobody. That was the only way he could get somewhere. Like a lot of the others.

A few children who were involved with the Free German and Free Austrian left-wing movements were keen to go back and to start rebuilding their shattered countries. Miriam married a Turkish musician from Vienna and, as a member of the Free German movement, was listed in 1946 to return to Berlin with the first group of 300 people. She left in the October of that year. But elsewhere in the ranks of the RCM, nationalism was frail.

Marta and Inge called. Both girls seem adamant in wanting to return to Austria and are very peeved at the obstructions they feel we are putting in their way . . . We suggested that it was their attitude that might be at the root of these obstructions, and in any case I did not feel the Movement had any wish to stop their eventual re-emigration. It was merely a question of appropriate time.

Four months later, in March 1947:

Marta called. Said that she and Inge had now seriously reconsidered the question of repatriation. They had heard from friends in Austria of the difficulties experienced in finding work and of the conditions prevailing there . . . she now realises we were right in impeding their return.

Then there were those, like Max Hutton, who returned but lived to regret it.

> I wanted to stay in England originally; I could never imagine going back to Germany. My sister had been to visit my mother and she suggested that I should see her too. It was not so easy at that time to visit Germany – you had to get a military permit. I arrived in Germany in 1949 and you can't imagine how things looked. It was simply dreadful. Everything was flat. No paint on the buildings and everyone in drab, worn clothing. It was really awful. But seeing my mother was quite an event for me and it touched me more than I had expected. Time passed by quickly and I decided to stay a little longer. I wound up staying for many years. I started working (my job in London was not very remunerative) and after a couple of years I built up my own business and I did very well.
>
> I had difficulties at first. You looked at people and wondered what he had done during the war and, even now, I often have doubts about people. Germans are curious people. They don't want to think or hear about what happened. They push it aside as if it never happened. They have no way of thinking clearly about things.
>
> I stayed with my mother; she had married again to a man who before the war had been a wholesaler. So I started working for him. I sold shoes to the retail trade, acting as an agent. He was an old man and needed help. In the end, I took over the firm and changed it completely.
>
> After a while, I realised my mother was inventing things, telling me lies. I could not take anything she told me at face value. She told me things that put me apart from other people and afterwards I found out they weren't true. She told me things about my father which couldn't have been true.
>
> I sometimes have a bad conscience for having come back; I think morally I should not have come back. I did it for selfish reasons because I saw a better chance to make a better living. If my mother hadn't been here, I wouldn't have thought about it.

The typical reaction of those who lost their family links with their first home was to try to block out the memories. One technique was to go all out for a new identity, to become more British than the British. As one young man responded to an inquiry about his nationality: 'I am as British as you are. In fact, I am more so because I chose it. I am double British.'

But however hard they tried, the shadow of earlier times remained – and remains to this day. Sometimes it shows in little things, like Claire Barrington's dread of journeys:

> I have felt this anxiety all through my life; I never prepare for holidays, I don't like holidays, I don't like suitcases or railway stations or booking tickets. I am always frightened of missing trains. I am always hours early when I am going somewhere . . .

Or Angela Carpos's dislike of card games:

> When I was staying with my grandmother in Germany, there was a very old Jewish man of eighty-two who taught me to play cards. He was dragged away one day. I still can't play cards today. My friends can't understand why I won't join in a game.

Margaret Olmer has always been a collector.

> My daughter, when she was eight, said: 'You have all these bits of china, aren't you greedy?' But I told myself I was trying to replace all these things that people have taken from me. Also, I had four children. I had a drive to give back to myself, to society and to my people. I never felt any desire for violent revenge – just a tremendous desire to succeed here. I see it in so many people. They have replaced tenfold what was taken from them. They came from such shortages and came with nothing.

And there are those, like Harry Katz, who have shut themselves off from a world that can no longer be trusted.

> After the war, I tried through the Red Cross to trace our parents and our sister. Maybe through a miracle they might be alive somewhere. But of course, being in the Warsaw ghetto, none of them were. There was just my brother and myself. When he was demobbed, the war started in Palestine and so he went there to volunteer. I took it for granted that when he came out of the army we would do something together; maybe get a place together or maybe start a little workshop. But he went straight to Palestine, so I hardly had any contact with him. I was practically alone for most of my life. I have difficulty making contact with people – perhaps because of my childhood – and it has kept on to the present day. I am still a bachelor and most of my friends are those I knew as a child fifty years ago. I keep myself to myself, partly because I have trouble talking – a speech impediment – and it has kept me away

from social gatherings. It has been a handicap all my life, but perhaps I have been using it as an excuse.

Over the years, the line on Germany has softened. Returning to Berlin, Peter Prager found himself thinking of his own experiences in a wider context.

> I didn't feel any hatred . . . as a young boy I often felt it was a pity I was a Jew and that I couldn't be like the others. Perhaps if I had not been a Jew I would have done exactly like the others – I would have been like my classmates. Those who hate the Germans have to consider what they would have done in their place. It doesn't excuse the Germans, but it does mean that you have to examine how the Nazis came to power. The Allies are not entirely blameless, the way they treated Germany after the First World War.

Whenever he visits Germany or Austria, Leslie Brent tends to treat everyone over the age of sixty with a certain suspicion.

> It's impossible to know what a person's thoughts and actions were during the Nazi era. But I have learnt to draw a distinction between Germans of that age group and the younger Germans I have met . . . Clearly the young German generation has quite a hard time of it, their problem being to come to grips with what their parents did or did not do, and I have a great deal of sympathy for them because it must be a very hard cross to bear.

Rediscovering their origins has not been the easiest experience for any of the child refugees. When, after the war, one girl met relatives from Berlin, she found she could not bring herself to speak a single word of German.

> It took me some time to sort myself out. But then I realised it was a very good thing that I did the journey. My sister had to do all the translations. The language did return when I went back to Germany in 1951, but this caused a lot of confusion in me.

Kurt Weinburg returned to the village of Werther and to his father's cigar-making business in 1950, but never quite relearned the art of socialising.

I could not go into a crowd of Germans. I could not go into a restaurant or a hotel. When I went to buy tobacco in south-west Germany and had to stay overnight, I put up in the smallest hotel I could find to avoid company. But then I had to listen to a party of Germans singing their hearts out. I had nightmares. I was eager to get back to my private room in our former home, or back in England. I just couldn't face it. I did visit certain people who I knew had been active trade unionists or really genuine friends of the Jewish families, but all the other German people I met, the first thing they said was how much they had suffered during the war and how courageous they had been. But you could count on one hand the numbers of families who took food to my relatives. That was real courage.

Until recently, a busy and absorbing professional life afforded Professor Leslie Brent the luxury of not thinking too deeply on the question 'Why me?' He felt 'quite irrationally', as he explains, an element of guilt at being the only one of his immediate family to survive.

But I didn't find or make the time for pondering, or perhaps I simply wasn't ready for it.

The opportunity for reflection came when he was invited to lecture to the Polish Academy of Sciences. On a drive from Krakow to Wrozlaw, his host turned to him:

'Oh, by the way, we will be travelling within twenty kilometres of Auschwitz. It is now a memorial which we Poles keep as a terrible reminder. Perhaps you would like to visit.' I was very much taken aback as I have always regarded it as the camp in which my family died. I said I didn't want to go back and explained to him why. Then, as we were drawing nearer I felt a strange compulsion to go . . .

In Auschwitz there is enough left to give one a pretty realistic idea of what it must have been like – the perimeter fence is there with the watchtowers and the gate, over which is written, incredibly, *Arbeit macht frei* (Work makes you free). None of the huts are left but the brick foundations and the chimney stack of each hut remain. So there are rows and rows of chimney stacks. I left some flowers. It was the first time I had wept uncontrollably in mourning for my family.

Leslie Brent has come to terms with his past, in so far as that is possible. Accompanied by his wife and son he has recently visited the town of his birth, now in Poland.

> There are moments when I think about all this when I become overwhelmed with sorrow. But time has made it easier. I can now look back with a little more serenity.

Others, not so fortunate, are still puzzling on the nature of their true selves. At the *Kindertransporte* reunion in June 1989, the predicament was shared but not resolved.

> I came over at the age of three and a half. I still don't know where I belong. I was brought up in the Midlands. I went to a Christian school. I was no longer considered German, I was not considered English. I certainly wasn't Jewish – my Jewish background was not nurtured. I am neither German nor English. I am neither Gentile nor Jew. I would like to know what is my identity?

By late 1947, the RCM was running short of money, voluntary workers and the will to go on. The Movement was still responsible for nearly 7000 youngsters, but less than a third were under eighteen and, of these, none were dependent on Bloomsbury House for any function that could not equally well be carried out by another charity.

The obvious choice for a friendly takeover was the Central British Fund whose finances had kept the RCM going when government funding was at its tightest. Talks began in the summer of 1948 with Otto Schiff, the begetter of all the wartime refugee organisations, heading the negotiations for the CBF. There was little to discuss. The RCM cash assets, some £4000, were just enough to cover the outstanding CBF debt. Office space was soon reallocated; so too were the staff who wanted to stay on. Dorothy Hardisty was ready to retire, Elaine Blond had already resigned and Lola Hahn-Warburg stayed only to see through the merger, though the last two remained active in the CBF's Jewish refugee work to the ends of their lives.

The RCM closed its files in December 1948. But, as we have seen, it was not the end of the story. Even today, fifty years on, there is still a long way to go before the final chapter is written. Let Herta Stanton, from Vienna, speak for the ten thousand:

> I go back for holidays. My husband loves it, but I never say who I am or what I am. I am British, I have come from England on holiday, finish. But I still want to go to Vienna; there is something about it I can't explain. I have a funny feeling about it. When we go back to Austria and the mountains start to appear, I feel choked. But I am afraid to go for fear of what may be said to me and what I would have to answer. I couldn't keep quiet.
>
> A friend went to Vienna last year. His family had a big toy shop in the middle of the city – I knew it well – and next door was a leather shop. The leather shop was still there and my friend recognised the owner. He said, 'Don't you know me? I'm Gustav.' The man stared at him. 'What, you are alive? They should have killed all of them.' That was his reception. He says he'll never go back to Vienna again.
>
> Another year, my eldest brother was in Vienna and he went to a cafe where my father used to go. As he sat down, an old waiter came to the table and said, 'Black coffee and whipped cream?' My brother said, yes, but how did he know? 'Oh, you're not Herr Pollak?' My brother said he was Herr Pollak's son. It was the same waiter who used to serve my father every day. The old man cried. Vienna is a funny place, lots of black and white, such contrasts, and I think I am still influenced by it. I am a product of it.

Bibliography

Bach, H. I., *The German Jew – a Synthesis of Judaism and Western Civilisation 1730–1930* (OUP, 1984)

Beller, Stephen, *Vienna and the Jews 1867–1938* (Cambridge, 1989)

Bentwich, Norman, *They Found Refuge* (Cresset Press, 1956)

Bentwich, Norman, *Wanderer Between Two Worlds* (Cresset Press, 1941)

Darton, Lawrence, *Friends Committee for Refugees and Aliens 1933–1950* (Society of Friends, 1951)

Eliahm, Elanth (ed.), *Memories of Sir Wyndham Deedes* (published privately, 1958)

Gassman-Sherr, Rosalie, *The Story of the Federation of Women Zionists of Great Britain and Ireland 1918–1968* (Federation of Women Zionists, 1968)

Gedye, G. R., *Fallen Bastions* (Victor Gollancz, 1939)

George, Margaret, *The Hollow Men* (Weidenfeld & Nicolson, 1984)

Gershon, Karen (ed.), *We Came as Children* (Victor Gollancz, 1966)

Gillman, Peter and Levi, *Collar the Lot* (Quartet, 1980)

Gissing, Vera, *Pearls of Childhood* (Robson Books, 1988)

Gorell, Lord, *One Man, Many Parts* (Odhams, 1956)

Josephs, Zoe, *Survivors – Jewish Refugees in Birmingham* (Meridian Books, 1988)

Palmer, Alan, *The East End* (John Murray, 1989)

Presland, John (pseudonym of Gladys Bendit), *A Great Adventure* (RCM, 1944)

Reid, Douglas, *Insanity Fair* (Jonathan Cape, 1938)

Samuel, Viscount, *Memoirs* (Cresset Press, 1945)

Segall, Lore, *Other People's Houses* (Bodley Head, 1958)

Shepherd, Naomi, *Wilfred Israel, German Jewry's Secret Ambassador* (Weidenfeld & Nicolson, 1984)

Sherman, A. J., *Island Refuge – Britain and the Refugees from the Third Reich 1933–1939* (Paul Elek, 1973)

Stein, Leonard and Aronsfeld, C. C. (eds.), *Leonard G. Montefiore* (The Wiener Library, 1964)

Sykes, Christopher, *Crossroads to Israel* (Collins, 1965)

Tartakower, Arieh and Grossman, Kurt R., *The Jewish Refugee* (New York Institute of Jewish Affairs, 1944)

Wedgewood, C. V., *The Last of the Radicals – Josiah Wedgewood MP* (Jonathan Cape, 1951)

Wicks, Ben, *No Time to Wave Goodbye* (Bloomsbury, 1988)

Zürndorfer, Hannele, *The Ninth of November* (Quartet, 1983)

Index